The Japanese Writing System

SECOND LANGUAGE ACQUISITION

Series Editors: **Professor David Singleton**, *University of Pannonia, Hungary* and Fellow Emeritus, *Trinity College, Dublin, Ireland* and **Dr Simone E. Pfenninger**, *University of Salzburg, Austria*

This series brings together titles dealing with a variety of aspects of language acquisition and processing in situations where a language or languages other than the native language is involved. Second language is thus interpreted in its broadest possible sense. The volumes included in the series all offer in their different ways, on the one hand, exposition and discussion of empirical findings and, on the other, some degree of theoretical reflection. In this latter connection, no particular theoretical stance is privileged in the series; nor is any relevant perspective – sociolinguistic, psycholinguistic, neurolinguistic, etc. – deemed out of place. The intended readership of the series includes final-year undergraduates working on second language acquisition projects, postgraduate students involved in second language acquisition research, and researchers, teachers and policy-makers in general whose interests include a second language acquisition component.

Full details of all the books in this series and of all our other publications can be found on http://www.multilingual-matters.com, or by writing to Multilingual Matters, St Nicholas House, 31-34 High Street, Bristol BS1 2AW, UK.

SECOND LANGUAGE ACQUISITION: 116

The Japanese Writing System

Challenges, Strategies and Self-regulation for Learning *Kanji*

Heath Rose

MULTILINGUAL MATTERS
Bristol • Blue Ridge Summit

DOI: 10.21832/ROSE8156

Library of Congress Cataloging in Publication Data
A catalog record for this book is available from the Library of Congress.
Names: Rose, Heath, author.
Title: The Japanese Writing System: Challenges, Strategies and Self-regulation for Learning Kanji/Heath Rose.
Description: Multilingual Matters: Bristol; Blue Ridge Summit, [2017] | Series: Second Language Acquisition: 116
   Includes bibliographical references and index.
Identifiers: LCCN 2017000272| ISBN 9781783098156 (hbk : alk. paper) | ISBN 9781783098149 (pbk : alk. paper) | ISBN 9781783098187 (kindle) | ISBN 9781783098170 (Epub)
Subjects: LCSH: Japanese language—Writing. | Chinese characters—Japan. | Japanese language—Study and teaching—Foreign students.
Classification: LCC PL528 .R67 2017 | DDC 495.6/82421—dc23 LC record available at https://lccn.loc.gov/2017000272

British Library Cataloguing in Publication Data
A catalogue entry for this book is available from the British Library.

ISBN-13: 978-1-78309-815-6 (hbk)
ISBN-13: 978-1-78309-814-9 (pbk)

Multilingual Matters
UK: St Nicholas House, 31-34 High Street, Bristol BS1 2AW, UK.
USA: NBN, Blue Ridge Summit, PA, USA.

Website: www.multilingual-matters.com
Twitter: Multi_Ling_Mat
Facebook: https://www.facebook.com/multilingualmatters
Blog: www.channelviewpublications.wordpress.com

Copyright © 2017 Heath Rose.

All rights reserved. No part of this work may be reproduced in any form or by any means without permission in writing from the publisher.

The policy of Multilingual Matters/Channel View Publications is to use papers that are natural, renewable and recyclable products, made from wood grown in sustainable forests. In the manufacturing process of our books, and to further support our policy, preference is given to printers that have FSC and PEFC Chain of Custody certification. The FSC and/or PEFC logos will appear on those books where full certification has been granted to the printer concerned.

Typeset by Nova Techset Private Limited, Bengaluru and Chennai, India.

Contents

Figures and Tables	ix
Preface	xi
About the Author	xvii

Part 1: Issues Surrounding Japanese Language Acquisition

1	Introduction	3
	An Overview of Japanese Language Education	3
	Why a Book on Learning Japanese Writing?	6
	Original Research Used in this Book	10
	Significance of the Research Showcased in this Book	13
2	The Japanese Writing System	14
	Components of the Japanese Writing System	14
	Implications	22
3	Cognitive Challenges in Learning the Japanese Writing System	25
	A Brief Introduction to Cognitive Processes	25
	Cognitive Processes in Reading and Writing Japanese	28
	Implications	31

Part 2: Cognitive Strategies

4	Cognitive Learning Strategies	37
	A Brief Introduction to Cognitive Learning Strategies	37
	Kanji Learning Strategies	42
	Implications	43
5	Visual Association	47
	Pictorial Association	49
	Symbolic Association	52
	Other Types of Whole *Kanji* Association	55
	Implications	56

v

6	Component Analysis	59
	Component Analysis Strategies	60
	Implications	65
7	Mnemonics	68
	Research into the Effectiveness of Mnemonic Strategies	70
	Implications	75

Part 3: Psychology and Self-regulation

8	Learner Psychology, Self-regulation and Language Learning	81
	Self-regulation as an Alternative to Language Learner Strategy Research	81
	Dörnyei's Model of Self-regulation	83
	Self-regulation as an Additive to Language Learning Strategy Research	85
	Self-regulating Capacity of *Kanji* Learning	86
	Implications	90
9	Metacognition and Language Learning	93
	Planning Learning	94
	Evaluating Learning	97
	Collaborative Learning	98
	Metacognitive Control Strategies	100
	Implications	101
10	Goal Setting and Commitment Control Strategies	104
	Commitment Control Strategies	104
	Typical Goals and Benchmarks for Japanese Study	107
	Commitment Control of Participants in *The Self-regulation Study*	110
	Implications	115
11	Affective Factors in *Kanji* Learning	118
	Emotion and Affective Factors in Self-regulation	118
	Emotion Control in *The Self-regulation Study*	119
	Implications	122

Part 4: Implications

12	Implications for Learners	129
	Challenges Faced by Japanese Language Learners	129
	A Learner's Lament: Why Can't the Japanese Writing System be Simplified?	130
	How to be a Better Learner: Strategies to Overcome Challenges	134

13	Implications for Instructors	139
	Issues Surrounding the Order of Teaching Japanese Writing	139
	How to be a Better Teacher: Advice to Support Second Language Learners	140
	Strategy Instruction in the Classroom	149
14	Implications for Researchers	153
	Recommendations for Further Japanese SLA Research	153
	Recommended Conceptual Frameworks for Use in Future Research	160
	Recommended Methods of Data Collection for Use in Future Research	162
	Conclusion	166
	Glossary	168
	References	173
	Index	180

Figures and Tables

Figures

Figure 1.1	Outbound tourists from Japan	4
Figure 1.2	Students traveling to Japan for study purposes	6
Figure 2.1	An excerpt to illustrate the scripts of the Japanese writing system	15
Figure 5.1	Example of pictorial association strategy for learning *hiragana*	48
Figure 5.2	Etymological depictions of *kanji*	50
Figure 5.3	Example of symbolic association of a *kanji*	54
Figure 12.1	A breakdown in self-regulation for learning *kanji* of a Japanese language learner	137
Figure 14.1	Theoretical framework for *kanji* strategy research	161

Tables

Table 1.1	Number of Japanese language learners	5
Table 2.1	Fifty sounds of Japanese: Represented by *hiragana*	16
Table 2.2	Romanization systems for Japanese	18
Table 2.3	Examples of *kanji* types	20
Table 4.1	An inventory of cognitive and metacognitive *kanji* learning strategies	44
Table 5.1	Errors according to *kanji* type (*The Intervention Study*)	51
Table 5.2	List of *kanji* taught in each year of elementary school in Japan	53
Table 6.1	Examples of *kanji* graphemes	60
Table 6.2	List of *kanji* radical types	60
Table 8.1	Criticisms of language learning strategies	82
Table 8.2	Issues with the field of language learning strategies	82
Table 8.3	Self-regulatory capacity for learning vocabulary	87

Table 8.4	Self-regulatory capacity for learning *kanji* (*SRCKanji*)	88
Table 8.5	Interview guide for investigating self-regulation in *kanji* learning	89
Table 10.1	*Kanji* knowledge recommended at each level of the Japanese Language Proficiency Test	108
Table 10.2	Examples of goal levels of participants in *The Self-regulation Study*	111
Table 13.1	Fast food menu to illustrate use of *katakana*	142
Table 13.2	Fast food menu *romaji* gloss	143
Table 13.3	*Kanji* ordered by frequency	146
Table 13.4	*Kanji* ordered by simplicity	147
Table 13.5	*Kanji* ordered by meaning groups	148
Table 13.6	Use of component analysis by an illustrative case in *The Strategies Study*	151

Preface

This book showcases the Japanese writing system, focusing on the challenges it poses for the second language learner, the second language teacher and applied linguistic researchers who are interested in implications for Second Language Acquisition (SLA). It is the result of more than 13 years of research into the teaching and learning of Japanese, however, my positioning of the Japanese writing system in this volume is more than an academic one; the idea to begin research into the SLA of Japanese – and particularly its writing system – grew from my own struggles with learning the language, as well as my struggles in teaching it.

A Personal Rationale

I first began learning Japanese as a high school student in a rural town in Queensland, Australia. My town was very small and the high school could only offer the bare minimum of core subjects that schools needed to offer. Language was usually compulsory for all first year high school students, but when I entered high school in 1989, the German teacher had left and was yet to be replaced, resulting in my grade missing the opportunity to learn a language. I had always had an interest in languages – I suspected I might be quite good at them – so I dabbled a bit in self-study of Japanese via cassettes and workbooks. I had chosen Japanese because, at the time, the rhetoric in Australia was that Japanese was the most useful language to learn due to our growing trade and economic ties with Japan. In addition, Europe seemed very distant from Australia to my 14-year-old self, so I did not have the same interest in German or French, as I could not see an immediate opportunity to use these languages in my future. When I entered Years 11 and 12 in high school, the state education system required students to undertake six eligible high school subjects, of which just five were used to calculate university entrance scores. Thus, I took the opportunity to drop one eligible subject in favor of learning Japanese via distance education. I studied the high school curriculum via a distance education module and had a one-hour speaking lesson over the phone with a wonderfully generous teacher who was based in the nearest school that offered Japanese. I struggled with the learning of Japanese in this manner; I found it hard to stay motivated and to regulate my study time. As a result, I scraped through with the lowest possible pass on my senior certificate.

This trend continued throughout my university studies, where I was placed in classes with high achieving language learners. I discovered that the students who decided to major in language at university were the ones who had an aptitude for language learning and had received A grades in their high school language class. In my second year of language studies, we were placed with students who had already spent a year abroad. I was consistently at the bottom of the class in terms of my grades and terrified to speak the language in front of others. It seemed I was not that good at learning language after all.

My one reprieve in those Japanese language classes were the *kanji* classes, which were treated separately from grammar and spoken instruction. In these classes I found I could keep up with the more proficient students, with some hard work. In fact, some of these students, who had amazing proficiency in the oral language, struggled immensely in the written language. It was my first encounter of educated people, who could speak Japanese at an advanced and fluent level, but were functionally illiterate. In the future, I would find many learners like this throughout Japan, and indeed became one of them myself for a number of years.

After I finished a teacher training degree, I decided to move to Japan before I would inflict my entirely home grown version of the Japanese language on unsuspecting learners. I had made it through the course based on my written literacy and textbook grammar, which compensated for my atrocious incompetence in the spoken language. I enjoyed using the spoken language in Japan and my proficiency skyrocketed in my first year there. In 1999, I took the National Japanese Language Proficiency Test of Level 2, which I passed with ease; my strength was still the *kanji* section, in which I had received an almost perfect score. I felt guilty that I had not pushed myself to take the Level 1 at the time. I was shocked to find that a classmate of mine, whose Japanese was far superior to mine, had failed. Her weakness, it emerged, was the *kanji* component of the test. Soon after in my Japanese class, I took an unofficial version of Level 1, and happily found that I was able to pass. I stopped formal study, as I was content with my ability in the language, but I continued to use Japanese every day. A year later, I took the Level 1 test and scored very poorly. Despite using Japanese every day for that year, it seemed that my ability in the language had decreased, more specifically, my written ability in the language had declined. Listening comprehension, which I used to score poorly at, had become my strong point; however, my *kanji* knowledge seemed to be worse than the year before. I was shocked at the thought that I could be immersed in a language in Japan and have my written proficiency drop. Although it is unsurprising to me now, at the time it only first dawned on me that the written Japanese language and the spoken Japanese language were completely separate beasts; it was possible to advance in one and decline in the other.

The following year, I returned to Australia to take up a job teaching Japanese at a primary school in the Sydney area and also moved into research. I conducted some research at the school into the teaching of strategies to students to learn *kanji* more efficiently; this was a topic that emerged as a point of interest in my own experiences where some learners seemed to systematically apply strategies to their learning, while other learners struggled with a proficiency in the written language that was much lower than what was reflected in their spoken abilities. After continuing research into Australian primary learners of Japanese for a further year, I returned to Japan to take up a university teaching position and collect data from Japanese language learners in Japan. I lived in Japan for eight years, more than double that of my previous experience; however, each year I saw my written abilities in the language decline due to the lack of time I had to devote to the review of *kanji* in light of my work and research commitments. I was fast becoming one of the subjects in my study; I was becoming a learner who was struggling with the written language despite a retained level of oral proficiency. Written Japanese – once my strong point – was becoming a weakness due to years of neglect.

Eventually, I completed a large-scale project that investigated the struggles encountered by learners of the Japanese writing system and the strategies they deployed to combat these obstacles. It is from this research and subsequent research, that this book is written; however, it is also written from multiple viewpoints, which center around my experiences as a learner of Japanese, then an instructor of Japanese and later a researcher of Japanese SLA. The Japanese Writing System has been documented as one of the most linguistically complex of the world's writing systems. It is both phonological (sound based) and morphological (meaning based). In its representation of linguistic units, the writing system is simultaneously morphographic (characters depicting meaning), syllabic (characters depicting syllables) and alphabetic (characters depicting phonemes), a phenomenon that does not occur in any other written language. Even its morphographic component (*kanji*) is complex, with multiple interpretations, multiple readings and multiple components, which give clue to its meaning, phonology or in many cases, neither.

Despite the difficultly of the written Japanese language for the second language learner, a book has never been written documenting the fascinating processes involved in acquiring it. In my own research, I needed to draw upon numerous research articles on the issues surrounding learning the Japanese writing system, because a single volume on the topic had not been written. Thus, this book aims to fill this gap and presents research into the Japanese writing system and into SLA alongside my own studies into the strategic learning of written Japanese. The book aims to interpret this research in terms of the implications for Japanese language learners, Japanese language instructors and SLA researchers, in line with my personal rationale for writing it from these multiple perspectives.

Overview of the Book

The book is set out in 14 chapters contained within four parts. Each chapter focuses on a separate aspect of either the Japanese writing system, or facets of acquiring it as a second language. Each chapter highlights previous and original research surrounding the study of written Japanese and concludes with a brief discussion of the implications of the content of the chapter for the Japanese language learner, the Japanese language instructor and the Japanese language researcher. In framing the book in this way, people with various vested interests in the topic of Japanese language learning can access this knowledge and apply it to their own situation.

The first part introduces the Japanese writing system and provides an overview of key components of the system, which each have an influence on how the language is learned. This part provides a discussion of the linguistic aspects of the language, as well as the cognitive challenges learners face in acquiring it. The first chapter positions the book in terms of providing a background to the learning of Japanese as a foreign language and the challenges it poses for SLA. Chapter 2 of the book deals with general background information regarding *kanji*. This includes an examination of the origin of the Japanese writing system and the categorization of *kanji* into types based on this origin. Chapter 3 looks at the fundamental differences between the memorization of a written script, which is based on morphographic symbols of meaning, as opposed to alphabetic scripts, which are based on phonology. The chapter focuses on different processing skills involved when reading Japanese. Based on these differences, the chapter outlines the challenges this poses for SLA. An understanding of written Japanese from this standpoint has implications for learners, instructors and researchers, all of which are separately presented and discussed in each chapter.

Part 2 of the book examines the cognitive aspects of the acquisition of the Japanese writing system by second language learners. It opens with Chapter 4, which outlines current theories underpinning language cognition and cognitive learning strategies. This chapter provides an overview of current thinking in the fields of cognitive science and applied linguistics, and frames this theory in the context of Japanese language learning. Chapter 5 reviews research findings in the area of visual association strategies, that is, memorizing script by visual clues including pictographic, ideographic and mnemonic associations. It draws on data from a number of studies original studies conducted in the area of cognitive learning strategies in its illustration of successful and unsuccessful examples of cognitive association in the *kanji*-learning task. However, visual association will also be explored in the learning of *kana*, as this is a popular teaching and learning method used in Japanese language classes around the world. Chapter 6 covers notions of component vs holistic approaches to *kanji* learning, which have been investigated by numerous studies. It also examines learning using radical-based systems of classification (meaning-based stems of *kanji*). This is followed by Chapter 7, which examines the use of mnemonic devices when learning *kana* and *kanji*. Mnemonic devices in Japanese language learning are popularized by a number of commercial books on *kanji* learning, and this chapter aims to examine the benefits of such devices on learning, as well as to debunk myths purported by proponents of this approach.

The third part of the book explores the notion of regulating one's learning when studying Japanese. Learning *kanji* is a laborious task that is only managed successfully by the highly motivated and self-regulated learner. This part of the book, therefore, will examine the strategies that research has shown to be useful for students to control motivation when learning *kanji*. This part opens with Chapter 8, which provides an overview of self-regulation and discusses its usefulness as a framework to explore struggles learners face in second language learning. This chapter provides an overview of modern-day theories of learner psychology and frames this theory in the context of Japanese language learning. Chapter 9 explores issues surrounding metacognition in terms of memory retrieval practice, visual memorization techniques and the role stroke order plays in *kanji* memorization. This chapter examines metacognition in terms of strategies learners apply to take control over their learning, as well as the underlying capacity some learners have to manage to task of *kanji* learning, juxtaposed against the struggles other learners face in SLA. Chapter 10 discusses goal setting in Japanese language learning and the notion of segmenting the learning process. This is an important topic in Japanese SLA, where the path to literacy in Japanese is a lifelong process. Without the setting and reassessing of short and long-term goals the Japanese language learner can easily lose direction. This is followed by Chapter 11, which explores the effect of affect (emotion) and interest in Japanese language learning. This chapter discusses issues of stress, disillusionment and loss of self-efficacy in Japanese language learning. It also discusses the obstacle of boredom in the *kanji*-learning task and the detrimental effects these psychological matters have on the language learner. The regulation of the level of satisfaction learners get when learning *kanji* is particularly important seeing as many students view the constant study and review of *kanji* as a boring and laborious task.

The final part of the book will draw conclusions for the reader based on the research presented in the preceding sections. In the spirit of previous chapters, it frames these conclusions and suggestions according to the three target readers: Japanese language learners, Japanese language instructors and Japanese language researchers. Chapter 12 focuses the language learner. It summarizes the strategies that research has shown successful learners of Japanese have used when not only learning *kanji*, but also when maintaining motivation to learn, and provides advice on how to become a better learner of Japanese. It also discusses the arguments surrounding the simplification of the Japanese writing system. Chapter 13 focuses on the language instructor. It discusses the implications of research on classroom practices and gives advice on how to better support students struggling with this complex script. The chapter also touches on issues surrounding the order *kanji* are presented in class, and issues surrounding strategy instruction. Chapter 14 focuses on the SLA researcher. It summarizes limitations of current research in the field and presents topics that are in need of future investigation. It also makes suggestions on constructing valid and reliable theoretical and methodological frameworks for these studies and discusses suitable research instruments to examine Japanese second language learning.

Developing and maintaining literacy in the Japanese language is a long learning process, but it need not be as painful for the student and the instructor as it sometimes feels. Similarly, there are many areas researchers can continue to study that will further highlight ways in which the magnitude of the *kanji*-learning task can be reduced. This book, therefore, makes a contribution not only to our academic understanding of Japanese language learning, but also in its provision of advice for the Japanese language student, instructor and researcher alike.

About the Author

Heath Rose is Associate Professor of Applied Linguistics in the Department of Education at The University of Oxford. Before moving to Oxford, he taught applied linguistics at Trinity College Dublin, where he was a committee member of the Trinity Centre for Asian Studies and was the Director of the Centre of English Language Learning and Teaching.

Heath's introduction to the Japanese language was as a high-school student in Queensland, Australia. This interest grew and prompted him to travel to Japan on a short-term exchange, and then to undertake a Bachelor of Arts in Asian Studies upon his return. He then trained as a high school English and Japanese teacher at The University of Queensland and started his career as a language teacher in Australia. He taught high-school level Japanese in Brisbane and later in a primary school in Sydney. He also taught English language in Japan for 11 years, while improving his Japanese and carrying out research.

Heath holds a Masters of Education in Second Language Teaching and a Doctor of Philosophy (PhD) in Education from The University of Sydney. His research into Japanese as a foreign language first examined the learning of the Japanese writing system by primary-aged learners and then later focused on research on university-aged learners who were studying in Japan.

Heath has published extensively in applied linguistics. He has articles published in international journals such as *Applied Linguistics*, *Modern Language Journal* and *Foreign Language Annals*. He edited a special issue of *Language Learning in Higher Education* on the teaching and learning of East Asian languages. He is co-author of a number of books on Global Englishes, including *Introducing Global Englishes* (Routledge, 2015) and *Global Englishes for Language Teaching* (Cambridge University Press, forthcoming). He is also co-editor of *Doing Research in Applied Linguistics* (Routledge, 2017)

Although Heath is now mostly involved in English language teacher training and lives outside of Japan, he maintains a research interest in the learning of Japanese as a foreign language.

This book was made possible due to research time and research funds received through a Marie Curie Career Integration Grant (FP7-PEOPLE-2012-CIG – 333171).

Part 1

Issues Surrounding Japanese Language Acquisition

1 Introduction

An Overview of Japanese Language Education

The teaching and learning of Japanese language around the world is a relatively new area of study compared to traditional European languages, with most programs being established within the last 40 years. As such, relative to other European languages, little is known in regard to how it is acquired as a second language. Unlike the learning of European languages by other European language speakers, the learning of East Asian languages has predominantly developed after the Second World War. Interest in the learning of the Japanese language in Western countries was largely due to globalization, which brought the East and the West closer together economically and politically. Japanese language education first grew from the increasing economic strength of Japan, beginning in the late 1970s and early 1980s. One driving force for language education growth was in response to an increase in tourism from Japan around the world. With a stronger economy came an increase in population mobility, which brought European language speaking nations such as France, the UK, the USA and Australia into direct contact with large numbers of Japanese tourists for the first time. The numbers of outbound tourists leaving Japan during this economic boom skyrocketed, as can be seen in Figure 1.1.

Also during this time, the global economy saw an influx of trade with Japan and closer economic and political relationships. In the 1970s, Japan grew to be the world's third largest economy and the nation soon became the second largest economy by 1980. With the growth of Japan on the global stage, the need to learn Japanese as a foreign language naturally grew. Nations such as Australia and the USA were quicker than others to fill a need for Japanese language programs, perhaps due to strong Pacific trade ties.

Interestingly, despite its recent entry among language study options, Japanese language education around the world has boomed (Bramley & Hanamura, 1998). Notably in the USA, Australia, New Zealand and the UK, the number of students enrolled in Japanese courses increased dramatically in the 1980s and 1990s, leading to the growth of Japanese language programs at the university level (Komiya-Samimy & Tabuse, 1992). In Australia, for

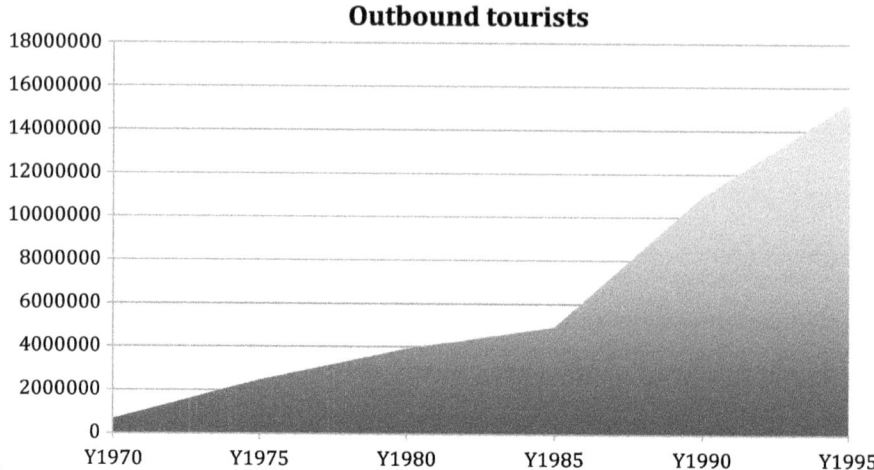

Figure 1.1 Outbound tourists from Japan
Source: Japan Ministry of Justice

example, Japanese quickly rose to prominence due to state government initiatives such as those by Education Queensland, which elevated Japanese as a major language study option in Queensland's public schools in the 1980s. Much of this push by governments in the 1980s to learn Japanese was due to financial incentives related the booming tourism and economic trade associated with Japan at the time.

Furthermore, Japan was viewed as a traditionally a monolingual, monoethnic and monocultural country (Noguchi & Fotos, 2001), with 98% of the population categorized as ethnically Japanese (Suzuki, 2006). Thus, there was a much larger perceived language barrier to overcome when conducting business with Japan as opposed to other Asian economic powers at the time, such as in Hong Kong and Singapore where English was widely used as the lingua franca of certain segments of education and governance. It was, therefore, deemed more desirable for students to learn Japanese in order to take advantage of these economic benefits compared to other Asian market countries, where English was more widely understood and used (e.g. Singapore, Malaysia and Hong Kong). For these reasons, the major driving force in the boom of Japanese education was largely due to government educational policy in countries that wanted to increase economic trade with Japan.

When the bubble economy of Japan burst, so did some of the driving forces for governments to promote Japanese language education. In the 1990s and 2000s, other languages such as Korean and Chinese rose to prominence for the very same reason that Japanese was promoted in the 1980s. These days we can see a similar situation to Japanese language education in the 1980s occurring in the push to learn Mandarin Chinese as a foreign language, in response to China's rise as the current second largest global economy.

Despite the economic shift in focus, however, Japanese language education has continued to boom around the world, although students' current reasons for wanting to learn it as a foreign language are no longer wholly centered on economic reasons. With the economic rise to prominence of Japan in the 1980s came an increase in cultural interest in Japan. The younger generation around the world, who had grown up knowing Japan as a world economic power, were also exposed to cultural aspects of Japan. This exposure in turn sparked interest in travel to Japan and interest in learning the Japanese language and culture. More recently, the world is witnessing an explosion of interest in anime and manga around the world, further fueling the younger generation's desire to learn the Japanese language and to go to Japan to study and experience Japan first-hand.

Evidence of the continued boom in Japanese language learning can be found by examination of the number of students taking the Japanese language proficiency test each year, which is an international, standard test of Japanese ability. The number of examinees in 1993 was 80,000, compared to 270,000 in 2003 and 560,000 in 2008 (Japan Foundation, 2009). Recent statistics from the Japan Foundation's Survey Report on Japanese-Language Education Abroad (Japan Foundation, 2013) also highlight an increase in Japanese language studies around the world. Table 1.1 shows the top 10 countries by Japanese language learners, with the change from 2009 to 2012 shown.

In conjunction with this increase in the number of students studying Japanese language, there has been an increase in the number of students travelling to Japan to study, as shown in Figure 1.2.

The Japanese Ministry of Education reported the number of foreign students (rounded to the nearest 1000) studying within Japan in 2003 numbered 109,000, compared with just 50,000 in 1993 and 10,000 in 1983

Table 1.1 Number of Japanese language learners

		2009	2012	Change (%)
1	China	827,171	1,046,490	27
2	Indonesia	716,353	872,411	22
3	Korea	964,014	840,187	−13
4	Australia	275,710	296,672	8
5	Taiwan	247,641	233,417	−6
6	USA	141,244	155,939	10
7	Thailand	78,802	129,616	65
8	Vietnam	44,272	46,762	6
9	Malaysia	22,856	33,077	45
10	Philippines	22,362	32,418	45

Source: Japan Foundation (2013).

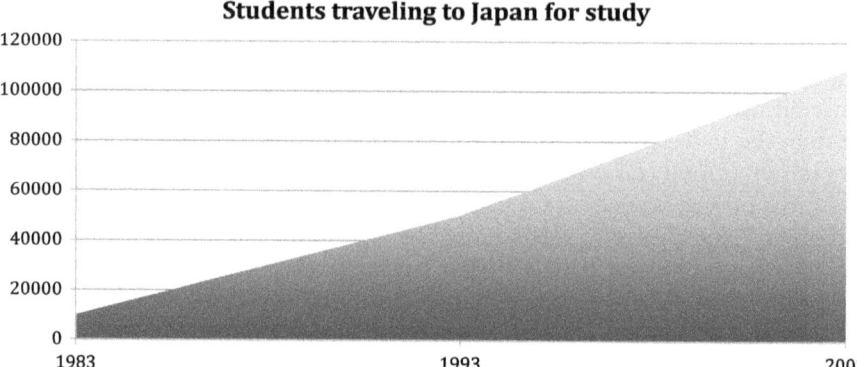

Figure 1.2 Students traveling to Japan for study purposes
Source: Japan Ministry of Education

(MEXT, 2004). Of these 109,000 foreign students in 2003, 7000 were students at Japanese universities on short-term language programs of less than a year for the purpose of intensive language and cultural study (MEXT, 2004). In 2005, this number increased again to 122,000 (Guruz, 2008). Furthermore, a recent initiative by Japan's Ministry of Education plans to increase the number of foreign students in Japanese universities to 300,000 by the year 2020 (Shimauchi, 2009). Thus, it is clear that Japanese language education is an area of continued growth both in and outside of Japan. This growth in the teaching of Japanese language has also brought about a growth in educational research concerning the learning of Japanese as a foreign language, especially in the field of SLA, which has allowed us to better understand how students learn Japanese (Bramley & Hanamura, 1998).

Why a Book on Learning Japanese Writing?

Despite this surge in Japanese language education, there have been a number of studies that have highlighted students' difficulties in learning Japanese, which are linked to a higher attrition rate in Japanese language programs, especially if the students come from an English-speaking background (Kato, 2000, 2002). Hatasa (1989) and Dwyer (1997), for example, have found university students of Japanese are progressing more slowly in language development than students of other languages in terms of overall proficiency. A study by Walton (1993) reported that it took students of Japanese three times as long to acquire the same level of proficiency as more commonly taught languages such as French, German or Spanish. More recently, Everson (2011) used a study of language training required for State Department employees (Jackson & Malone, 2009) to suggest languages such as Japanese and Chinese take at least four times as long to acquire than European languages. Dwyer (1997) also found students of Japanese were not reading as much as students of European languages and suggested the problem appeared to be the insurmountable barriers posed by the Japanese writing system.

The Japanese writing system is particularly complex from a linguistic perspective. Generally speaking, the world's writing systems fall within three categories: morphographic scripts, syllabic scripts and alphabetic scripts.

Morphographic scripts represent morphemes in a language. A morpheme is the smallest unit of meaning that a word can be broken into. For example, the word *black* contains one morpheme. The word *blackboard* contains two: *black* and *board*, which each hold a meaning. The word *unease* also contains two morphemes: *un* and *ease*. Even though *un* is not an word in itself, it does hold meaning; it assigns the negative from to the morpheme which follows it. An example of a modern morphographic script is Chinese *hanzi*. This system of writing began as a logographic script (symbols representing words), and then later evolved into a morphographic script as more complex language required written representation. Even though historically most of the world's writing systems originated as logographs, Chinese is one of the few morphographic writing systems remaining (although in modern Chinese, many characters represent language phonologically). In Chinese, one morpheme is represented by one character. For example, the *hanzi* for *unease* contains too characters [不安], one representing the negative *un* and the other representing *ease*.

Syllabic scripts represent syllables in the language (a syllabic script is often referred to as a sy syllabary). A syllable is the articulation of a single segment of uninterrupted sound, which includes a vowel, and often is preceded and/or succeeded by a consonant. The Japanese word *maguro*, contains three syllables *ma*, *gu* and *ro*. Thus, a syllabic script would need three separate characters to represent this word, one for each syllable. Japanese *katakana* is an example of a syllabic script, and thus the word *maguro* can be represented with three symbols: マグロ. Other well-known syllabaries include the historical Linear B, the Cherokee syllabary and the Vai syllabary.

Alphabetic scripts represent phonemes in a language. A phoneme is the smallest unit of sound that is distinguishable in speech. Most alphabetic scripts use one letter to represent a single sound. A well-known alphabet is the one in which this book is written, the Roman alphabet, which was developed to represent the Latin language. A word like *agenda*, for example, contains six phonemes, each represented by a letter. Interestingly, because the Roman alphabet was borrowed for the English language, the fit is not as exact (a phenomenon we will return to in the next chapter). We do not have enough letters in the Roman alphabet to represent all phonemes in the English language. To fit the English language, we would need at least six additional letters to represent vowels and we would need to repurpose other letters to represent those sounds that have no corresponding letter, such as the initial phonemes in the words <u>th</u>ink, <u>th</u>ey, <u>g</u>enre and <u>sh</u>eet.

As mentioned, the writing systems used to represent major world languages generally fall within one of these three groups. Mandarin and Cantonese are morphographic. English, Russian and Korean (Hangul) are alphabetic. Syllabic scripts are less common in representing modern languages, but ancient languages such as Mayan and Sumerian used syllabaries. Japanese, on the other hand, is highly unusual because of the fact that it uses a morphographic script, two syllabic scripts and an alphabetic script, side-by-side, to represent the language: *kanji* (morphographic), two forms of *kana* (syllabic) and *romaji* (alphabetic). In terms of the challenges this complex writing system causes learners in SLA, *kanji* appears to be the most difficult of these four scripts. Due to its representation of the morphemes in a language, rather than the phonology of a language, *kanji* is furthest removed from the writing systems that most of the world's learners are used to (except, of course, Chinese language speakers). Each *kanji* often has multiple *readings,* or ways of pronouncing a single character, depending on its context and use. Learners must know 2000 *kanji* to be functionally literate in the Japanese language. It is for this reason, that *kanji* will be the main focus of this book.

It is widely documented that Japanese foreign language learners struggle with the mastery of the Japanese written language, particularly if their first language's script is alphabetic (Rose & Harbon, 2013; Shimizu, 1995, 1999; Toyoda, 1998, 2000; Toyoda & Kubota, 2001). Many teachers and learners, therefore, seek assistance in order to help students of Japanese to overcome the barrier to literacy that not being able to read creates for learners of the language. Research into the second language learning of *kanji*, usually falls into three categories:

(1) The examination of learning strategies that successful learners use to memorize this difficult script.
(2) The examination of cognitive processes involved when learners of phonological writing systems encounter morphographic representations of language for the first time.
(3) The examination of self-directed learning (or self-regulation) utilized by learners in this arduous learning task.

This books aims to explore each of these areas in depth, to paint a full picture of the SLA of the Japanese written language.

This book is also intended as an important resource to summarize recent research on the topic of learning the Japanese writing system in terms of strategies students can use to learn this complex script. Language learning strategies are defined as specific actions, behaviors, steps or techniques that students use to improve their skills in a second language (Oxford, 2001). Research has also suggested that we examine learners' capacity to regulate the study of language and control their motivation to learn (see, for example, Dörnyei, 2005; Dörnyei & Skehan, 2003; Tseng *et al.*, 2006). This book uses notions of learning strategies to examine the cognitive processes involved when memorizing and learning *kanji*, as it is a useful way to explore the mental activities and actions that learners deploy to learn more effectively. In terms of the psychological and behavioral aspects of learning, the book uses the framework of self-regulation. Self-regulation refers to the degree to which learners are active participants in their own learning and are proactive in their pursuit of language learning (Dörnyei, 2005). Thus, in terms of language learning, self-regulation culminates in the strategies students use to control motivation to learn, which Dörnyei (2005) terms as *motivation control strategies*. This book, therefore, examines the topic of *kanji* learning within these parameters of cognition, psychology and behavior.

In the past 30 years, there have been numerous and often singular research projects that examine many facets of learning the Japanese writing system in second language learning contexts. However, as of yet, there exists no single resource that ties this research together to give a clear picture of what previous studies have shown. This book also heavily draws upon my own research into *kanji* learning strategies that has spanned the past 10 years and covers Japanese language learning from elementary school to the university level. In this respect, the book is primarily a valuable resource for researchers of Japanese language education.

Furthermore, this book aims at making these research findings accessible to the Japanese language learner and instructor. Often, learners are bewildered by the task of *kanji* learning and, research has indicated that the attitudes of teachers towards teaching *kanji* and their own teaching strategies are multidimensional and complex (Shimizu & Green, 2002). Both teachers and learners are often told conflicting stories about strategies that work and do not work. A market that has been flooded with books that claim to teach students to learn *kanji* using 'simple' strategies does not help this situation. These books claim that *kanji* can be learned by mastering a singular 'foolproof' strategy such as the use of mnemonics devices (or stories) to help them remember *kanji* and their components. My research has shown these books can do more damage than good to the Japanese language learner, when they discover that mastering *kanji* is a much more complex task than is claimed, and a singular strategy to learn all *kanji* is clearly insufficient (Rose, 2013; see also Chapter 7, this volume). On the contrary, this book shows the learning and teaching of *kanji* is a complex and demanding task for the learner and instructor. Therefore, this book aims at dissecting what research has actually shown regarding *kanji* learning and disseminating it in easy to understand terms so that learners and instructors can be more aware of the strategies and processes needed to further improve their written proficiency in the Japanese language. This book integrates a number of my own original studies into Japanese language learning with modern research in order to provide a full picture of the complexity of studying the Japanese writing system.

Original Research Used in this Book

This book draws on studies into the learning of the Japanese writing system by non-Japanese learners. These studies have been conducted over the past 30 years when Japanese began to grow as a foreign language option in Western countries. The book also draws on examples from three original studies conducted by the author over the past 13 years. Some results of these studies have been published elsewhere (see Rose, 2003, 2012b, 2013; Rose & Harbon, 2013), but much of the data generated in these studies will be reported here for the first time. Throughout the book, I aim to clearly indicate through in-text citations when data are drawn from previously published research, in the same way that any published research would be referred to. In cases where the book refers to particular studies (e.g. *The Intervention Study*, *The Strategies Study* and *The Self-regulation Study*), it can be assumed that the results of these studies are discussed here for the first time. The three studies are outlined below.

The Intervention Study

The first study involved single case research into the learning strategies used by a class of Year 6 students in a Sydney elementary school, who were studying Japanese as a foreign language. Single-case research follows a similar design as experimental research, as Nunan (1994) explains:

> The difference between experimental research and single case research is that experimental studies typically involve comparing two or more groups, while single-case research, like the case study, involves a single individual or group and does not attempt to set up experimental and control groups. (Nunan, 1994: 82)

The study aimed to answer the following research questions:

(1) What *kanji* learning strategies do primary school age Japanese as a foreign language learners use when memorizing *kanji*?
(2) Can *kanji* learning strategies observed in successful language learners be taught to less successful learners to improve learning ability?

In this study, the participants were given 20 minutes to memorize a list of unknown *kanji* and to complete a questionnaire in which they reported the learning strategies they had used. The first part of the questionnaire had students self-report strategy use according to an inventory of known strategies used by learners of Japanese as a foreign language. The second part of the questionnaire asked them to specifically explain how they had tried to memorize each of the *kanji*. After an hour, students were given a *kanji* test to measure the success rate that they had remembered the list of *kanji*. Those students who had remembered all *kanji* in the list were identified as the most successful learners and those students who had recalled the fewest *kanji* were identified as the least successful learners. Three of the most successful learners and two of the least successful learners were interviewed in order to have them elaborate on the learning strategies used.

One week later, the students were given a second list of *kanji* and were instructed to learn them for 20 minutes according to the successful learning strategies that were observed in the first stage of the study. As with the first stage of the experiment, students were given a questionnaire and then a *kanji* test one hour later in order to measure differences between learning processes and success rates between the first and second stages of the research. Data from both stages were compared to answer the second research question regarding whether learning strategies could be taught for learner success. Some aspects of the first study were published in the *Journal for the Modern Teachers Association of Australia* (Rose, 2003), but most of the data from this study will be referred to in this book for the first time.

The Strategies Study

The second study took place at two universities in Japan, and followed the learning of a group of participants over a year-long exchange. In regard to the Japanese language curriculum, students at both universities had one 90-minute lesson per week of *kanji* instruction. In this class, students were taught weekly lists of *kanji*, engaged in learning activities (namely the learning of *kanji* compounds, *kanji* writing practice and *kanji* review) and they sat regular bi-weekly *kanji* tests. The students were divided into six levels at both universities ranging from complete beginner to advanced and the study aimed to include students from the full range of proficiency. Participants included 17 students; although this number was later reduced to 12 cases in order examine even numbers of participants who exhibited strategic behavior. Grenfell and Macaro (2007: 15) argue, 'it is theoretically possible to be a "good" beginner language learner and a "poor" advanced learner', so this was also taken into account when reducing the number of participants in order that potential successful and unsuccessful learners were included in the mix. All students were on a year-long language exchange from their usual full time studies at American, Australian or UK universities; seven were American, one was Australian, one British and the remaining three were nationals of Thailand, the Philippines and Burma, who were enrolled in American universities.

This study aimed to answer the following two questions:

(1) In terms of learning strategies, how do learners of Japanese from alphabetic language backgrounds learn *kanji*?
(2) How do these learning patterns develop over a year of *kanji* instruction, which includes a raised awareness of strategies due to participation in the project?

In the study, participants took part in an initial interview to ascertain their use of *kanji* learning strategies. A self-report inventory of *kanji* strategy use was also used to quantitatively measure strategies used. After this initial interview, students took part in bi-weekly interviews that coincided with *kanji* tests taken by the students. In the interviews, participants were asked to elaborate on how they had approached the *kanji*-learning task, leading up to these *kanji* tests. The interview also included a stimulated recall task, where participants were asked to review that week's list of *kanji* and to re-take the *kanji* test in front of the researcher, while voicing out loud their cognitive processes to explain how they had remembered and recalled each of the *kanji*. Mackey and Gass (2005: 226) define stimulated recall as 'an introspective technique for gathering data that can yield insights into a learner's thought processes during language learning experiences. Learners are asked to introspect while viewing or hearing stimulus to prompt their recollections'.

Over the course of the 10 interviews, the study revealed patterns in how students approached the *kanji* learning task, as well as changes in learning techniques over time. Some results of this study were presented in a paper (Rose, 2013), which only examined one of several strategies for learning *kanji*. Most of the results from this study will be referred to in Part 2 of this book for the first time.

The Self-regulation Study

The third study used the same participants in *The Strategies Study*, but examined a separate aspect of the learning process, that of self-regulation. The participants were interviewed 10 times throughout the year in order to provide insight into the issues surrounding self-regulation of *kanji* learning. The interview questions were derived from focus groups with two groups of five students during a pilot study. This method followed that used in a study by Tseng *et al.* (2006), which examined self-regulation in vocabulary learning, a process not dissimilar to the learning of *kanji*.

The study aimed to answer two questions:

(1) In terms of self-regulation, how do learners of Japanese from alphabetic language backgrounds learn *kanji*?
(2) How does self-regulation develop over a year of *kanji* instruction?

This provided insight into the struggles of students learning the Japanese writing system from various perspectives including challenges in setting goals, controlling procrastination, dealing with emotional aspects connected to learning Japanese, as well as negotiating the time-consuming and arduous task of learning lists of hundreds of *kanji*. Some results from the study have been reported in Rose and Harbon (2013), but most of the findings are reported for the first time in Part 3 of this book.

Significance of the Research Showcased in this Book

To sum up, this book aims to make a significant contribution to SLA research in the following ways. First, the research in this book will help to move the field of language learning strategy research in a new direction by incorporating self-regulation into its theoretical framework, a movement supported by many scholars in the field (e.g. see Gao, 2006; Rose, 2012b; Tseng *et al.*, 2006). Second, it draws on data yielded by data collection instruments such as stimulated recall tasks and interviews in its in-depth qualitative approach. This follows recommendations of critics of learning strategy research (e.g. see Dörnyei, 2005; Woodrow, 2005) to adopt more qualitative approaches. Although the aim of the book is not to present a lot of research data, some excerpts from the studies will be drawn upon throughout the book to illustrate various points. The research in the book takes a context-specific approach in its data collection, embracing the cultural and environmental influences on learning. This move is supported by recommendations of scholars such as Woodrow (2005) and Takeuchi *et al.* (2007), who argue that any research into language learner strategies must take into account the contextual influences on learning for language learning tasks. The book also approaches the issue of *kanji* learning using an original theoretical framework (Rose, 2012b), which is based on the researcher's original past published research (Rose, 2012a; Rose & Harbon, 2013). Furthermore, the research in the book explores the learning of the Japanese writing system by native English speakers, which will help further our understanding of SLA in a field saturated with studies of learning English as a second or foreign language. Finally, the focus of this book, and its inclusion in an SLA series that is heavily focused on English SLA, will help to diversify the field's understanding of the acquisition of languages other than English.

2 The Japanese Writing System

This chapter will review literature on the Japanese written language. First, the components of the Japanese writing system will be defined in terms of its use in representing the Japanese language. The chapter will also outline ways to classify *kanji* in terms of its origin and linguistic representation. Linguistic representation of *kanji* has direct implications on the Japanese language learner, as an understanding of different *kanji* types has implications on the types of strategies that will be more effective to learn each type of *kanji*. Furthermore, an understanding of *kanji* classification will combat the erroneous belief held by many beginner learners of Japanese that all *kanji* are pictographic representations of their meaning. We will discover, in fact, that very few *kanji* are pure pictographs.

Components of the Japanese Writing System

The complexity of the Japanese writing system owes much to its historical development in representing the language. Currently there are five scripts that comprise the Japanese writing system:

(1) *Kanji*: a morphographic script that were adopted from Chinese.
(2) *Hiragana*: a syllabic script that were created from *kanji*.
(3) *Katakana*: a syllabic script that represent language in the same way as *hiragana*, but for the purposes of representing 'foreign' loan words.
(4) *Romaji*: an alphabetic script used in modern-day Japanese for stylistic purposes.
(5) Arabic numerals: a script used to represent numbers in the same way that it is used in the English language.

These five scripts are used interchangeably in the Japanese writing system as can be seen in Figure 2.1, which is an excerpt taken from a Wikipedia article on Ireland (https://ja.wikipedia.org/wiki/ireland). In the figure, *katakana* is underlined with a straight line, *hiragana* is underlined with a wavy line, *Romaji* and Arabic numerals are italicized and *kanji* is unmarked.

> アイルランド共和国（アイルランドきょうわこく、アイルランド語: *Éire*、英語: *Ireland*）、またはアイルランドは、北大西洋のアイルランド島に存在する立憲共和制国家である。北東に英国北 アイルランドと接する。首都はアイルランド島中東部の都市ダブリン。ナショナルカラーは緑。独立時の経緯によりアイルランド島の北東部北アイルランド六州は英国を構成するが、アイルランド共和国は *1998* 年のベルファスト合意以前は全島の領有権を主張していた。2005 年の英エコノミスト誌の調査では最も住みやすい国に選出されている。

Figure 2.1 An excerpt to illustrate the scripts of the Japanese writing system

As Taylor and Taylor (1995: 295) point out, 'all these various types of script originated elsewhere and have been adopted and adapted by the Japanese over hundreds of years'. Each element of the Japanese writing system will be discussed in turn in this chapter, in terms of its historical emergence and modern-day usage.

Hiragana and *Katakana*

Hiragana and *katakana* are the two syllabaries of the Japanese language. A syllabary is a type of script that represents the syllables of a language (usually an isolated vowel sound, or a consonant + vowel sound). Historically, many writing systems of the world started out as syllabaries and were adapted into alphabets when the need to represent complex consonant structures emerged in a language. English, for example, would not be a good language to represent with a syllabic script due to the complex combination of consonant strings that exist (think of the number of sounds that exist in the single syllable of the word 'strengths' in English). Japanese, however, mostly follows a systematic syllabic structure that comprises single consonant and vowel sounds. In the following description, I have chosen not to use phonetic symbols to describe the phonemes in the Japanese language, but instead have chosen the depictions of these vowel and consonant sounds as they appear in *romaji*. This decision was made so that the connection between the phonemes and the writing system is more apparent to the reader, many of whom may not be familiar with phonetic symbols.

Only the final consonant of /n/ in Japanese (e.g. in the suffix *san*) and the glottal stop depicted by a double /t/ (e.g. *wakatta*) prevent the Japanese language from being perfectly depicted by a pure syllabary. As a result, the Japanese language is comprised of five vowel sounds (/a/, /i/, /e/, /o/, /u/) in combination with its consonantal sounds. In Japan, these sound combinations are often depicted in a *hiragana* chart called *gojuon* [五十音], literally 'fifty sounds' of the Japanese language. However, this is a bit misleading as there are actually in excess of 100 such sounds. These sounds comprise of the five vowel sounds listed above in combination with 14 consonantal sounds /k/, /g/, /s/, /z/, /t/, /d/, /n/, /h/, /p/, /b/, /m/, /y/, /r/, /w/, plus the need for a single consonant /n/ and symbol for a glottal stop. But, not all combinations exist in the Japanese language, such as the absence of a /ye/ and /yi/ sound, and the absence of a /we/, /wi/ and /wu/ sound. There are also 30 glide combinations of three vowel sounds (/a/, /o/, /u/) with /my/, /ny/, /ky/, /gy/, /hy/, /by/, /py/, /chy/, /jy/ and /ry/. Also, other sounds have shifted over time in vernacular Japanese, such as a /shi/ sound replacing the /si/ combination, a /chi/ sound replacing the /ti/ combination, a /fu/ sound replacing the /hu/ combination and a /tsu/ replacing /tu/. As such, a total of 102 individual syllabic symbols would be needed to represent the syllables of the Japanese language, making it a very suitable language for a syllabary (English would need in excess of 15,000 such symbols to represent all of its syllables). The *hiragana* and *katakana*, however, reduce this number of symbols to just 46 by adding discourse markers that indicate a change in voiced consonants. For example, the syllables /ku/ and /gu/ are written using the same symbol, with an addition of a diacritic or discourse marker on the latter as in く and ぐ. The same diacritic [``] is also used to change the initial /s/ to /z/, /t/ to /d/ and /h/ to /b/, as in the examples of [sa] and [za], [ta] and [da] and [ha] and [ba]. A different diacritic [O] is used to change the initial /h/ to a /p/ (see Table 2.1 for this reduced table).

Table 2.1 Fifty sounds of Japanese: Represented by *hiragana*

	–	k	s	t	n	h	m	y	r	other
a	あ	か	さ	た	な	は	ま	や	ら	わ
i	い	き	し*	ち*	に	ひ	み		り	
u	う	く	す	つ*	ぬ	ふ*	む	ゆ	る	を
e	え	け	せ	て	ね	へ	め		れ	
o	お	こ	そ	と	の	ほ	も	よ	ろ	ん
Diacritic ``		g	z	d		b				
Diacritic O						p				

Furthermore, the glide sounds are depicted with the addition of a small /ya/, /yo/ or /yu/ symbol to cut down on the need for 30 additional letters in the syllabary, for example, /kya/ is represented by the /ki/ + small /ya/ (きゃ) and /nyu/ is represented by /ni/ + small /yu/ (にゅ), and so forth. Finally, the glottal stop is represented through the repurposing of the /tsu/ (つ) symbol, but in smaller form, as in the word wakatta [分かった]. The end result is a 46 letter syllabary (plus four obsolete combinations) that represents all sounds in the Japanese language, thus the notion of the 50 sounds in Japanese has emerged.

Romaji

The name of the script is borrowed from this origin: ローマ字 [*romaji*], literally *Roman letters*. Movements to write Japanese in *romaji* gained momentum after the Meiji restoration on the grounds that it would improve education and literacy, and help Japan modernize (Gottlieb, 2010). All children in Japan today learn to read and write Japanese in the Roman alphabet and it is considered to be a useful phonetic script, which is used to complement, rather than replace other scripts in the writing system. Despite being universally understood, it is very rare to find samples of the Japanese language written exclusively in *romaji*; if people want to write the Japanese language phonetically, it is usually done so through *kana*. However, despite its recent prevalence, the use of *romaji* in Japan dates back to at least the Meiji era, where there were some unsuccessful movements to abolish the complicated Japanese writing system for *romaji*, although these movements were largely academic and failed to catch on in wider society.

In more recent times, computers brought about an increase in writing in *romaji*, where the Japanese language is entered into a word processor in *romaji*, before being converted into *kanji* and *kana*. The system proved to be a useful way to type in *kanji* for the first time, as typesetting before the computer era was often a time-consuming and painstakingly slow process. Other recent computing developments have seen many Japanese people move to touch screen systems on smart phones that allow the user to rapidly select *kana*, by touching on a key which represents the initial sound of a syllable and swiping up, down, left or right for the corresponding vowel sound. Thus, the era of typing Japanese in *romaji* may be short-lived for some devices, which are adapting to new technology very quickly. For the time being, however, typing *kanji* into computers via a *romaji* keyboard remains the most prevalent method.

The use of *romaji* in fields of creative design is thriving in Japan. *Romaji* is often used on signs, magazine covers, t-shirts and merchandise. Company logos and slogans often incorporate *romaji* into them, as well as in advertisements. The decision to use *romaji* is often a stylistic, rather than linguistic, choice; however, in 2002, the Ministry of Justice approved the use of *romaji* in the registration of Japanese company names, which removed a rule that had prevailed since 1893 (Gottlieb, 2010), indicating that *romaji* is making further inroads into realms of usages where it was once excluded.

Another common domain for the use of *romaji* is to represent words of Japanese origin into English, for example, proper names and food items in materials made for tourists would be written in *romaji*. However, even this is not a simple task, due to different spelling standards of Romanization over time. Variants of conventions of Romanization exist, which mainly fall into three systems:

(1) The Hepburn system, developed by an American missionary, and later standardized by American organizations, and thus widely used by foreign speakers of Japanese.

(2) Nihon-shiki [Japanese style], developed in the late 1800s as a way to write the Japanese language in the roman alphabet.
(3) Kunrei-shiki [cabinet decree style], which aimed to standardize Nihon-shiki Romanization.

The major differences between the three styles are depictions of *kana*, which fall outside the perfect consonant plus vowel syllabary, for example:

- *Kana* that represent glides before the vowel (e.g. To<u>kyo</u>, <u>nyu</u>shi and <u>ryo</u>ri).
- *Kana* that represent an elongated vowel sound (e.g. Oosaka).
- *Kana* that fall outside the standard pronunciation of the initial consonant in the syllabary set (e.g. fu as opposed to hu; shi as opposed to si; tsu as opposed to tu; chi as opposed to ti).

Table 2.2 shows example words with different romanization to illustrate the key differences between the three systems. Furthermore, variants also exist outside of these categories. The initial おお combination, which is common in Japanese names, can be represented by Oh, Oo or Ō. The final sound in the above example of company head [しゃちょう] can be also be depicted as ou, in addition to ō or ô. Indeed, when typing it into a computer, many programs require this sound to be entered as ou, even though it does not fall into any of the Romanization standards in Table 2.2.

Generally speaking, the Hepburn system is most useful for learners wanting an accurate phonological representation of the Japanese language. To illustrate, the ちぢみ example below accurately describes to the reader that the middle syllable in the word is pronounced *ji*. A beginner learner, who encounters the Nihonshiki or Kunreishiki versions of this word, would most likely be led to produce the incorrect pronunciation of the word. However, the Hepburn system does not portray to the learner whether the middle *kana* for the word *chijimi* would be じ or ぢ, which might then cause confusion when writing the *kana*. For these reasons, teachers are often keen to have learners read and write in *kana* very early on in the learning process, to avoid such inconsistencies.

Table 2.2 Romanization systems for Japanese

English	Kana	Hepburn	Kunreishiki	Nihonshiki
Mount Fuji	ふじさん	fujisan	hujisan	hujisan
Company head	しゃちょう	shachō	syatyô	syatyô
Continue	つづく	tsuzuku	tuzuku	tuduku
Grammatical marker	を	o	wo	o
Korean pancake	ちぢみ	chijimi	tizimi	Tidimi

However, a lack of understanding of Romanization systems for the Japanese language may cause confusion later down the line, if learners need to draw on this knowledge. Anecdotally speaking, I learned to read and write *kana* very early on in my acquisition of Japanese. Thus, years on, when I began typing in Japanese, I got very frustrated with my inability to type infrequently used *kana* such as ち or づ. A lack of knowledge of the *nihonshiki* and *kunreishiki* versions of *romaji*, prevented me from fully understanding which combinations of roman letters I needed to enter to convert into the correct *kana*.

Kanji: The backbone of the writing system

Kanji are morphographic characters that originated in China and were introduced to Japan with Buddhism between the 4th and 7th centuries. *Kanji* can be defined as: 'graphic symbol[s] representing a lexical morpheme with no systematic relationship to the corresponding spoken sounds, each morpheme being represented by a specifically shaped character' (Paradis *et al.*, 1985). From its historical beginnings, there were many problems with the adoption of the Chinese writing system to represent the Japanese language. The two languages are not only syntactically and grammatically different, but also are written using a different word order. Chinese characters are well-suited to represent content words, but in the Japanese language where adjectives and verb endings conjugate according to grammatical context and tense, Chinese characters were an impossible match with Japanese language construction.

However, these problems were at first ignored and Chinese characters were the sole script in Japan until two forms of syllabary (*kana*), were created out of *kanji* during the 9th century, when it was realized that *kanji* alone were inadequate to represent the Japanese language. It was also thought that a less educated population, including women at the time, would be able to use the *kana* to write the Japanese language. Although *kana* could technically be used in place of *kanji*, over time it has instead been used in tandem with *kanji* as a way to fill grammatical gaps in the language that existed because the Chinese-based writing system could not represent the Japanese language appropriately due to this fundamental grammatical difference.

Although *kanji* were supplemented by *kana*, they still remain the backbone of the Japanese writing system today, with approximately 10,000 *kanji* in use in the Japanese written language (Taylor & Taylor, 1995). Of these 10,000 *kanji*, however, only 2000 of the most frequently occurring *kanji* are needed to function as literate members of Japanese society (Chikamatsu, 2005). These 2000 *kanji* account for 99% of the *kanji* occurring in printed matter, thus 'it is conventionally thought that Japanese adults need to know 2000 *kanji* to read Japanese newspapers or published materials in Japan' (Chikamatsu, 2005: 73). Foreign students of the Japanese language, therefore, also need to master these 2000 *kanji* to be able to read the Japanese language at a functionally literate level.

Although *kanji* are described as being pictorial representations of meaning, the majority of these 2000 essential *kanji* are not pictographs. In general terms, there are three major categories of *kanji* that are easily distinguishable:

(1) pictorial characters: 'stylised representations of the object they represent';
(2) abstract characters: 'arbitrary symbols for words'; and
(3) combination characters: 'the synthesis of two characters (or components) into one'.

(Paradis *et al.*, 1985: 26)

For further illustration, Table 2.3 contains basic examples of each *kanji* type with explanations of each character's features.

This, however, is a somewhat overly simplistic categorization of *kanji*. Many scholars refer to a traditional categorization system that includes six types of *kanji* based on actual etymology. Early records of this system can be found in the manuscript 説文解字 [Setsumonkaiji], which was a 2nd century Chinese dictionary from the Han Dynasty era. These types are:

(1) Shokeimoji (pictographs): Pictorial representations of meaning.
(2) Shijimoji (logograms): Symbolic representation of abstract ideas.
(3) Kaiimoji (ideographs): A combination of pictographic components.
(4) Keiseimoji (semasio-phonetic ideographs): A combination of components, of which one gives a clue to the original Chinese pronunciation or meaning.
(5) Tenchuumoji (derivative characters): *Kanji* that have been derived from an original concept that has been disassociated.
(6) Kashamoji (phonetic loan characters): *Kanji* that have been adopted into current usage for phonetic reasons.

Although this six-type classification system is a more accurate depiction of *kanji* type, for the beginning *kanji* learner, the three basic types are

Table 2.3 Examples of *kanji* types

Kanji	*Meaning*	Kanji *type*	*Explanation*
木	tree	Pictorial	Stylized representation of a tree.
田	rice field	Pictorial	Stylized representation of a rice field.
赤	red	Abstract	Abstract symbol for the color red.
万	10,000	Abstract	Abstract symbol for the number 10,000.
飲	drink	Combination	A synthesis of characters, including the *kanji* 食 and 欠.
語	language	Combination	A synthesis of characters, including the *kanji* for speak 言, mouth 口 and the number 5 五.

probably sufficient enough to differentiate between *kanji* types, without causing too much confusion and creating unnecessary complexity to the already complex task of *kanji* learning.

It is also necessary to point out the fundamental differences between Chinese characters and Japanese *kanji*. First, it is important to emphasize that although their origins came from the same script 1500 years ago, and most of the Japanese characters are recognizable by Chinese language speakers, the two scripts are mutually unintelligible due to 1500 years of use and development in two mutually unintelligible languages. While it is true that a Japanese language speaker may be able to understand menus, signs and succeed in limited communication with a Chinese speaker in written form, this is the nature of a script that is based on representation of content words, and should not be mistaken as indication that that the written languages are mutually understandable. In fact, these similarities should not be treated any differently from an English speaker being able to understand an Italian menu or being able to pick up the gist of simple communication in Italian due to the influence of Latin in both languages. Indeed, Italian and English are more closely related than Japanese and Chinese, which come from completely different language families. In fact, in this respect, English is closer to Hindi, than Japanese is to Chinese.

Second, in mainland China the written characters have been simplified in an effort to ease the burden placed on the population to reach and maintain literacy in the language. This means that the physical form of Chinese characters has deviated somewhat from *kanji*. Some examples of this simplification would be the *kanji* for electricity 電 → 电; for gate 門 → 门; and for wind 風 → 风. In addition to this, Japan has made notable attempts to simplify the writing system, but instead of simplifying the physical appearance of the characters, simplification has mostly been carried out by limiting the number of *kanji* used. The Japanese government has limited official *kanji* to 2136 characters, which represent the number of characters needed to be literate in Japanese; however, in actual usage, this number is in fact higher, and many students learn and use *kanji* outside of this official list.

A further issue with the Japanese writing system is that *kanji* have become more complicated due to the manner in which they were historically used to represent the Japanese language. As was discussed earlier in the chapter, there were issues of applying the written script from China to the new language of Japanese, which is syntactically and grammatically different from the writing system's host language. The result of this mix-and-match approach is the current situation, where *kanji* can be read in numerous ways in the Japanese language. Many *kanji* have both an *on-yomi* (Chinese reading) and a *kun-yomi* (Japanese reading), although the label of 'Chinese reading' is somewhat misleading because on-yomi is in fact a Japanese reading of Chinese origin, and is usually different from how the *kanji* would be read in modern-day Chinese. The distinction of on-yomi and kun-yomi occurred due to the usage of *kanji* to represent Japanese language with characters originally read in Chinese. Kun-yomi emerged after *kanji* had been used for centuries to read and write in the Chinese language in Japan. Kun-yomi were created as alternative readings to the *kanji* later, when writers began to represent concepts in the Japanese language using the original Japanese word that had existed before introduction of Chinese. As a result, a *kanji* often has a kun-yomi and an on-yomi, such as *yama* and *san* for the *kanji* for mountain 山.

In reality, however, a *kanji* can have many more than two readings due to the variety of ways in which it has been used over time, such as the *kanji* 下, which can be read according to two different on-yomi (*ka* and *ge*), and three different kun-yomi (*sagaru/sageru*, *shita* and *kudasaru*). In addition to this, in cases where the Japanese language has one word for a concept applied to different contexts, different *kanji* are used due to a historical distinction in Chinese or traditional Japanese. An example of this is the Japanese word for hot (*atsui*), which has two different *kanji* depending on whether the word refers to something that is hot to touch [熱い] or the temperature [暑い]. Another example is the Japanese word to fix (*naosu*), which can be written as 治す or 直す, depending whether it refers to fix or heal an illness, or fix or mend an object. Thus, as a result of the complex history and usage of *kanji* in the Japanese language over time, the Japanese written language has also become extremely complex. The barriers that these complexities pose to the second language learner are immense.

Implications

Implications for the Japanese language learner

The historical origins of the Japanese writing system, and particularly the classification of *kanji* types, have a direct impact on the Japanese language learner in terms of how they view this script. When many students begin studying Japanese, they erroneously believe all *kanji* are pictographic representations of meaning, or at least have origins that have developed from pictographic representations. This leads to a situation where they apply a pictographic strategy to all *kanji* they encounter, often drawing or creating associations that require vast stretches of the imagination. That is to say, when learning the *kanji* for tree [木] which is an actual pictograph or *shokeimoji*, an association of the *kanji* to the shape of a tree appears to be a natural strategy. As the student encounters other non-pictographic *kanji*, however, this type of strategy will become less effective. For example, it would not be recommended to associate the shape of the *kanji* 鍵 with its meaning of key. As this *kanji* is a *kaiimoji* or combination *kanji*, a strategy that allows the learner to examine the components of the *kanji* for meaning will be much more effective. A study by Mori (1999), for example, showed a degree of success in learners deciphering unknown *kanji* when components were semantically semi-transparent. For the more advanced learner, a *keiseimoji* or seimo-phonetic ideograph would perhaps best be associated with its sound rather than its meaning, seeing as it is specifically marked for phonetic purposes. The Japanese character powder [粉], for example, contains a character on the left, which ties it to its meaning of rice (powder was originally made from rice), and a character to its right, which gives a clue that the pronunciation of the character is *fun*, identical to how the left character is pronounced in isolation [分].

Therefore, the *kanji* learner must be aware of the variety of *kanji* types that exist when developing strategies to learn them. Some strategies covered in Part 2 of this book will prove more effective for different *kanji* types. By using strategies that are best suited for each *kanji* type, the learner can greatly reduce the cognitive energy spent on *kanji* learning.

In addition to *kanji* types, the student must navigate multiple readings of *kanji* according to the written context. This is where many students struggle. Students initially associate *kanji* with the kun-yomi because association with the Japanese word is usually apparent, as the kun-yomi is most often the Japanese word for the object it represents. That is, when encountering the *kanji* for mountain [山], a student will associate it with the reading *yama*, as that will be the familiar vocabulary for mountain. In many cases the student will ignore the on-yomi of *san* and dismiss it as irrelevant as the necessity of this reading will not become apparent until the student expands their Japanese vocabulary to include words that call on the on-yomi, such as summit [山頂, *sancho*], range [山脈, *sanmyaku*] and volcano 火山 [*kazan*].

Implications for the Japanese language instructor

As a Japanese instructor, we struggle to introduce *kanji* in creative and meaningful ways to our students. The complex nature and origins of *kanji* need not be a barrier to the teaching of *kanji*, but instead be a tool to help students become more aware of the cultural significance of *kanji*. Previous research has shown that those students who take an interest in the cultural traditions of *kanji* are better learners of *kanji*. Some of this can be attributed to a heightened awareness of the types of *kanji* that exist. By sparking students' cultural curiosity in *kanji* we not only increase their motivation to learn, but we also give them the historical and cultural understanding of *kanji*, which will enable them to understand the script better and more accurately choose the correct strategies to learn them.

In regard to *kanji* type, the instructor can use the type of *kanji* to steer students toward appropriate strategies to better memorize them. Research suggests instructors avoid forcing students to learn in a particular way, in favor of raising their awareness of the strategies they are able to use if they choose to (Macaro, 2001), as each individual learns in uniquely different ways. In raising awareness that various strategies exist in order to memorize different *kanji* and their multiple readings, teachers can help ease the burden of *kanji* learning from the beginning.

Implications for the Japanese language researcher

The classification of *kanji* as outlined in this part is widely accepted in the literature. The examination of strategies that students use to study *kanji* is also an area that has received much attention by researchers in the last 20 years. Surprisingly, there has been little to no research that links the two. Often, researchers have looked at *kanji* learning strategies without considering the impact that *kanji* type has on strategy use. These studies typically involve students studying lists of *kanji* and reporting on strategies used to study them, for purposes of comparing the effectiveness of strategies with each other, rather than comparing the effectiveness of strategies used according to *kanji* type. The variable of *kanji* classification on strategy use is undeniable, and thus it is an area that could be researched using quantitative measures of large groups of students reporting on strategy use for large lists of *kanji* and then having the data analyzed with *kanji* classification being a variable when looking at strategies employed. Such research will provide a much more in-depth look at how strategies are adapted according to *kanji* classification.

An understanding of *kanji* type is also necessary to account for differences in how students approach lists of *kanji* in experiments. That is, if to one group you give students a higher percentage of pictorial *kanji* than to another, then your research instrument is going to yield invalid data due to the ease with which a pictorial strategy will be applied. It seems like an obvious flaw in research design, but it is one that has been made repeatedly in previously published research papers that claim one strategy is more widely used or more successfully employed than another.

3 Cognitive Challenges in Learning the Japanese Writing System

This chapter will explore the cognitive challenges in learning the Japanese writing system, in particular the cognitive processes involved in memorizing a morphographic script, a task that is of particular difficulty for students of alphabetic language backgrounds. *Kanji*, unlike alphabetic writing systems, do not represent the phonology of a language (well, not usually; as we learned in the preceding chapter, some *kanji* do, in fact, represent the phonology of the Japanese language). They therefore require rather different cognitive processes to decode them when reading. Many beginner learners first use a phonological processing system when learning *kanji*, which causes difficulties in learning, as they soon discover the reading skills they are accustomed to in their first languages do not apply to written Japanese. This chapter will explore the different processes involved when learning a character-based system and discuss implications this has for the Japanese language learner, instructor and researcher. It will begin, however, with a brief introduction to cognitive processes in general, in order to better understand how these processes come into play when learners face the task of memorizing a writing system that contains so many novel characters, many of which can be read in multiple ways.

A Brief Introduction to Cognitive Processes

Cognitive models of SLA examine the learning of language along similar lines to the integration of any new pieces of information into the memory. That is, SLA occurs through the receiving, processing, storing and retrieving of new knowledge into existing memory structures. Increased proficiency in the language is the result of not only more language being successfully integrated into the memory, but also the ease with which this language can be retrieved from memory stores. If a learner no longer has to think about retrieving language (whether it is in the form of vocabulary, language chunks or grammatical knowledge), the recall process has become effortless and automatic. In cognitive theory, this automaticity can be described as processes that have shifted from declarative knowledge (knowing about the language) to procedural knowledge (automatically knowing how to use it). Let us do a simple experiment to illustrate the difference between the two.

Answer the question:
What is the sixth planet from the sun in our solar system?

If you do not need to recall the order of our planets on a regular basis, you probably had to think for a few seconds to find the answer. Some of you may have even needed to count the planets in their order from the Sun or to use a mnemonic strategy (story or rhyme) learned in school to retrieve the correct answer. This is because this information is part of most people's declarative knowledge; it is something we all know about, but it is also something we have to actively retrieve from our memories with some effort.

Procedural knowledge is different, as illustrated by the next question.

Answer the question:
Which way do you turn a lid to open a jar: clockwise or anticlockwise?

In order to answer this question, you probably had to pretend to perform the action yourself. This is because this is part of our procedural knowledge. It is something that you automatically know without having to think about. After all, when was the last time you opened a jar and had to think of which way to turn the lid?

These examples show us the different ways in which information (including language) is stored. As people build up proficiency in a language, more of this knowledge transfers from declarative knowledge (trying to think of the right word) to procedural knowledge (using the word without thinking). The examples also highlight the differences between controlled mental processing (which is slow, deliberate and effortful) to automatic mental processing (which is fast, efficient and effortless). Information only becomes part of our procedural knowledge after it has been integrated and used so many times that we no longer have to search for where it is stored. Proceduralization of knowledge of a second language is the ultimate outcome of second language learners and it is a goal that is difficult to attain.

Some learners may find after heavy use of a language in familiar situations, that certain uses of the language have become proceduralized. This is particularly true of frequently used language structures and vocabulary. However, unrehearsed and unfamiliar language exchanges may still require effort. For example, I would find an exchange in the supermarket with the cashier to be an automatic process to do in my second language, having rehearsed the structures many times. However, going into the city office to discuss my taxes might still require effortful retrieval of the necessary vocabulary items and polite sentence structures. This book is mainly interested in the challenges of learning at the beginning stages of memorizing – that is, how learners memorize the Japanese writing system from the outset of learning – so we need to first examine the initial mental processes involved when learning new linguistic items.

Memory encoding refers to links we make between new information and known information in our long-term memory. The long-term memory is the place where all permanent (or semi-permanent) information is stored. The success with which this information is stored is dependent on initial encoding and the strength of the memory trace to retrieve this information. A memory trace refers to your link to the information.

Associations are often semantically connected, although all types of unpredictable and creative associations can be made. Memory retrieval refers to the process whereby information in our memory is retrieved. A failure to recall information is either a failure of encoding ('I do not remember that at all'); or a failure of retrieval ('Oh, that is right!').

In the field of cognition, there has been notable research into the concept of memory strategies. Memory strategies can be defined as 'deliberate, goal-oriented behaviours used to improve memory' (Matlin, 2005: 503). A further definition is the mental activities that are designed to improve one's coding and retrieval (Herrmann *et al.*, 2002), sometimes referred to as retrieval practice. Retrieval practice refers the practice of locating and accessing this information, by spending time actively learning and reviewing materials over multiple study sessions (Matlin, 2005). Continuous retrieval practice is thought to improve the memory trace of stored information. Moreover, if this retrieval practice occurs often enough, the process will become increasingly automatic and gradually become part of our procedural knowledge.

In regard to encoding information, research into memory strategies provides a strong theoretical basis on which to examine Japanese writing system memorization and recall. First, 'research of levels of processing show that you recall information more accurately if you encode it at a deep level, rather than a shallow level' (Matlin, 2005: 506). By relating new information with other associations, images or experiences, the encoding becomes more meaningful and it is more likely to be remembered (Roediger *et al.*, 2002). On the other hand, repetition or rote learning 'is an extremely poor technique for memorization' (Payne & Wegner, 1992: 91), as it encodes at a much shallower level. Regarding retrieval and retrieval practice, cognitive theory suggests the amount learned is affected by the total time devoted to learning (Baddeley, 1997). Although, Matlin (2005: 175), qualifies this by saying 'keep in mind, however, that 1 hour spent actively learning the material – using deep levels of processing – will usually be more helpful than 2 hours in which your eyes simply drift across the pages'.

Another useful concept of encoding in cognitive science is that of memory schema. Memory schema is the network of linked information in our memories that is usually based on our own experiences and knowledge of how things are connected in the world. The representation of new object, for example, is often based on the type of object that they are, the parts that they tend to have and their typical properties. In terms of language learning, new items of vocabulary will often be powerfully linked with items that share similar properties or fit together in a way that seems logical with our understanding of the world. In terms of learning *kanji*, this could mean that we automatically make associations of new *kanji* with images we associate with its meaning or sound, with items that form part of the same category (e.g. colors with colors), items that look similar or contain similar radicals of components. Such links are a natural way our mind makes connections between new and known information.

Cognitive Processes in Reading and Writing Japanese

One area that has interested researchers is the effect of orthography on an ability to learn to read and write. It is thought that a deep orthography such as *kanji* causes different problems than a shallow orthography. A shallow orthography refers to a transparent writing system, where one is able to decode the writing system to either sound or meaning in a consistent way. Usually, shallow orthographies have a somewhat neat one-to-one relationship between a letter and a sound. Greek and Spanish would be considered to have a shallow orthography, as would Japanese *kana* and *romaji*. A deep orthography refers to a complex script in terms of the relationships between symbols used in the writing system and the sounds or meanings they represent. Often a learner will need to know irregularities in rules and patterns in order to successfully decode the language in its written from. English would be an example of a deep orthography (with numerous spelling irregularities and rules), as would *kanji* (with irregular correspondences to their readings and meanings).

A study by Ellis *et al.* (2004) compared the reading processes of children reading in *hiragana*, English, Greek and *kanji*. They found that reading in *hiragana* and Greek caused fewer reading errors, fewer instances where children were unable to extract any meaning from unknown words and had higher rates of reading comprehension at young ages. This is due to the nature of the *hiragana* script for the Japanese language and the Greek alphabet for the Greek language, where the letters represent sound in unambiguous ways. According to the authors, 'the regularity of symbol-sound mappings makes *hiragana* an exceptionally transparent orthography' (Ellis *et al.*, 2004: 443). Greek is also very transparent in its symbol to sound mapping, although less so than *hiragana*. English on the other hand, uses 26 letters to represent 44 phonemes and its orthography is very ambiguous in its representation of the actual phonology of the language. *Kanji* is a different system entirely and its representation of language is very unambiguous if all of the *kanji* are known. If a *kanji* is not known, however, the reader has very few clues to try to decode meaning, as there is no way to 'sound-out' a morphographic script (unless they contain phonetic components, such as phonetic-seismographs. Thus, it is not surprising that the Ellis *et al.* (2004) study found *kanji* to be most difficult for learners to read reliably, and that there were high rates of no-responses to unknown *kanji*. Children in their study were three times less likely to read words in *kanji* correctly, compared to *hiragana*. Likewise, instances where children were unable to even make a guess at the word (and therefore produce no response) were 1% for words in *hiragana*, but 66% for *kanji*. The results of the study showed that children learning a writing system like *kanji* have considerably larger hurdles to overcome in becoming literate in the language than for children learning more opaque writing systems such as Greek.

Nevertheless, Japan does have one of the world's highest literacy rates, despite its difficult script, but this does not mean the road to literacy is easy; this high literacy rate is more a reflection on the Japanese educational system, than the simplicity of the writing system. In fact, there is considerable evidence to suggest that literacy in Japanese, even for the native speaker, is a lifelong task. As an example, Chikamatsu (2005) has explored the phenomenon of 'tip-of-the-pen', which seems to be a unique occurrence for users of writing systems that include morphographic scripts. The term is derived from the phrase in English of 'tip of the tongue' used to describe the phenomenon of a word that is unable to be recalled; or is more precisely on the fringe of one's memory just out of reach of recollection. A cognitive definition of this phenomenon is 'The tip-of-the-tongue state (TOT) is the feeling that accompanies temporary inaccessibility of an item that a person is trying to retrieve' (Schwartz & Metcalfe, 2011: 737). Tip of the tongue, therefore, describes the feeling of being unable to recall this piece of information that one would ordinarily expect to be able to recall without effort; it is a failure of memory retrieval of an item that has been retrieved successfully on numerous occasions in the past. The tip-of-the-pen describes a similar occurrence when a writer is unable to produce a *kanji* due to it being on the fringe of recollection. Many writers may find themselves stopped mid-sentence, with their pens poised waiting for recollection of how to write a *kanji*.

Furthermore, some writers might suffer tip of the pen mid-*kanji*, with one component written and another component remaining inaccessible. The tip-of-the-pen phenomenon is of relevance here, as it is related to a failure of retrieval and is often due to a lack of retrieval practice. Interestingly, the phenomenon of tip of the pen is becoming rife in the Japanese native speaker population due to the proliferation of computers in writing. Users of the Japanese language are no longer required to frequently reproduce *kanji* in writing, but rather type phonetically and then chose the correct *kanji* on a computer or handheld electronic device. Therefore, writing *kanji* has become more of a receptive, rather than a productive, practice. When native Japanese speakers have to physically write *kanji* with pen and paper, more and more speakers are finding they are unable to recall the *kanji* with the necessary accuracy to produce them correctly. Even if writing a *kanji* was once part of a person's procedural memory (having written them many times in their school years), later in life the same people are finding that knowledge of a *kanji* has reverted back to their declarative memory. Thus, the processes needed to produce *kanji* that previously had been effortless, have since become slower and more effortful.

If native Japanese speakers are having difficulty in maintaining knowledge of their writing system, surely this is bad news for the second language learner. Such phenomena indicate that for the second language learner, continued retrieval practice is necessary to maintain the same level of literacy in Japanese. Learning to read and write in Japanese is not as simple as learning a new skill and retaining it through reading, as it is for English. Instead, being functionally literate in Japanese requires more deliberate, methodical encoding, and continuous effortful retrieval practice, lest the new literacy skills may soon fade from memory.

Another area that has interested researchers is the difficulties second language learners have when shifting from a written language background that is based on phonology to a written language background based on meaning. Some studies, such as Chikamatsu (1996), have shown that second language learners from an alphabetic language background (e.g. English speakers) tend to look for phonological clues when encoding Japanese writing than those from morphographic language backgrounds. It is thought that students from phonological language backgrounds first try to deploy phonological reading strategies for *kanji*, before realizing that they do not work. Some researchers have argued that students need assistance in shifting their mental processes from phonological to semantic.

At this point, however, it is also important to emphasize research that has found the importance of sound in reading and writing *kanji*, a point which is often de-emphasized in the discussion of *kanji* as a morphographic script. Horodeck (1989: i) writes that:

> It is widely acknowledged that *kanji* is 'ideographic', meaning that the symbols used to write [*kanji*] stand for meanings, not sounds, and therefore are designed and employed in ways fundamentally different from the symbols used in most other writing systems.

While this is illustrative of a pervasive assumption in linguistics, that morphographic scripts are processed according to meaning, and not sound, Horodeck aimed to test whether this was actually the case. Horodeck examined errors in writing *kanji* by native Japanese speakers in university examinations. This study highlighted 495 errors in more than 2400 examinations, which were then analyzed according to whether the error was based on a phonological misunderstanding (e.g. when a writer would replace a *kanji* with one that resembles the same sound), or a semantic misunderstanding (e.g. when a writer would replace a *kanji* with one that contains similar semantic links or radicals). Horodeck argued that analyzing this type of error would reveal whether readers and writers of *kanji* were using phonological or semantic processes. Results of the study revealed evidence that many *kanji* were written according to their phonological properties rather than their semantic properties. This is a very interesting finding considering the prevailing assumption in linguistics that morphographic scripts are not read according to the same cognitive processes as alphabetic and syllabic scripts.

Horodeck also took his study a step further, and examined whether the same errors were present in reading. In the second stage of his study, Horodeck required native Japanese speakers to read text containing incorrect *kanji*. When the incorrect *kanji* matched the phonology of the correct *kanji*, the error would often go unnoticed by the reader. Such results also point to the importance of phonological processing skills when reading and writing *kanji*.

Following on from Horodeck's findings, Sayeg (1996) also points to the importance of sound in processing *kanji*. She argues from her own experiences as a second language learner of Japanese that the reading of a *kanji* is just as, if not more, important that the meaning of the *kanji*. She argues that the reading of a *kanji* should be introduced first, followed by the meaning, which is different to how *kanji* are presented to most language learners. Learners are often encouraged to make these semantic links before exploring the reading of *kanji*. Sayeg (1996) argues that more emphasis could be made on phonology when learning *kanji* and – more importantly – when developing reading proficiency. Evidence suggests, therefore, that the importance of the phonological aspects of *kanji* should not be downplayed in the language classroom.

Implications

Implications for the Japanese language learner

A knowledge of cognitive processing, memorization and reading processes have clear impacts on the Japanese language learner in terms of how they memorize the various scripts, and how they learn to read and write. In terms of memorization, the Japanese language learner must effectively memorize 2000 *kanji* to reach functional literacy. Many of these *kanji* have multiple readings. The types of links made in the learner's schema not only need to involve the encoding of new *kanji* to their meaning, but also to their pronunciation, which is not an easy task. In my own studies (e.g. Rose & Harbon, 2013), I have found that advanced learners of Japanese have to spend a considerable amount of time merely maintaining their current knowledge of *kanji* and that without repetitive retrieval practice, previously known *kanji* may be forgotten as the memory trace deteriorates.

This chapter has shown the importance of deep encoding if memorization is to be successful. The good news here is that cognitive theory shows that encoding according to meaning tends to be a more powerful link in comparison to sound (see Matlin, 2005). Such evidence bodes well for a morphographic script, which is inherently representative of meaning. However, disregard to the reading of a *kanji* has its own pitfalls, as another study of mine (Rose, 2013) has shown that learners who focus solely of meaning are able to recall the abstract meaning of *kanji*, but cannot read it aloud or understand it in combinations with other *kanji*. In such cases, the meaning is often only abstractly linked when used in the written language, especially when it forms only part of the meaning of a particular word. Strategies to better memorize and recall *kanji* are of utmost importance and the following part aims to explore these cognitive and metacognitive strategies in much more detail.

Implications for the Japanese language instructor

The mental processes involved in the learning of morphographic characters have obvious implications for teachers of Japanese in terms of how *kanji* are presented to students. As connections with meaning appear to be most effective in terms of retention (according to cognitive theory, semantic associations are very powerful), it is important for learners to make meaningful links with new *kanji*. Second language acquisition, in the case of learning the written form of the Japanese language, needs to take a departure from those tactics used in the process of first language acquisition. Native Japanese speakers begin to learn *kanji* after they are already fully functional in the spoken language. Thus, the links between newly learned *kanji* are more easily made to known vocabulary in the language and thus the learner can focus on making meaningful connections with the *kanji*'s form. In contrast, the second language learner often learns the writing system in tandem with the spoken form. Thus, for many learners, the *kanji* and the vocabulary item it represents are taught in the same lesson at same moment in the curriculum. I strongly believe, based on an understanding of schema, that this is a mistake. Without a firmly entrenched anchor of vocabulary in the target language, a learner is left with no other choice but to associate it with its more abstract and less reliable equivalent concepts in their native language.

Opportunities to learn *kanji* in context are lost and situations like that in my 2013 study arise, where students invest a considerable amount of time learning *kanji* meanings, but are left with the result of being unable to read the *kanji* in the target language. To ensure a deeper encoding of *kanji* and opportunities for effective retrieval practice, spoken language acquisition has to be given a priority in order to build knowledge of the linguistic items in Japanese, before the *kanji* for these words are then introduced. In not, a learner must simultaneously learn two connected items without an appropriately activated schema.

Furthermore, research suggests that activities for retrieval practice that have been borrowed from first language acquisition, such as making students write out a *kanji* repetitively may prove far less successful for the second language learner. Some studies have shown that repetitive writing is the preferred format of teaching *kanji* in American classrooms (Shimizu & Green, 2002), even though other studies into the learning of *kanji* have shown that repetitive writing is one of the least effective memorization techniques (Toyoda & Kubota, 2001). This is no doubt due to the shallowness of repetitive writing as an encoding technique. Thus, instructors need to consider the effectiveness of current classroom activities used to teach Japanese writing and ensure they make sense from a cognitive perspective. Those activities which encourage the learner to make meaningful links with firmly known and understood concepts will prove to be of greater benefit than those that encourage superficial or short-term memorization.

Implications for the Japanese language researcher

Considering that very few languages use a morphographic script in the world today (Chinese and Japanese, and to a lesser extent Korean), there have been very few studies into the cognitive processes involved when learning to read and write in these languages as a second language learner. For Japanese – even more so than Chinese – the cognitive processes involved in learning a writing system that constantly jumps between a morphographic script and a phonetic script should be of primary interest to researchers, but it remains severely under researched. The SLA of written English on the other hand is saturated with studies into the learning process, from reading studies, writing studies and vocabulary acquisition. This has caused an imbalance in the way in which we understand the reading and writing process in the field of SLA. The *Journal of Second Language Writing*, for example, states that it is:

> devoted to publishing theoretically grounded reports of research and discussions that represent a contribution to current understandings of central issues in second and foreign language writing and writing instruction. Some areas of interest are personal characteristics and attitudes of L2 writers, L2 writers' composing processes, features of L2 writers' texts, readers' responses to L2 writing, assessment/evaluation of L2 writing, contexts (cultural, social, political, institutional) for L2 writing, and any other topic clearly relevant to L2 writing theory, research, or instruction.

However, a look at the articles presented there quickly reveals that almost all studies center around L2 learning of English. Some articles, in their abstracts, even neglect to mention the language they focus on is English, and merely state that they examine 'L2 learning'; it is only noted later in the articles that the focus of their research included sample entirely made up of L2 English learners. The focus of English is so pervasive in second language learning research, that often conclusions are drawn from L2 English writing research that are generalized across all L2 writing contexts. Simply put, the focus on English as a second language by researchers has unfairly skewed the published research in this field and I would argue that the field of applied linguistics needs to boost research volume on languages other than English for a full understanding of L2 writing to be achieved.

A second direction for the researcher in the field of L2 Japanese learning stems from new technology that has greatly improved the methods in which we can examine the cognitive processes involved in the reading process. Eye-tracking technology has offered an opportunity to examine what parts of a *kanji* learners focus on to derive meaning and also the role of context in deciphering less familiar *kanji*. This opportunity has, as yet, scarcely been taken. The implications for further research into the learning of a morphographic script as a second language learner are not only immense, but also absolutely necessary to level the playing field in our understanding of how people learn written languages, and not just alphabetic scripts.

Part 2
Cognitive Strategies

4 Cognitive Learning Strategies

Part 2 of this book explores the notion of cognitive language learning strategies. Each chapter in this part focuses on one category of strategy use that research has shown to be of great importance to learners of Japanese when studying *kanji*. These strategies include:

(1) Making visual associations between new *kanji* and known pictures, symbols, scripts and so forth.
(2) Using mnemonics, which involve the creation of stories to remember *kanji* meanings.
(3) Analyzing components of the *kanji* in order to derive meaning.

As with all of the chapters in this book, research will be presented, followed by implications of this research for the *kanji* learner, instructor and researcher. This first chapter in Part 2, however, aims to provide the reader with an overview of language learning strategies (sometimes referred to as the broader term, language learner strategies) in order to illustrate its relevance to the task of learning Japanese as a second language.

A Brief Introduction to Cognitive Learning Strategies

It has long been observed that processes for acquiring a second language vary according to the individual learner. The use of effective learning strategies may account for some of this variation. The effect that learning strategies can have on language learning has been closely examined over the last 35 years. In seminal research in this field (Rubin, 1975: 41) it was observed:

> The differential success of second/foreign language learners suggests a need to examine in detail what strategies successful language learners employ. In addition to the need of research on this topic, it is suggested that teachers can already begin to help their less successful students to improve their performance by paying more attention to learner strategies already seen as productive.

More recently, Gass and Selinker (2009: 439) make the following claim in their introduction to learning strategies:

> A common observation is that not only are some language learners more successful than others, but also that good language learners sometimes do different things than poorer language learners. The term commonly used in second language acquisition literature to refer to what learners do that underlies these differences is *learning strategies*.

Researchers have argued that learning strategies promote learning by aiding the acquisition, storage and retrieval of information (Govea de Arce, 2001; Oxford, 2001). In addition to this, Oxford (2001: 166) states that learning strategies make learning 'easier, faster, more enjoyable, more self-directed, more effective and more transferable to new situations'. Learning strategies, therefore, are seen as tools that language learners can use to accelerate or aid their second language learning.

The definition of language learning strategies has developed over the years since Rubin's original investigation in the field. Rubin (1981: 42) defines language-learning strategies as 'the techniques or devices that a learner may use to acquire language'. A further definition is 'the special thoughts or behaviors that individuals use to help them comprehend, learn, or retain new information' (O'Malley & Chamot, 1990: 1). A more recent definition of language learning strategies posited by Cohen (2007: 31) involves the following attributes:

> Strategies can be classified as a conscious mental activity. They must contain not only an action but a goal (or an intention) and a learning situation. Whereas a mental action might be subconscious, an action with a goal/intention and related to a learning situation can only be conscious.

Therefore, language learner strategies are processes and actions that are consciously deployed by language learners to help them to learn or use a language more effectively.

After Rubin's (1975) examination of learning strategies, research began to investigate a wide range of different strategies for different aspects of language learning, such as overall strategies, vocabulary learning strategies, cognitive strategies and social strategies (e.g. see Bialystok, 1979; Hosenfeld, 1976; Naiman *et al.*, 1975; Selinger, 1977). The need for a classification system of newly identified strategies emerging from this research soon became apparent, leading to the development of the first taxonomy of language learning strategies by Rubin (1981). This was the first movement toward the grouping of strategies; however, Grenfell and Macaro (2007: 11) have since observed Rubin's taxonomy was a list of 'what might be termed academic or study skills'.

Research continued into the 1980s, with particular emphasis on cognitive strategies for English as a Second Language (ESL) learning (e.g. see Chamot & Kupper, 1989; Chamot & O'Malley, 1987; O'Malley *et al.*, 1985a, 1985b), leading to the O'Malley and Chamot classification of language learning strategies (O'Malley & Chamot, 1990). O'Malley and Chamot positioned language learning strategies within a cognitive framework based on cognitive theories and 'provided a theoretical background to much language learning strategy research at the time' (Grenfell & Macaro, 2007: 16). The O'Malley and Chamot classification included three broad categories, which are described below:

(1) Metacognitive strategies, which involved thinking about (or knowledge of) the learning process, planning for learning, monitoring learning while it is taking place, or self-evaluation of learning after the task had been completed.
(2) Cognitive strategies, which invoked mental manipulation or transformation of materials or tasks, intended to enhance comprehension, acquisition, or retention.
(3) Social/affective strategies, which consisted of using social interactions to assist in the comprehension, learning or retention of information. As well as the mental control over personal affect that interfered with learning.
(from O'Malley & Chamot, 1990: 229–232)

O'Malley and Chamot's (1990) classification system borrowed heavily from concepts in cognitive psychology, particularly drawing on the work of Anderson (1985). Anderson's work particularly focused on the cognitive and metacognitive aspects of the human memory, examining notions such as encoding and retrieval of new information (including words), attention to language input, and language comprehension and processing. As such, research conducted within this framework, was less concerned with social/affective strategies, as evidenced by the following claim by its creators:

> Affective strategies are of less interest in an analysis such as ours which attempts to portray strategies in a cognitive theory. For the purposes of discussion, however, we present a classification scheme that includes the full range of strategies identified in the literature. (O'Malley & Chamot, 1990: 44)

This ad hoc nature of the third category of this classification system has since been criticized as 'a miscellaneous category that appears to have been introduced simply to accommodate all the strategies that did not fit into the first two types' (Dörnyei, 2005: 168). It is for this reason that this book explores the psychological aspects of language learning under the framework of self-regulation in a separate section, and explores the cognitive and metacognitive aspects of learning strategies in this section. Setting aside terminology issues for now, it is clear that some interesting concepts can be found in the notion of cognitive theory in learning strategy conceptualizations, which may be of relevance to the SLA of the Japanese language.

O'Malley and Chamot's (1990) model highlighted some important cognitive strategies used by language learners when learning vocabulary that may also be applicable to *kanji* memorization. They were the use of *imagery*, which is the use of 'visual images to understand and remember new information', *grouping*, which involves the classification of words or concepts according to their attributes or meanings, repetition of new words, and *elaboration*, which involves 'relating new information to prior knowledge, relating different parts of new information to each other, or making meaningful personal associations with new information' (O'Malley & Chamot, 1990: 36). Drawing on Anderson's (1985) cognitive theory, O'Malley and Chamot's research also examined the memorization process through activation and memory traces. In Nyikos and Fan's (2007: 260) review of research into vocabulary strategies, we can find many of these concepts in research in the 1990s to the present day under categories such as 'repetition strategies' and 'associative strategies'.

Despite these moves to integrate cognitive theory with language learning strategies, by 1990, O'Malley and Chamot's classification system had been overshadowed by Oxford's taxonomy (Oxford, 1990), which expanded on previous classifications and added the Strategy Inventory of Language Learning (SILL), a questionnaire that could be used by learners to measure their own strategy use and to increase their awareness of language learning strategies utilized by other language learners.

Although the Oxford model and the SILL have been subject to criticism since its first development, an explosion of research was conducted under its theoretical framework throughout the 1990s. In fact, in a recent review of research methods in strategy research, it was stated that the SILL is 'without doubt the most widely used instrument in language learner strategy research' (White *et al.*, 2007: 95). Grenfell and Macaro (2007) also estimated that the SILL has been used to assess the strategy use of more than 10,000 learners around the world; therefore, much of what researchers know about learning strategies is within Oxford's paradigm. Thus, an overview of some of this research will help inform our understanding of second language learning for the Japanese written language.

Since the establishment of models of language learning strategies, there have been numerous studies that have examined a relationship between learning strategies and learner achievement in studying language in general. A study by Clark (1999) found the use of cognitive strategies by university-aged language learners was associated with high achievement on proficiency exams, while the infrequent use of cognitive strategies was associated with low achievement. Doering (2001: 1), in her study of eighth grade French immersion students, found successful language learners 'used a greater number and wider range of strategies than less effective learners'.

A comprehensive analysis of a number of studies into language learning strategies by O'Malley and Chamot (1990: 128), also found 'more effective students used learning strategies more often and had a wider repertoire of learning strategies than did less effective students'. These findings are supported by Oxford (2001: 167) who states: 'Research shows that greater strategy use is often related to higher levels of language proficiency'. In a recent evaluation of strategy research over the previous 30 years, Grenfell and Macaro (2007: 15) offered the following assessment:

> Successful and highly motivated learners adopted more strategies, especially those involving planning, evaluation and monitoring. Poorly motivated pupils, on the other hand, employed a limited set of strategies and were less ready to act strategically.

Thus, research suggests a link between strategy use and achievement, an indication that more effective *kanji* learners may also employ a greater number and wider range of *kanji* learning strategies.

Learning strategy research has also suggested that there are numerous other factors besides language proficiency that can affect strategy choice. In a 1989 study, Oxford and Nyikos (1989) found factors such as a student's motivation to have a powerful influence on the choice of learning strategy, far more so than language proficiency in speaking, reading, writing or listening. Other factors that affected learning strategy choice were: the student's major; the length of time he or she had been studying the language; and whether the student was learning the language as an elective or was required to do so (Oxford & Nyikos, 1989). The findings of Oxford and Nyikos's study are very significant because, in terms of its sample size, 'it is the largest completed study of language learning strategies' at the time (Oxford & Nyikos, 1989: 291). Subsequent studies examined differences between strategy use and personality and gender (Ehrman & Oxford, 1989), task-type and cognitive aptitude (Oxford & Ehrman, 1995) and learner anxiety and cultural background (Oxford, 1998; Oxford & Ehrman, 1995). Collectively, these past studies suggested learning strategies are not exclusively deployed by all learners in a generalizable way. A more recent review of strategies has suggested that out of all variables, motivation has the strongest relationship to strategy use (Oxford & Schramm, 2007). This assessment is also supported by other researchers who argue there is a consensus in the field that motivated learners not only use a wider range of strategies, but use these strategies more frequently (Takeuchi *et al.*, 2007).

In summary, language learning strategy theory suggests that more efficient learners use a greater number and wider range of strategies. Research also suggests a connection between strategy use and language achievement. Over time, theory has been qualified by findings that strategy choice is affected by a number of variables with indications that students use a variety of different strategies to achieve language aims. In addition to this, previous research indicates that language learning strategies differ according to variables such as motivation (Oxford & Schramm, 2007) and that these factors must be accounted for. Previous language learning strategy research has provided a useful base on which to build the research that examines Japanese language learning, but does not consider the task of *kanji* learning in enough depth to apply directly to the task of learning the Japanese writing system. We have seen from previous chapters that kanji learning is quite different from the learning of other aspects of language. The number and complexity of *kanji* in particular indicate they remain an obstacle for many learners from alphabetic writing systems backgrounds. Furthermore, models of language learning strategies have been subject to criticism (see Dörnyei, 2005; Dörnyei & Ryan, 2015; Skehan, 1989) since its original conception, and thus a more watertight, and context specific framework is necessary to focus on the particular task of *kanji* learning.

Kanji Learning Strategies

Through think-aloud interviews with Australian university students of Japanese, Bourke (1996) compiled the Strategy Inventory for Learning *Kanji* (SILK). Her study identified 15 categories of learning strategies. In *kanji* recollection, Bourke found the most commonly used strategy was relating the shape of the *kanji* to its meaning and the second most common strategy was to examine the radical. The radical is a component of the *kanji* by which it is grouped with other *kanji* according to its shape, meaning or sound. Her study also found:

> The most successful students in the *kanji* recall tasks were the ones who used the highest number and widest variety of strategies [which] concurs with the claim by Oxford (1989: 199) that more effective students use strategies more 'consciously, purposefully, appropriately and frequently than do less able students'. (Bourke, 1996: 131)

Her study concluded that the type and complexity of the *kanji* and the proficiency of the learner greatly influenced strategy choice. That is, she found pictorial strategies to be helpful to beginner students, but more complicated *kanji* needed to be broken down into meaningful components for these students as they progressed through their language development. She emphasised that students need guidance from teachers in their initial exposure to *kanji*:

> Students need help in the initial stages to change from a holistic approach to *kanji* to a more analytical approach and build up their knowledge of the meaning of component elements. (Bourke, 1996: 226)

Fujiyoshi (1996) used Bourke's (1996) study as a basis to test whether Bourke's results could be reproduced in observations of advanced learners of Japanese at the university level. Fujiyoshi (1996) examined the learning strategies of six university students and concluded that, while *kanji* recollection strategies concurred with Bourke's findings, strategy use varied according to individual subjects, which is in accordance with Oxford and Nyikos's (1989) findings that individual differences affect strategy choice.

In my own research, I used Bourke's (1996) SILK and adapted it based on *kanji* learning research studies that occurred after its creation, which resulted in an inventory of known and codified cognitive and metacognitive strategies applied to the task of *kanji* learning. This inventory, like Bourke's SILK, was intended for data collection purposes and could be used by learners to self-report the strategies they used when memorizing *kanji*. These strategies are listed in Table 4.1 and this inventory was used as the basis of a questionnaire for *The Strategies Study* in order to elicit data on the strategies used by learners to memorize *kanji*.

Generally speaking, the strategies listed in the categories A to E focus on the cognitive aspects of strategic learning and those listed in F, G and H focus on the metacognitive aspects of *kanji* learning. That is, those listed in the first part are strategies to more deeply encode *kanji* into one's memory, and those listed in the latter part are designed to strengthen the memory trace through effective retrieval practice.

In summary, language learning strategy theory suggests that more efficient learners use a greater number and wider range of strategies. Research also suggests a connection between strategy use and language achievement. Over time, theory has been qualified by findings that strategy choice is affected by a number of variables with indications that students use a variety of different strategies to achieve language aims. In addition to this, previous research indicates that these *kanji* learning strategies differ according to variables such as motivation, and that these factors must be accounted for.

Implications

Implications for the Japanese language learner

Knowledge of language learning strategy theory has clear implications for the Japanese language learner. Many learners who are bewildered by the task of *kanji* learning often develop their own set of individual learning strategies based on little more than trial and error, or based on recommendations from external sources such as other learners, teachers, Internet sources and books. The act of seeking out learning strategies that have been codified and researched can be of direct use to learners. Research has shown that even exposure to a questionnaire that depicts possible strategies can provide learners

Table 4.1 An inventory of cognitive and metacognitive *kanji* learning strategies

A	*Association*
A1	I create associations between the *kanji* and a picture related to its meaning
A2	I create associations between the new *kanji* and other *kanji* I already know
A2	I create associations between the new *kanji* and *katakana*
A3	I create associations between the new *kanji* and other known symbols or letters
A4	I create associations between the new *kanji* and letters of the alphabet
A5	I associate *kanji* with other *kanji* from the same meaning group
A6	I associate *kanji* with *kanji* that mean the opposite
A7	I associate *kanji* with other *kanji* that look different but have the same reading
A8	I associate *kanji* with other *kanji* that look the same but have a different reading
A9	I compare and contrast *kanji* that look similar so as not to confuse them
A10	I associate *kanji* with the Japanese reading first and then the meaning
A11	I associate *kanji* with the meaning in English then the Japanese reading
B	*Stories*
B1	I make up my own stories according to what the *kanji* looks like to me
B2	I make up my own stories according to the component elements of the *kanji*
B3	I use stories told to me by my teacher or in reference books
B4	I use rhyme to remember *kanji*
C	*Component analysis*
C1	I group the *kanji* with other *kanji* containing the same components or radical
C2	I remember the radical first and it helps me remember the *kanji*
C3	I break the *kanji* into smaller parts and use these to remember the *kanji*
C4	I associate the *kanji* with the meaning of one or more of its components
D	*Visual/emotional response*
D1	I visualize the *kanji* in my head and transfer the image to paper
D2	I remember what it looked like on the page where I learned it
D3	I associate *kanji* with other *kanji* in the sequence or list I first learned it in
D4	I place the new *kanji* in a sentence and remember it in that context
D5	I remember the *kanji* by the way it feels to write it
E	*Stroke order*
E1	I remember *kanji* because I have committed the stroke order to memory
E2	If I remember the first stroke, the rest comes naturally
F	*Planning your learning (metacognitive strategies)*
F1	I have a set time each day/week which I spend learning *kanji*
F2	I use flashcards to repeatedly practice *kanji*
F3	I write out *kanji* many times until I know them
F4	I use a computer program to practice *kanji*

Table 4.1 An inventory of cognitive and metacognitive *kanji* learning strategies (*continued*)

F	Planning your learning (metacognitive strategies)
F5	I use *kanji* as often as I can (e.g. in class notes, homework assignments etc.)
F6	I try to find better ways of learning *kanji* from books or by talking to others
F7	I use other *kanji* resources additional to those required in my course
F8	I set myself goals and objectives for what I wish to achieve each week
F9	I set myself a long-term goal for how many *kanji* I want to learn
G	Evaluating your learning (metacognitive strategies)
G1	I test myself
G2	I relearn or focus on *kanji* I have trouble with
G3	I keep a separate list of *kanji* I have trouble remembering for easy reference
G4	I focus on *kanji* that are likely to come up in an exam
G5	I test myself regularly on old *kanji* so I don't forget them
H	Working with others (metacognitive strategies)
H1	I study with others, practicing together
H2	I ask another person to test me

with clarity as to what has been empirically proven to work for other learners. Thus, learners might find benefit in exploring strategy research, or even talking to peers about the strategies that work for them. Such activities can arm learners with a richer repertoire of strategies to apply to their own learning.

Furthermore, research has shown that learners who actively deploy a wider range of carefully selected strategies are more successful. This fact highlights to learners the pitfalls of a one-size-fits-all learning regime that is often perpetuated in study materials (a notion we will return to in Chapter 6). In short, there is no one magical strategy that a learner can apply to all *kanji* to successfully become a fluent reader and writer in the language.

Implications for the Japanese language instructor

Instructors are in a unique position to raise awareness of language learning strategies of their learners, and can help support learners in building up an effective repertoire of strategies for future use. According to White *et al.* (2007), the simple act of showing students a list of strategies can raise awareness for adult learners, as they will immediately be exposed to new ideas to carry out the learning process. Instructors also have to be aware that strategy use is highly individualized and just because a particularly strategy has proved useful for them, does not mean that their students will find the same use from applying the same strategies in their learning. In my study (Rose, 2013), I found equal numbers of learners who rejected strategies taught to them by their teachers as learners who accepted and used them. The teacher's role in learner strategy training, therefore, is to raise awareness and encourage learners to explore new ways of learning, without forcing strategies upon their students or presenting their own preferred strategy as the only options available.

Implications for the Japanese language researcher

The field of language learning strategies has been unevenly skewed with research into the learning of English as second language. As learning strategy research has become more task-focused and more context-dependent, sub-areas of research such as language learning strategies in vocabulary acquisition have become highly researched fields. However, the current research into vocabulary acquisition and second language writing has paid little attention to the challenges of learning languages other than English. Barriers that the Japanese writing system poses in vocabulary acquisition have scarcely been explored. Language learning strategies in the learning of morphographic scripts in severely under researched, which is even more shocking considering the barriers to SLA are considerably larger and thus the need for such strategies would logically be more profound. The opportunities for the applied linguistic researcher in this domain are currently wide open.

5 Visual Association

One of the most common strategies that learners employ when memorizing new scripts are visual association strategies. Visual association strategies are strategies in which the *kanji* being learned is associated with its physical form. As outlined in the previous section (see p. 28 on schema), the mind is constantly looking for ways to integrate new knowledge with existing knowledge of the world around us. It looks to make connections between new and known information. The previous chapter also touched on the fact that visual links are a powerful way in which people can memorize new information into one's schema. In O'Malley and Chamot's (1990) work, for example, the use of imagery was an effective way for learners to integrate knew information such as vocabulary into a learner's memory stores. Such work is supported by cognitive psychology, which also shows that strong memory links can be achieved through use of visual imagery (e.g. see Anderson, 2005; Matlin, 2005). Thus, to make connections between the appearance of a new letter with our understanding of other scripts, images and known concepts not only seems logical, but also extremely effective in terms of storing them into our memories.

The first script that most learners of Japanese encounter is *hiragana*. This script is often taught early in Japanese curricula, because it is viewed as an important, but relatively simple, script. Knowledge of *hiragana* (an extremely accurate symbol-to-sound script) allows learners to read and write entirely in Japanese in just 46 discrete symbols. A second script of *katakana*, usually quickly follows in the curriculum, as this script quickly allows students access to the some 10% of Japanese vocabulary that are borrowed from foreign languages, especially from English. In fact, some curricula in Australia encourage the learning of *katakana* first, as it allows students to access new vocabulary more quickly, as unknown words written in *katakana* are more likely to be deciphered by students because of knowledge of English, compared to unknown words written in *hiragana*, for which the learner has no prior linguistic knowledge to provide them with clues.

The 46 letters of *hiragana*, and the corresponding letters of *katakana*, are often taught through a visual association strategy, which I will illustrate with reference to a number of commercial materials. A famous series used in Australia in the 1970s and 1980s purported it was possible to learn *hiragana* in 48 minutes (Quackenbush & Mieko, 1999), at least at a receptive level. Personally, I remember using these materials to learn *hiragana* and *katakana* in 1990, when I taught myself *hiragana* and *katakana* one evening after school. The series uses visual association when presenting each letter to the learner in the form of pictures super-imposed over the kana. The *hiragana* for あ for example, had a picture of an antenna on a roof superimposed on it, and encouraged the learner to associate its sound of 'a' with 'antenna'. The books also encouraged students to compare similar *hiragana* so as not to confuse them. For example, る was taught with a picture of a 'ruby' inside the enclosed loop of the letter, encouraging the association of 'ru' for 'ruby'. Immediately following this, ろ was introduced to the learner with the visualization that a 'robber had stolen the ruby', thus encouraging the link between 'ro' and 'robber' (see Figure 5.1). Such visual association was extremely powerful, and indeed I still remember these stories today, some 25 years later. Obviously these techniques focus on the encoding aspect of memorization only, and if these memory traces are not strengthened through retrieval practice, knowledge would soon deteriorate.

Thus, contrary to the previous chapter, which discussed the importance of using a repertoire of strategies for effective learning, it is quite possible to learn *kana* using one systematic strategy. Much of this is due to the simplicity in which these letters represent the phonology of the Japanese letters (remember the Ellis *et al.* (2004) study in Chapter 3, which showed *hiragana* to be one of the most transparent symbol-to-sound mapped scripts of the world). *Kanji,* on the other hand, are not so simple and a visual association

Figure 5.1 Example of pictorial association strategy for learning *hiragana*

to sound strategy would be insufficient to learn all 2000 characters, which take on different meanings in different combinations and often have different readings or pronunciations depending on use.

Beginner learners of Japanese often think visual association means the connection of the characters to a pictographic representation of meaning, much like in our *kana* examples. However, visual associations are much more than this and can involve the following:

(1) Pictorial association: associating *kanji* with pictures.
(2) Symbolic association: associating *kanji* with symbols including Japanese *hiragana* and *katakana* scripts, English alphabet and other commonly used symbols, such as for numbers, currency, mathematics and so forth.
(3) Whole *kanji* association: associating *kanji* with other *kanji*, either by:
 (i) meaning (*kanji* with similar meaning);
 (ii) appearance (*kanji* that look similar);
 (iii) sounds (*kanji* with the same sound).

Each of these associations will be discussed separately in this section.

Pictorial Association

When many students encounter *kanji* for the first time, they immediately are drawn to making pictorial associations with the shape of the *kanji* and the object that they represent. Indeed, this impulse is so strong that many students in the beginning stages of *kanji* learning erroneously believe all *kanji* are pictographic representations of meaning. Much of this has to do with the fact that simple *kanji* that represent simple vocabulary items are the first to appear in textbooks, due to the simplicity of their forms. This is coupled with the fact that these *kanji* are also some of the most frequently occurring in written texts. Teachers often intensify this connection by showing students the etymology of these *kanji* from pictures to their modern forms, such as those shown in Figure 5.2.

As a result, pictorial association is the most commonly used strategy by beginner learners, which is supported by research in the field of *kanji* learning strategy research (Bourke, 1996; Toyoda, 1998). In fact, the study of elementary school-aged learners of Japanese in Australia in *The Intervention Study* showed pictorial association was the preferred strategy for memorization, and was employed 56% of the time. This study revealed that learners uniformly applied a pictorial association strategy without any prompting from the researcher. That is, when learners were faced with the task of memorizing a list of unknown *kanji* for the first time (for most of these learners, this task was the first time they had to study *kanji* as part of their Japanese language classes), they automatically looked for pictures in the *kanji* to link

50 Part 2: Cognitive Strategies

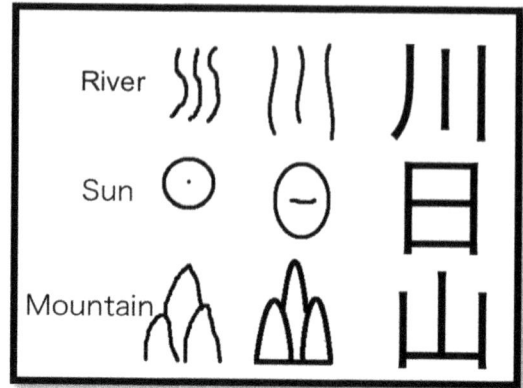

Figure 5.2 Etymological depictions of *kanji*

with the meaning. This is an indication of a pervasive belief, even in younger learners, that *kanji* are pictographic representations. Examples from this study include a learner remembering:

- 雨 as 'rain, because it kind of looks like rain coming down' (Learner Stimulated Recall, *The Intervention Study*);
- as 'mountain, because it looked like a mountain when you joined the things' (Learner Stimulated Recall, *The Intervention Study*);
- as 'river, because rivers are long and they're kind of like, um, streams and rivers so I thought it's river' (Learner Stimulated Recall, *The Intervention Study*).

The stimulated recall data also revealed a lot of nonsensical pictorial associations, where the learner tried to memorize the shapes in the *kanji* without regard to its meaning. Examples of this include remembering river [川] as 'three stripes', language [語] as having 'two boxes at the bottom' and I [私] as 'a nose thingy' (Learner Stimulated Recall, *The Intervention Study*). Although students successfully remembered each of these *kanji* in the stimulated recall and the test, I am doubtful whether they would actually recall the *kanji* in a delayed post-test. However, a delayed post-test was not included in the research design for ethical reasons, thus this assumption of mine is merely conjecture.

The Intervention Study also found that as a result of an over-reliance on pictorial associations, there was an imbalance between the type of *kanji* that were successfully recalled by these students in their *kanji* tests. The study found that on average, 58% of students recalled compound *kanji* correctly, compared to 70% for abstract *kanji* and 99% for pictorial *kanji*. These results indicate that students in this beginning stage were relying too heavily on pictorial strategies and had not developed a repertoire of strategies to deal with *kanji* that were not pictorial representations of meaning. A summary of the results of *The Intervention Study* by *kanji* type are listed in Table 5.1.

A study by Paxton (2015) concurs with the results from *The Intervention Study* (Rose, 2003), that students found pictorial *kanji* easier to learn than other *kanji* types, perhaps due to the ease with which a pictorial learning strategy could be applied. His study revealed that 75% of learners found pictographs 'very easy' to learn (and a further 17% found them 'easy'). This was in stark opposition to the same learners' views of *kanji* that contained multiple components, which only 7% of learners stated were 'very easy' to learn. Such findings suggest that pictorial associations are of great value to a learner, but only for the learning of pictographic *kanji*. This also supports my conclusions from *The Intervention Study*, that pictorial association strategies, while useful for pictographic *kanji*, were less successful for other *kanji* types.

In *The Strategies Study*, the *kanji* learning strategies of university-aged students of varying proficiency levels highlighted a danger of applying pictorial association strategies to more advanced *kanji*. An example of this was a student who chose to interpret the *kanji* 感 meaning 'feelings' as looking like 'a squashed insect'. In such cases the visual association is disconnected with the meaning of the *kanji* and as a result the student more often than not was unable to successfully recall the actual meaning of the *kanji*.

This study also revealed that in the more advanced stages of *kanji* learning, students still reported that they used pictorial association when learning *kanji*. However, during stimulated recall sessions, where these students were asked to verbalize how they memorized and recalled *kanji* learned in the previous week, there was very little evidence of pictorial association. A result of this study was that pictorial association is the most over-reported strategy by intermediate and advanced learners, perhaps because they relied so heavily on the strategy in the beginning stages of *kanji* learning, that the gradual lack of application as their proficiency progressed had gone unnoticed.

If we examine *kanji* type according to the usual order *kanji* are presented to learners, it is not surprising that pictorial association is so powerful in the beginning stages of *kanji* learning, but then quickly diminishes in its usefulness as a learner encounters more *kanji*. For example, in the order *kanji* are introduced in the Japanese school system, the majority of *kanji* first learned are pictographic *kanji*. Almost half of the *kanji* taught in Year One of

Table 5.1 Errors according to *kanji* type (*The Intervention Study*)

Kanji *type*	Number of kanji in pre-test	Total number of errors made	Errors made per kanji
Pictographic	7	2	0.29
Compound	6	63	10.50
Abstract	7	53	7.57

elementary school are pictographic. Thirty percent of Year Two *kanji* are pictographs. However, by Year Three, pictographs represent less than 15% of *kanji* and in later years of study pictographs represent very few newly learned *kanji*. Thus, *kanji* learned in initial years of Japanese language study may be unrepresentative of *kanji* as a whole and learners may have a false sense of the importance and usefulness of pictorial association for *kanji* learning in the long term. Table 5.2 gives a list of *kanji* according the year of introduction in Japan's primary school syllabus.

Thus, in conclusion, research highlights the importance of pictorial association in the beginning stages of learning when student exposure to pictographic *kanji* is large. Research also warns of the dangers of continuing to apply such a strategy as a student progresses in literacy and the strategy loses its ability to make a significant connection between a *kanji* and its meaning.

Symbolic Association

Symbolic association is the association of *kanji* with existing symbols, whether they are numerals, alphabetic letters, Japanese *kana*, shapes or signs.

In *The Strategies Study* it was found students recorded some usage of this association strategy, although these associations were far less frequent than pictorial associations. Also, as with pictorial association, the strategies were less observable as a students' proficiency progressed.

As an example of association with a symbol by a student in this study was the association the *kanji* 千 as looking like a yen symbol [¥], as shown in Figure 5.3. Another example was the association of 十 with a cross and 赤 as a nurse with a (red) cross on her hat, both of which provide further examples of association with symbols and shapes (the last example uses symbolic association in conjunction with a mnemonic device, a strategy discussed in Chapter 6).

Even though associations were made with shapes, *The Strategies Study* revealed that symbolic association was more often made with Japanese *kana*, or more precisely *katakana*. For example, students often identified *katakana* shapes within the *kanji*, such as:

- ム in 始 or 広;
- タ in 多 or 夕;
- カ in 力 or 勉;
- タ and ト in 外.

These associations are often made with visual appearance alone and therefore do not aim to make a connection with the *kanji*'s meaning without use a mnemonic device, which will be discussed in the following chapter. Students do, however, report that by identifying these *katakana* within the *kanji*, they are more easily able to reproduce the *kanji* in written form due to

Table 5.2 List of *kanji* taught in each year of elementary school in Japan

Year	Kanji
One	一右雨円王音下火花貝学気九休玉金空月犬見五口校左三山子四千字糸耳草車手十出女小上森人天水正生青夕石千白八文名本立力竹中虫町日田土二日入年赤百木目林六(80字)
Two	引羽雲園遠何夏家歌画回会海絵外角楽活間丸岩顔汽記帰弓科牛京強教兄形計元言原作古午岩顔汽記帰弓科牛京強教兄形計元言原作古午後語工姉公思交寺光自社谷近合国黒今才細食地止市矢親図数西声星行室首線計書多少台色同心新茶昼鳥長買朝晴雪前電春刀太体頭同池知南肉馬売昼直店風分聞東東方北答妹道読内鳴毛門夜野友通父曜光米米歩母頭北毎万明(160字)
Three	悪安暗医委意育員院飲運泳駅央横屋温化荷界開階寒感漢館岸起期客究急級宮去橋業局仕死銀区苦具君係軽式決研球幸守港根祭皿拾終世集始指歯詩次実写章乗申酒神炭曲進習柱昔重宿所暑助消商都待植身題談着注丁全送想息体鉄対豆第島湯短動品農調箱相追定庭族坂命投氷筆登表等童部配倍平返勉緑面役問油由秒病負葉福物流旅両列皮悲美(200字)薬遊羊予服様落練 和 陽
Four	愛案以衣位囲胃印英栄億加果課芽械害街各覚完官管関観願希喜季季紀機議改救給挙好漁共協鏡競極訓軍察径景旗結建残改固史司候航康告差菜最材初浅殺景欠散健試賞氏成試児治辞席借種祝順初松笑残倉士照統特孫清静単積仲説祝節戦然唱巣側賞堂働別良省達置失兆飯飛停選典徒灯統兵陸隊念敗梅博末必票的伝努労粉利料毒包望牧満脈民標夫副 特辺便法冷連老民無不要粉陸変輪類令例歴 録(200字)勇要養特料量
Five	圧移因永営衛易益液演応往桜恩可仮価河過賀快解格刊幹慣眼寄規技義逆旧居許境均禁句確経額件険検現個故久厚耕師鉱興示似混査再災採修在財在減殺護枝酸志条鉱師資織示制性識質舎謝授術際招絶承銭祖素状状情像増測燃政勢退精税態責設張評貧余武総銅導独任率損判貸肥非備迷綿預復布領(185字)燃弁破墓報豊防暴務夢余容略留編仏保能

(Continued)

54   Part 2: Cognitive Strategies

Table 5.2 List of *kanji* taught in each year of elementary school in Japan *(continued)*

Year	Kanji
Six	異 遺 域 宇 映 延 沿 我 灰 拡 革 閣 割 株 干 巻 看 簡 危 机 揮 貴 疑 吸 供 胸 郷 勤 筋 系 敬 警 劇 激 穴 絹 権 憲 源 厳 己 呼 誤 后 孝 皇 紅 降 鋼 刻 穀 骨 困 砂 座 済 裁 策 冊 蚕 至 私 姿 視 詞 誌 磁 射 捨 尺 若 樹 収 宗 就 衆 従 縦 縮 熟 純 処 署 諸 除 将 傷 障 城 蒸 針 仁 垂 推 寸 盛 聖 誠 宣 専 泉 洗 染 善 奏 窓 創 装 層 操 蔵 臓 存 尊 宅 担 探 誕 段 暖 値 宙 忠 著 庁 頂 潮 賃 痛 展 討 党 糖 届 難 乳 認 納 脳 派 拝 背 肺 俳 班 晩 否 批 秘 腹 奮 並 陛 閉 片 補 暮 宝 訪 亡 忘 棒 枚 幕 密 盟 模 訳 郵 優 幼 欲 翌 乱 卵 覧 裏 律 臨 朗 論（181字）

Source: Ministry of Education, Culture, Sports, Science and Technology, Japan, from http://www.mext.go.jp/a_menu/shotou/new-cs/youryou/syo/koku/001.htm (last accessed 4/10/2016).

Figure 5.3 Example of symbolic association of a *kanji*

these clues. In addition, in some cases students are able to use these associations with *katakana* to connect to the reading of the *kanji*, such as *ta* and 多 or *soto* in 外; although, these opportunities were somewhat rare in the data I collected in *The Intervention Study* and *The Strategies Study*.

Instances of associations with symbols of the English alphabet were even rarer and almost exclusively with the association of particular letters with particular reoccurring components in *kanji* such as 阝 for the English letter B. My research has shown many students disagree with the association of *kanji* with the alphabet as it connects two very separate writing systems and therefore opens the door to confusing cognitive processes. However, *The Strategies Study* did highlight some examples of successful association with the alphabet, in cases where learners saw an opportunity to associate a letter of the alphabet in a meaningful way. An example of this included a student who took the opportunity to make the association with the letter B and the 阝 in 部 to provide a clue that the *kanji* was pronounced *bu*, starting with the letter B.

Other Types of Whole *Kanji* Association

Kanji learners also, in general, group *kanji* according to those that looked the same or are part of a similar meaning, although in most instances this is done through comparison of similar components, a strategy that will be examined in Chapter 7. An example of an association of whole *kanji* would be a strategy used to differentiate between similar looking *kanji* so as not to confuse them. This strategy is similar to examples in the opening section of the chapter which highlighted to learners the similarities and differences between る and ろ. *The Strategies Study* highlighted a few examples of this strategy in action. For example, one participant associated the *kanji* for car [車] with ride [乗], in order to remember their differences. Another participant differentiated between younger sister and older sister, remembering the former, as having a 'more girly skirt' on the right component, to differentiate it from the square shape on the similar component in older sister. In addition to their similar appearance, these examples also have a semantic link, which will be discussed next; however, not all similar looking *kanji* have a semantic link and are often differentiated by learners according to shape alone. Examples from stimulated recall sessions in *The Intervention Study* and *The Strategies Study* include:

- the *kanji* for six [穴] and hole [六];
- the *kanji* for island [島], bird [鳥], and horse [馬];
- the *kanji* for person [人] and enter [入];
- the *kanji* for thousand [千] and dry [干];
- the *kanji* for spicy [辛] and happy [幸];
- the *kanji* for north [北] and compare [比];
- the *kanji* for man [士] and earth [土].

Many of the *kanji* (but not all) come from separate origins and do not share a common comment, etymology or semantic connection, and thus are linked in the memory according to shape alone, so as not to accidentally misread them as similar looking *kanji*.

A second type of whole *kanji* association involves the grouping of *kanji* that are part of a similar meaning group, such as 母 (mother), 父 (father), 兄 (older brother), 姉 (older sister), 弟 (younger brother) and 妹 (younger sister). Learners will also often associate *kanji* that are the opposite in meaning, such as 寒 (cold) and 暑 (hot), 白 (white) and 黒 (black), and 夜 (night) and 朝 (morning). Associations such as these are not made for the purpose of visual association with the *kanji* and its meaning, and in this way this strategy is not really a visualization strategy, but a way to store *kanji* in an appropriate schema in long-term memory. In fact we make associations such as this for any object we try to store in our memories and thus it is a good exercise to make conscious strategic choices to further strengthen the place of new *kanji* into logical, existing schema.

A third and more rarely used association of whole *kanji* with other *kanji* is to create cognitive links between two or more *kanji* that share the same reading so not to confuse them. Examples of this would include linking *kanji* such as 熱 (hot to touch), 暑 (hot temperature) and 厚 (thick), which are all pronounced *atsui*. This strategy is often only used when a learner has an extensive knowledge of vocabulary in Japanese and is obtaining literacy skills after developing their spoken ability. That is, they have a good knowledge of phonology in Japanese in their minds and are remembering *kanji* in order to represent the right words already in their memory structures.

Summary of association

In summary, research has shown students are prone to use visual associations, particularly in the beginning stages of learning. First, pictorial association seems to be a strategy that all Japanese language learners are aware of and heavily rely on during beginning stages of learning, when pictographic *kanji* are numerous. *The Strategies Study* showed that many students did not realize that they no longer applied this strategy at the intermediate to advanced stages of *kanji* knowledge. As a result, students may incorrectly self-report their use of this strategy, which has implications for researchers. Second, symbolic association is most common with Japanese *kana*, which is not surprising considering *kana* were originally derived from *kanji*, and thus associations between the two are more obvious than with the symbols of the roman alphabet, which students make far fewer associations with. Finally, research has revealed a wide range of associations with other *kanji* based on appearance, meaning and sound, although this was often carried out in a way that is evident in memorization in general and thus not isolated to *kanji* learning.

Implications

Implications for the *kanji* learner

It is important for the beginner *kanji* learner to use visual associations in the initial stages of *kanji* learning, in order to help them make the transition between making cognitive connections with meaning rather than sound. Any student who approaches *kanji* as they would an alphabetic script is destined for failure in the learning task, as such an approach would lead to frustrations at an inability to 'sound out' words when reading Japanese. In such cases, a visual association strategy will help to forge the connection between *kanji* being representative of sound.

In addition, seeing as the majority of *kanji* encountered in the initial stages of Japanese language learners are pictographic *kanji*, visual association strategies that connect *kanji* to this representation are an obvious choice. Indeed, *The Intervention Study* showed that pictorial association strategies were effective in memorizing a pictographic *kanji* 99% of the time (Rose, 2003), showing clear usefulness for this strategy at beginner levels. The advantages of such a strategy are clear, as long as the association is meaningful; however, only 3% of all *kanji* are *shokeimoji* (pictographs), which indicates that a visualization strategy has its clear limitations in terms of connecting all *kanji* to visual pictures.

Therefore, learners need to be aware of the usefulness of pictorial association strategies at the initial stages of learning and also the need to move away from this strategy as they encounter a higher frequency of *kanji* types, for which a more appropriate strategy should be applied.

Implications for the *kanji* instructor

It is important for instructors to understand the strengths and limitations of an approach to *kanji* learning that incorporates a visual association strategy. As this strategy is proven to be useful in the initial stages of *kanji* learning, instructors can incorporate strategy training into the *kanji* classroom. Many instructors do so through an examination of the etymology of these pictographic *kanji* (as shown in Figure 5.1), which also has the triple benefits of encouraging students to link *kanji* to its meaning, to move away from a phonological processing and also to spark historical and cultural interest in the script itself.

Despite the advantages of utilizing a visual association strategic approach to *kanji* instruction in the initial stages of Japanese language learning, the instructor must be aware of the limitations of such an approach. First, the teacher must make it clear to the students that such associations are useful for pictographic *kanji* and that the effectiveness of such an approach quickly diminishes as the *kanji* become more complex in physical appearance and in meaning. Second, the teacher must encourage students to only make meaningful connections. They should stress that even though a *kanji* may look like an unrelated object, such as looking like a 'squashed insect', it is only recommended to make a connection to an object associated with the meaning of the *kanji*, otherwise the connection will be meaningless. Finally, the teacher must be aware of the limitations of visual associations. As shown in *The Strategies Study*, advanced learners of *kanji* over-report use of pictorial *kanji* to the point of stating in questionnaires it is a strategy they almost always use, even though in fact it is one rarely applied at the advanced stages of Japanese language learning. The Japanese language instructor, like the advanced *kanji* learner, may fall into the trap of over-emphasizing the importance of this strategy in the classroom, thus further perpetuating the myth that visual associations is one of the most useful strategies in the Japanese language learners' repertoire.

Another aspect of applied linguistic research that an instructor should bear in mind is the importance of creating meaningful associations that would naturally exist in a learner's memory structures. For example, it would be logical to present *kanji* to learners that are part of the same schema. This would include presenting *kanji* for the days of the week at the same time, presenting *kanji* for colors and presenting *kanji* for conceptual notions such as emotions all at once. While this is follows the typical structure of many textbooks, I have seen some textbooks that present *kanji* according to other criteria, such as complexity, stroke order or frequency of use. In doing so, an opportunity is lost for the *kanji* to be integrated into the same schema of a learner's mind. For example, a textbook might refrain from teaching the *kanji* used for days of the week (曜), because it might be deemed as much more complex than the earth elements that are used in combination with it to represent each of the days (日・月・火・水・木・金・土). I would argue that we need to give learners more credit and that they are highly capable of memorizing complex *kanji* at a receptive and productive level in the early stages of learning. In many ways, the complexity of the *kanji* will stand out as a distinguishing factor, making it instantly recognizable when presented alongside the other simpler characters.

Implications for the researcher

Much previous research has emphasized the importance of visual association in the initial stages of *kanji* learning (see Bourke, 1996; Rose, 2003). There has also been research that argues the importance of moving away from a holistic approach to *kanji* study to one that enables examination of *kanji* components (see Flaherty & Noguchi, 1998; Toyoda, 1998; Toyoda & Kubota, 2001). Many of these studies, as mentioned in Chapter 2, do not truly isolate *kanji* type when examining strategy use. A study that conducted a more in-depth analysis of successful memorization and recall of *kanji* using visual association would further strengthen claims of the effectiveness of visual association strategies on pictorial *kanji* and ineffectiveness for other *kanji* types. I would suggest a controlled study that involves learners studying a range of *kanji* types under the controlled condition of applying a visual association strategy. These learners would then take a *kanji* test to identify which *kanji* were successfully memorized using the strategy. An analysis of the data would reveal which *kanji* types were remembered more effectively than others using this strategy. Naturally, other variables such as complexity of the *kanji* (e.g. stroke order), would also need to be accounted for. Such a study would provide valuable evidence that learners need to adjust their strategies according to the type of *kanji* they are learning.

6 Component Analysis

One cognitive strategy that has gained much attention in recent research is that of component analysis. *Kanji* components are also referred to as graphemes, which are the smallest unit a *kanji* can be broken down into. As the majority of *kanji* contain similar components/graphemes to other *kanji*, researchers argue that students need to develop awareness that complex *kanji* can be broken down into these smaller units. Toyoda (1998: 156) calls this understanding graphemic awareness, which can be described as 'awareness that *kanji* can be segmented into graphemes and that graphemes can be the subject of analysis'. Table 6.1 provides a few examples of commonly occurring *kanji*, which have been broken down into their graphemes.

In many cases, a radical is one of the graphemes in a *kanji*. A radical is a component of the *kanji* that is used to organize the *kanji* by grouping it with others that contain the root component. Many *kanji* dictionaries, for example, are provided with an index that organizes *kanji* according to radicals. There are seven types of radicals in *kanji* categorization, based on where they are positioned in the overall *kanji*:

(1) *Hen*, which appear on the left-hand side of a *kanji*.
(2) *Tsukuri*, which appear on the right-hand side of a *kanji*.
(3) *Kanmuri*, which appear in the top half of a *kanji*.
(4) *Ashi*, which appear in the bottom half of a *kanji*.
(5) *Kamae*, which enclose a *kanji*.
(6) *Tare*, which wrap around the top and side of a *kanji*.
(7) *Nyo*, which wrap around the side and bottom of a *kanji*.

Sometimes it is difficult for a learner to understand which part of the *kanji* is the radical, as it is not always obvious, even to a native speaker. Table 6.2 illustrates some examples of common radicals of each type listed above.

Radicals are often useful in accessing the meaning of the *kanji*, as radicals are connected to its root meaning. That is, *kanji* with the radical form 氵 often incorporate the root concept of *water*, such as in the *kanji* for *sweat* (汗), *swim* (泳), *lake* (湖) and *stream* (河). Some radicals are also used alongside graphemes that provide phonological clues, such as the radicals in 時, 寺, 峙 and 持.

Table 6.1 Examples of *kanji* graphemes

Kanji	Meaning	Graphemes
時	time	日・寺
部	part	立・口・阝
読	read	言・土・冗
校	school	木・亠・父

Table 6.2 List of *kanji* radical types

Type	Radical	Name	Examples
hen	犭	kemonohen	猫・狐・狙
tsukuri	刂	ritto	判・刊・型
kanmuri	宀	nabebuta	六・亡・夜
ashi	灬	rekka	点・熱・無
kamae	門	mongamae	聞・閉・開
tare	广	madare	庁・広・広
nyo	辶	shinnyo	近・達・速

Others seem to be more abstract in their representation of meaning, such as the *nabebutta* in Table 6.2, which occurs across seemingly unrelated (semantically or phonologically) *kanji,* such as in 六 (six), 亡 (death) and 夜 (evening).

Component Analysis Strategies

Component analysis is the act of breaking down *kanji* into its components (or graphemes) to assist in memorization. Component analysis is also useful in making connections with other *kanji* that contain the same component and can also assist the learner in making meaningful associations based on these connections. Component analysis strategies are probably the most widely applied strategies at the intermediate and advanced stages of Japanese language learning. The previous chapter highlighted the inherent illogicalness in trying to memorize *kanji* according to their whole form, as most *kanji* are not holistic representations of meaning, but contain combinations of semantic or phonetic components from which meaning is derived. Thus, it is logical that *kanji* are more effectively processed in a learner's memory according to these components, which can be compared and contrasted with *kanji* containing similar components in a learner's schema. It stands to reason, therefore, that students who are more acutely aware of the components of a *kanji* are able to better process them in their memories and recall them when reading.

In an early study of Japanese learners in Australia, Bourke (1996: 226) observed a higher degree of graphemic awareness as students encountered more complex *kanji*. She argued that 'as *kanji* becomes more complicated, it is helpful to break them into their component elements and relate these elements to their traditional meaning'. In a further study by Toyoda and Kubota (2001), 11 university students were tested for the learning strategies utilized to recall *kanji* and *kana*. Their study found that students who displayed graphemic awareness and analyzed the components of *kanji*, remembered more *kanji* than those who applied a pictorial, mnemonic or repetitive writing strategy.

Regarding the teaching of *kanji* and component analysis strategies, Flaherty and Noguchi (1998) examined the effectiveness of teaching *kanji* through component analysis compared to a holistic approach. Their study found that students in both second language and foreign language learning environments learned *kanji* more effectively through component analysis. This result, however, is not surprising considering only a small percentage of *kanji* are pictographic and the majority are compounds of two or more characters, as explained earlier.

In my own study, participants in general valued the importance of associating *kanji* using radicals, although some students were less convinced of the worth of learning *kanji* radicals at all. These differences in opinion are illustrated by some interview excerpts below:

Excerpt 6.1

> All the radicals that use the – the – all the *kanji* that use this (青) this sort of *kanji*, means blue, or calm. And they've all got that similar meaning of, you know, calm and blueness and clear skies, or whatever. (Learner Interview, *The Strategies Study*)

In this example, a student uses a radical to link to the underlying meaning of a *kanji*. Such a technique would only obviously be applicable to *kanji* whose radicals still connect to its overall meaning, which is the majority of *kanji*. Due to the evolution of *kanji* as a morphographic (meaning-based) script, many *kanji* do maintain a semantic connection to the radical's meaning. Other examples would include:

- the water radical (氵) in *kanji* such as *sweat* (汗), *swim* (泳), *lake* (湖) and *stream* (河);
- the gold radical (金) in *kanji* such as silver (銀), lead (鉛), iron (鉄) and copper (銅);
- the pathway/road radical (辶) in *kanji* such as *to chase* (追), *to return* (返), *to send* (送) and *to advance* (進).

In these examples, the radical provides a powerful link to the underlying root meaning of the *kanji*.

However, other participants in *The Strategies Study* reported that the reoccurring radicals caused some confusion, in that they could remember the radical in the *kanji* but 'freeze on the rest' due to the fact that the radical tended to be the easiest part of the *kanji* to remember and thus the most likely part to stick in their memory. Other participants discussed the usefulness of organizing known and new *kanji* according to radicals, but admitted this systematic style of study was time-consuming and thus difficult to keep up. Therefore, this study highlighted how learners use radicals to help trigger meaning and to remember *kanji*; however, the study also highlighted a problem encountered when the same radical appears in so many different *kanji*, that it becomes difficult to remember the non-radical components. Furthermore, the study showed that associating the *kanji* by radical alone was the cause of frustration. As learners encountered more and more *kanji* of the same radical, the systematic grouping of *kanji* soon became cumbersome and time-consuming, causing some participants in the study to abandon radical-based learning strategies.

Radicals are just one component of a *kanji* and numerous studies have shown that learners are more creative in their use of component analysis strategies and tend to use more imaginative associations with a *kanji*'s components in order to effectively memorize them. Learners in their innovative ways of thinking, are not bound by radicals alone and use non-radical components to trigger meaning. This creativity is also illustrated from the following excerpt from my study, where a learner discusses how he memorized the *kanji* for *language* (語):

Excerpt 6.2

But like I remember I was talking to you about the *kanji go* (語) and how the first part of it looked kind of like a different *kanji* (言). I don't remember what it was, but – and then the second part of it was the top half looked like go (五) as in the number, and then the bottom was kind of like a box (口) – yeah. It was like a box for each of them, so – you know, so – yeah. Breaking them up and remembering them that way. (Learner Interview, *The Strategies Study*)

Here, the participant explains how he dissects the *kanji* into segments and each of the segments fits into a 'box' that forms part of the *kanji*. That is, he breaks down 語 into the components 言, which he associates by meaning, and 五, which he associates by sound, and 口, for which he applies a pictorial association strategy of resembling a box. In this example, the learner is associating all three components in cognitively different ways: according to meaning (言), to sound and meaning (五) and pictorial association (口). Thus, component analysis here extends beyond semantic links, and is often used in tandem with other cognitive strategies.

In all my studies that examine learner cognition, one feature remains consistent in regards to use of component analysis strategies; in all cases, when component analysis is used by learners, it is used as a tool to break down a *kanji* into smaller parts so that another associative strategy can be used for memorization. That is, the components are then used to associate the *kanji* to pictures, symbols, radicals or other *kanji* through visual association or mnemonic devices to then connect them to their meaning or sound. A few examples from the stimulated recall sessions from *The Intervention Study* and *The Strategies Study* are listed below, to illustrate how this was carried out by some of the participants.

(1) *Govern* [治] was remembered as being just a couple of marks [氵] around what looks like *mu* [厶] and *mouth* [口].
(2) *Sea* [海] as a *field* [田] with *waves* [氵] splashing on it.
(3) *Autumn* [秋] was remembered by associating the *kanji* for *tree* [木] and *fire* [火], via a mnemonic that 'leaves turn red (like fire) in autumn'.
(4) *Rumor* [噂] was remembered as a *mouth* [口] with 'four horns sticking out everywhere and it's glued together because it keeps on trying to spread rumors'.

The first example uses component analysis, with pictorial association ('a couple of marks'), symbolic association (with the *katakana mu*) and association with other *kanji* (in the example of *kuchi*, meaning mouth). This example, while used successfully by the learner in the study, is somewhat problematic in that links to the meaning of the *kanji* are unclear through the association of the components, that is, I remain unconvinced that such as strategy would result in the long-term memorization of this *kanji* with its meaning *to govern*. The second example uses component analysis with a mnemonic to recall the meaning of *autumn*, explaining the *kanji* for *autumn* [秋] contains the *kanji* similar to *tree* [木] and the *kanji* for *fire* [火]. This type of component analysis is far more powerful in that *autumn* is associated with trees (a parent category of leaves), as well as the second component of *fire*. I would, therefore, be more strongly convinced that this type of strategy would result in more effective long-term memorization of this *kanji*. In fact, many of the mnemonic strategy examples that are presented in the following chapter will also be examples of component analysis. This is because learners often use mnemonic-based stories to connect a *kanji*'s components in an effective way to its meaning.

The third example uses component analysis in identifying the component *mouth* [口], but then uses pictorial association of *horns* [八] and a mnemonic to connect it to the meaning, *rumor* [噂]. This example is effective, but I would caution over the danger of this analysis becoming overly convoluted. As will be shown in the following chapter, convoluted associations can result in the learner losing the memory trace to its meaning. Moreover, such messy associations might also result it learners falsely recalling any number of other *kanji* that contain similar components. For example, the student could remember this association and falsely apply it to any *kanji* that contains both the mouth component and a component resembling 'horns', such as *vulgar* [俗], *blossom* [咲], *steeple* [塔] or *virtue/good* [善]. Nevertheless, this example still shows how learners use component analysis to break down *kanji* into parts so that then they could apply other strategies to these parts to facilitate their memorization, whether this was through pictorial association or mnemonic devices, or both.

Previous research has established that as learners encounter more *kanji*, graphemic awareness grows and students rely more on component analysis. The reasons for this are two-fold: first, at the more advanced level, *kanji* are rarely of the pictographic or abstract types and mostly of a compound *kanji* type (e.g. *kaiimoji* or *keiseimoji*) facilitating the breaking of them into their components. Second, as students memorize more *kanji*, they encounter *kanji* that share similar components, so the pool of components in which to compare and contrast *kanji* also grows.

Across all of my studies into *kanji* learning, I have consistently found that beginner learners, who have a small pool of known *kanji* in which to examine components, have difficulty in drawing meaningful associations between them. This is in contrast to more advanced learners, who encounter more *kanji* that share similar components, and for whom component analysis is not only the preferred cognitive learning strategy, but an essential one to advance to higher proficiency levels. The following interview statement from a participant in *The Strategies Study*, who was an intermediate-level proficiency participant, illustrates this.

Excerpt 6.3

> Right. Well, it's – I think it's easier to group them and to memorize the group than to memorize each – like one *kanji*, you know. I kind of like see it as like seeing the root of a word. You can – you know, if you know the root of the word, if you know the root of the *kanji*, it's easier to use it than it is – because I feel like you get a more natural understanding of the meaning, than – opposed if you just – just take, you know, two random *kanji* and memorize them. (Learner Interview, *The Strategies Study*)

This statement serves as an illustration from a learner's perspective of the benefits of component analysis when learning *kanji*, but also of the inherent limitations.

In summary, component analysis is a strategy that many learners embrace consciously, and that research shows to be absolutely essential to progress to the advanced stages of Japanese written proficiency. However, component analysis is just the first step in memorizing complex *kanji*, as the learner then must decide what to do with these components. Therefore, most learners will use component analysis with a range of other strategies, not only with the association of components with other *kanji*, but in accordance with a range of phonological, semantic and pictographic connections.

Implications

Implications for the *kanji* learner

Component analysis is not just a convenient way to group *kanji*, but a way of understanding the root meaning of the *kanji*, because those *kanji* that share similar root *kanji* or radical, also often share the same root meaning. Component analysis is also a convenient way to place new *kanji* with known *kanji* in a highly systematized way. In fact, by placing *kanji* into semantically or visually bound categories, learners are working within the way their minds naturally organize information in schemata, which will result in better memorization and more efficient recall. While at times the study of radicals or *kanji* components might seem to be time-consuming, it is an activity that will result in significant future success for the language learner.

There is some indication from my research that component analysis may be less useful for beginner learners of *kanji*, where the number of known *kanji* is so limited, so it is difficult to match similar components of new *kanji* and known *kanji*. These learners, therefore, might be unaware that a component in a new *kanji* might be very important in their future studies. I, myself, remember coming across the *kanji* for 語 early in my Japanese studies, as it is used in the word *Japanese*. At this stage I used a pictorial association of the left-side of the *kanji* [言] to look like a box with papers 'written in Japanese' piled on top. It was only later, when the character reappeared in other *kanji* such as *say* [言], *speak* [話] and *read* [読] that I switched to a semantically-situated component analysis strategy to associate that component with meaning connected to *language*. Some learners may believe that it could have been useful to know the components of a *kanji* from the outset. This is a tactic used by some commercial books that will be explored in the following chapter; however, I argue that if it is the only *kanji* a learner knows in which the component appears, it could potentially cause confusion, as the learner would often need to memorize the component meaning and the *kanji* meaning at the same time.

This is perhaps better illustrated by frequently occurring *kanji*, whose components are less-frequently used. Take for example the character for *alcohol* [酒], which is taught in grade three in Japanese schools and is one of the earlier *kanji* learned by adult learners as a second language. Learners should question whether the component 酉, which is a widely unused sign for *bird*, needs to be learned at all, especially considering it is not part of the *joyo kanji* and appears in so few frequently occurring *kanji*. In fact, a learner might be best to associate it with *alcohol,* as the next time they are likely to encounter it is when they learn the 1006th most frequently occurring *kanji* in the word for *drunk* [酔]. Thus, the learner has to weigh the amount of extra effort in learning the semantic origin of a *kanji*'s components with the benefit it will provide in the future. Certainly, frequently occurring components will be well-worth the effort, but less-frequently occurring ones may best be disregarded in favor of another strategic approach.

Implications for the *kanji* instructor

As mentioned in the previous section, learners may be unaware of the importance of *kanji* components, and the frequency in which they might occur in upcoming words. Thus, the teacher is in a unique position to highlight potentially useful components to the students when they first occur. For example, in one of the first *kanji* lessons, when students learn the character for *day/sun* [日], it might be useful for instructors to raise awareness of students of the future importance of this *kanji*. Teachers could prime students by telling them that they will see this *kanji* a lot in the future for words associated with *day/sun,* such as sun [陽], early [早], warm [温] and tomorrow [明], or day of the week [曜]. Teachers are in a better position than students to understand the importance of a component in *kanji* and thus can relay this importance to the students where necessary. This does not mean that component learning should precede the teaching of *kanji*. For example, the *kanji* for waterfall [滝] might likely precede the teaching of dragon [竜], as waterfall will far more likely to be used by adult learners than the dragon (unless, of course, the learner is a fan of the Japanese anime *Dragonball,* although *turtle* [亀] is more commonly seen in that series, as it is the *kanji* worn by the protagonist and the word *Dragonball* is written in *katakana*).

Implications for the researcher

While component analysis is clearly an important strategy for students of Japanese, it is a surprisingly under-researched one. A lot of teaching practices around components or radicals are based on a historical understanding of where *kanji* are derived from and how they have been traditionally organized. Many books, which encourage component analysis (see Heisig, 2007), are certainly not based on any empirical evidence that teaching and learning *kanji* via components is pedagogically sound.

Based on the strategies that learners report, we know that *kanji* are learned effectively by analyzing their parts, but researchers have an unclear understanding of how these strategies relate to the types of *kanji* being learned. We still do not fully understand the relationship between different ways of memorizing components and the level of success learners have in embedding them in their long term memory. Researchers are still unsure of the process involved when students overcome the difficulties in learning *kanji* whose components provide different clues, some abstract, some semantic and some phonetic. The field would benefit from in-depth experimental studies to test the effectiveness of component analysis according to different *kanji* types. Furthermore, there is a need for exploratory studies that systematically examine strategies deployed for specific *kanji*, so as to develop ways to better present these *kanji* to learners in textbooks.

7 Mnemonics

One cognitive strategy that has been highlighted in learning, teaching and researching of the Japanese language is the use of mnemonic strategies to memorize the written language. From a cognitive perspective, a mnemonic strategy is defined as 'a method for enhancing memory performance by giving the material to be remembered a meaningful interpretation' (Anderson, 2005: 461). A further definition is making associations between new and already known information through use of stories, phrases, verse or the like (Oxford, 2001). In terms of using these kinds of associations when memorizing the Japanese writing system, I would define mnemonic strategies as the use of stories or phrases to link written characters or letters to the meanings or sounds they represent. The use of mnemonics to study *kanji*, in particular, has been at the center of Japanese language-teaching practices, in that it is widely viewed as a useful strategy to get learners to memorize *kanji*. Mnemonics are often used in conjunction with pictorial association and component analysis strategies as a means to make meaningful links with the components found in *kanji*.

Mnemonic strategies have also been showcased in a number of commercial textbooks aimed at the Japanese language learner. Many of these textbooks claim mnemonic strategies to be the solution to the second language learner's struggle to master the large number of *kanji* needed to be learned in Japanese SLA. Some of these textbooks include:

- Heisig, J.W. (2007) *Remembering the Kanji (Vol. 1): A Systematic Guide to Reading Japanese Characters*. Honolulu: University of Hawaii Press.
- Heisig, J.W. (2008) *Remembering the Kanji (Vol. 2): A Systematic Guide to Reading Japanese Characters*. Honolulu: University of Hawaii Press.
- Henshall, K.G. (1988) *A Guide to Remembering Japanese Characters*. North Clarendon: Tuttle.
- Rowley, M. (1992) *Kanji Pict-O-Graphix: Over 1,000 Japanese Kanji and Kana Mnemonics*. Berkeley: Stone Bridge Press.
- Stout, M. and Hakone, K. (2011) *Basic Japanese Kanji (Vol. 1): High-Frequency Kanji at your Command*. North Clarendon: Tuttle.

Heisig's (2007) book, which is now in its 6th edition, is one of the more famous *kanji* learning books aimed at the Japanese language learner. The book organizes *kanji* learning into a systematic approach, which utilizes the various reoccurring graphemes found in *kanji*. As the previous chapter has outlined, a grapheme (Toyoda, 1998) or component (Flaherty & Noguchi, 1998) is used to describe the smallest meaningful unit that a *kanji* can be broken down into. Heisig (2007: 13) refers to these graphemes as 'primitive elements', which he defines as the reoccurring components that give clues to a *kanji*'s meaning. These components are then used to create mnemonic-based stories that connect the components to the *kanji*'s meaning. The author states that the process of creating stories might first embarrass students, due to the silliness or childishness of the stories, but this should not detract from the powerful effectiveness of utilizing a mnemonic approach to learning *kanji*. Heisig (2007: 7) is adamant in the preface to his book that using his approach can help students attain their goal of 'native proficiency in writing the Japanese characters'. In these books, *kanji* are presented alongside stories connecting *kanji* components to the *kanji*'s meaning, although the book is almost void of connections to how the *kanji* is pronounced in the Japanese language. An example is that 'while a mnemonic strategy may be used to connect the *kanji* 下 [below] to its meaning, the same mnemonic strategy provides no indication whether the *kanji* should be read *ge, shita, kuda, ka* or *sa*, all of which are possible' (Rose, 2013: 982). By the end of Heisig's (2008) second volume of *kanji* study, learners are weaned off the suggested mnemonics and encouraged to create their own. Only after all *kanji* are learned through linking the *kanji* with meaning, is the learner encouraged to go back to the beginning and repeat the process by linking the *kanji* to its sound. This is an obvious flaw in the system, which will be returned to later in this chapter.

Rowley's (1992) book, is similar to the Heisig volumes (2007, 2008), in that it uses a pictorial strategy alongside a mnemonic strategy. Similar to the strategies outlined in Chapter 5, this system involves relating the *kanji* or components to pictures of what they represent. This strategy seems to be obviously applicable to pictographic *kanji* or those that contain pictographic elements. For example, the *kanji* for *rest* [休], can be remembered quite easily by linking is pictographic components of *person* [人] and *tree* [木], as a 'person resting under a tree'. However, the fact is that most *kanji* components are not pictographic representations of meaning and are often symbolic or arbitrary. Thus, the more abstract or complex a *kanji* is, the less likely this type of mnemonic strategy may prove of any use to the learner. The author seems highly aware of the limitations to his own strategies, as he states 'Several common *kanji* have been excluded [from the book] because frankly I couldn't come up with a satisfactory visual or textual mnemonic' (Rowley, 1992: 8). A similar approach can be found in the Henshall (1998) publication. Notions of stretching mnemonic strategies to nonsensical situations by being overly reliant on pictorial links will also be returned to later in this chapter.

In the Stout and Hakone (2011) book, the authors seem to embrace the nonsensical, as they apply complicated mnemonic strategies to abstract *kanji*, despite seemingly simpler ways to make a meaningful connection. An example I have referred to elsewhere (Rose, 2013) is when the authors teach the *kanji* for the number 9, as a pictographic representation of 'a hand reaching something – nine is the number before reaching ten' (Stout & Hakone, 2011: 18). Here, the learner is not only encouraged to link a non-pictographic *kanji* with a picture of something completely disconnected to its meaning (a hand), but also is encouraged to use an abstract mnemonic strategy in order to connect a reaching hand with the meaning of the number 9. I would argue that such nonsensical use of mnemonics is not only ridiculous, but also potentially damaging to effective learning and logical memorization processes. This is an issue I will return to later in the chapter when discussing the notion of losing the meaning in overly complicated mnemonics.

Research into the Effectiveness of Mnemonic Strategies

Despite the large number of books that purport a mnemonic approach as essential to the learning of the Japanese written language, there is little evidence from research that exclusive use of such approaches accelerates SLA. In fact, none of these books offers any kind of empirical basis on which to support their convictions that a mnemonic approach to learning *kanji* is superior to other approaches. Indeed, the few studies that have examined the use of mnemonics have seemingly mixed results.

In one such study, Bourke (1996) found that component analysis was superior and more frequently used than any other approach, but when *kanji*, or *kanji* elements, were not meaningful to students, a mnemonic approach was helpful. This indicates that mnemonics can provide a solution to difficult to learn *kanji*, but are not the sole (or even preferred) approach used by learners. Such results concur with Toyoda's (1998) study, which found a mnemonic approach was ranked the second most widely used approach to learning *kanji*, after a component analysis approach. However, these results must be interpreted cautiously, as a component analysis strategy is not exclusive of a mnemonic strategy, and vice versa. That is, a mnemonic strategy is often used to relate the components of a *kanji* to its meaning and thus these strategies can be used in tandem; it is not the case that a learner will use one or the other.

In another study, Lu *et al.* (1999: 304) found students 'learned more of the *kanji* characters and their meanings when the *kanji* were presented using descriptive mnemonics'. This study, however, is limited in that it only compared the effects of learning *kanji* with mnemonics to learning *kanji* without them, which does not indicate their effectiveness compared to other strategies. Thus, this quasi-experimental study highlights the effectiveness of a mnemonic approach to learning, but the results are not easily generalizable to real learning environments where students often employ multiple strategies at the same time. Nevertheless, despite issues with interpreting the results of these studies, the above research points to a potential benefit to memorization of *kanji* offered by a mnemonic approach. Thus, there appears to be some value in claims that a mnemonic approach facilitates *kanji* learning.

Other reports into the use of mnemonics, however, found them to have no significant effect on a student's ability to memorize *kanji* (Sakai, 2004; Wang & Thomas, 1992). Sakai's (2004) study compared the learning of *kanji* through use of mnemonics with the learning of *kanji* through contextual clues and through rote memorization. Wang and Thomas' (1992) study compared the application of mnemonic strategies for learning *kanji* against the use of rote learning techniques when learning *kanji*. Both of these studies indicated that the use of mnemonics when learning *kanji* is limited and problematic if relied on too heavily. These studies did, however, compare mnemonic learning with non-cognitive strategy use (such as compensatory and metacognitive strategies), which is an unfair comparison as these strategies are not mutually exclusive and can both be employed at the same time. Specifically, using the theory covered in Chapter 4, we can see holes in these research designs. From a cognitive theory point of view, we understand that mnemonic strategies are used to enhance encoding of new information and rote learning retrieves this encoded information. Thus, these approaches are examining distinctly different parts of the memorization process and therefore should not be compared in an empirical study. Therefore, even though mnemonics have been explored in previous literature, mixed results indicate mnemonics to be one gray area worth further investigation.

Because of the gray areas in the potential usefulness of mnemonics in learning *kanji*, mnemonic strategy use was a key focal point in *The Intervention Study* and *The Strategies Study*, and has been reported in previously published work (Rose, 2003, 2013). In these studies, use of mnemonic strategies among participants varied from extreme frequency to conscious refusal to use them. As was to be expected, when a mnemonic was used, it was often used with other strategies such as pictographic association or, more commonly, component analysis; that is, the stories that participants made connected with the components of the *kanji*. Some examples of this are given below:

(1) The verb *taberu*. Yeah. It looks like a house. So, for me, I eat in a house, or I eat in a restaurant which is like a building. So I would always think of it as the building. (Stimulated Recall Task, *The Strategies Study*)
(2) Like I always remember this one as *Yasumu* because there's a person resting under a tree. And it's not really a story, but kind of – I know this is person, and I know this is tree. And I just try to picture the person under the tree, and know that that's relaxing. ...Or like *Suki*. I know that that's a mother and a child, and I say, what can be more pleasing

than a mother with her child? Like things like that. I don't – I don't make up stories so much as I try to read the pictograph. (Stimulated Recall Task, *The Strategies Study*)
(3) That's profit, so cutting down the stalk of rice for profit (Stimulated Recall Task, *The Strategies Study*)

In these examples, Participant 1 associates the *kanji* for *taberu* (食) as looking like a building using pictographic association. She then relates the meaning *to eat* through a mnemonic of *eating in a restaurant*, which is a type of building. Participant 2 connects the *kanji* for *rest* [休] to its meaning by making a story of its components of *tree* [木] and *person* [人] by thinking of *a person resting under a tree*. He gives another example of the *kanji* for *like*, having the components of a *mother* [女] and *child* [子], meaning *like* [好]. Having studied the etymology (origin of the written form) of the *kanji* compounds, Participant 3 uses a mnemonic to associate meaningful compounds to recall the meaning of *profit*, in the act of *harvesting rice for profit*. In the case of Participant 3, who used mnemonics with his study of etymology, he did not want to label his learning as using 'stories' because of the stigma attached that using stories is 'confabulated' (his words). He saw his own application of mnemonics based on etymology as very different to those outlined in the commercial textbooks which were confabulated in many ways, resulting in stories that bordered on the 'silly' or 'ridiculous'.

In the interview data of these studies, some participants made the distinction between meaningful mnemonics (relating the meaning to actual components that have meaning), and 'stories', which are less meaningful. In fact, in stimulated recall data there were very few instances where participants employed a mnemonic device that was not also based on an association of meaningful *kanji* compounds. There seemed to be a consensus among the group of participants that mnemonics were useful only when meaningful, otherwise they had limitations to language learning. Indeed, many of the participants in the interviews were very cognitively aware of the use of mnemonics as a strategy in *kanji* learning and many participants expressed opinions of limitations to studying *kanji* in this way or relying too heavily on them. Learners cited the difficultly in making up stories or the dangers in coming up with too convoluted interpretations, which confused the memorization process. On the other hand, other learners recognized that mnemonics were often ridiculous, but they served a purpose if they resulted in memorization of *kanji*, which is illustrated with the following excerpt from one learner.

Excerpt 7.1

At first it sounds ridiculous, if someone explains it to you. 'The bunny comes out of the hole, goes around. The *cat* chases it through the grass to the rice field'. But it still makes sense. I can remember *neko* [猫 – cat] because of that [story]. (Learner Interview, *The Strategies Study*)

In other data (Rose, 2013), one particular participant – referred to by the pseudonym Jacob – used mnemonics outlined in the Heisig books (2007, 2008) to memorize each and every *kanji*. As mentioned earlier, Heisig introduces the graphemes of a *kanji* first (which he refers to as 'primitive elements') and then uses these graphemes to construct stories to tie in with a *kanji*'s meaning. As learners advance and *kanji* become more complex and contain more graphemes, these stories become equally complex. In the stimulated recall data, Jacob used a mnemonic device in the form of a story from the Heisig books for almost every *kanji* recalled. As a result, the stories seemed to be quite illustrative of the 'confabulated' stories that other participants seemed to avoid. Jacob, in contrast, devotedly followed these stories whole-heartedly. In one stimulated recall session, Jacob explains the Heisig method for learning a complex *kanji*, in the excerpt below.

Excerpt 7.2

So, sometimes he'll [Heisig will] stick very closely to what you might find in the dictionary and sometimes he'll give it a meaning which it just – it's not connected but its memorable. So we've got the *kanji* here. And as it says, 'the picture in this *kanji* is not a pleasant one. It shows a large and fluffy Saint Bernard dog stretched out on the table all stuffed and stewed and garnished with vegetables – its paws in the air and an apple in its mouth. At each corner of the table sits an eager but empty mouth waiting for the utensils to arrive so the feast can begin'. Now, because that's such a ridiculous story, it's incredibly easy to remember. You've got these four mouths around the table, dog in the middle, with their utensils. So that's the kind of thing it's based on. So the more ridiculous, the better in remembering it. Some of them are a lot more obvious like exquisite is the women who are few. Extinguish of course you've got the spark and the water extinguishing the spark, so some of them are pretty simple. (Jacob T3 in Rose, 2013: 989)

In the interviews with Jacob, he reported applying Heisig's mnemonic approach to *kanji* learning in all of his study sessions. It became apparent that he used the stories to encode the *kanji* in his memory (through use of mnemonic devices to link graphemes to whole *kanji* and then to link this with the meaning of the word in his first language (English). He then applied a wide range of metacognitive strategies to engage in retrieval practice, but retrieval also involved the rehearsal of the mnemonics. For example, Jacob would make use of flashcards and test himself on the stories; he would audio record the stories onto a portable music player and listen to them before bed and on the train. As a result of this extensive training Jacob was able recite very detailed stories, which were often word-for-word recitals of the original Heisig versions, such as in the excerpt above.

The interviews revealed that the reason Jacob relied on such a systematic approach was that he believed it was the only way to achieve what he thought to be an unachievable goal of learning 2000+ *joyo kanji* before graduation. Jacob viewed the Heisig method as a 'magic bullet' that he could use to successfully 'learn the *kanji*' before the end of the year. After all, the author himself claimed the method worked; this motivated him to study and made his goals seem achievable.

As *The Strategies Study* was a longitudinal study, it gave scope to measure Jacob's progress and changing attitudes throughout this pivotal year. Jacob was very positive about the method at the beginning of the study and was pleased with the progress he was experiencing using the stories from Heisig; however, by the end of the year, Jacob was once again returning to the state of mind that his goals were not achievable. Moreover, he began to voice a waning faith in learning *kanji* in this way. The biggest problem Jacob experienced with the sole use of a mnemonic strategy was that the stories focused on link new *kanji* with their English meanings; however, many *kanji* at his advanced level rarely appeared by themselves and were more often used to create complex words in conjunction with other *kanji*. Unlike *kanji* at the beginning stages of Japanese language learning, which were often used to represent nouns, verbs and adjectives, *kanji* at the advanced stages were more abstract and their etymological meanings were not always related to their modern day uses. Thus, when Jacob encountered these *kanji* in reading materials he was able to successfully recognize the *kanji* recite the associated story and recall its abstract meaning, but this did not result in him being able to decode the *kanji* in the context of the sentence, especially when used in combination with other *kanji*.

A further limitation reported by Jacob was that the memorized the stories were entirely in English and thus he was unable to read the *kanji* in Japanese, as the Japanese reading of the *kanji* had not been part of the encoding process, nor the retrieval practice activities. This meant that Jacob could not read known *kanji* out loud or look them up in a phonetic dictionary. In short, although Jacob had memorized the meaning of the *kanji* very successfully using the Heisig approach, this method of study had not facilitated the learning of the pronunciation of each *kanji* in this process. At the end of the year, Jacob was disheartened with the notion of returning to the *kanji* that he had spent so long learning because he now realised he needed to incorporate phonological associations with each of them.

Finally, in the stimulated recall session, another limitation became apparent. Due to the confabulated nature of the stories, stimulated recall data highlighted that Jacob could often could recall the mnemonic in the form of a perfectly recited story, but then fail to recollect the meaning. I have referred to this phenomenon as 'losing the meaning in the mnemonic' (Rose, 2013), which I use to describe situations when a learner can recall the mnemonic-based story, but fail to remember the *kanji* it was connected with. This phenomenon of losing the meaning in mnemonic was observed in a number of stimulated recall sessions, not only by Jacob, but also by other participants who actively applied a mnemonic strategy. Cognitive theory can explain the cause of this phenomenon. In these cases, learners seemed to be encoding *kanji* using stories that were too far removed from the meaning of the *kanji*. An example can be seen below:

Excerpt 7.3
> Some of them are quite ridiculous. 'There's this monster on the ceiling that likes to eat nails and then spit them in people's heads'. I remember the story, but I can't remember the *kanji* right now. I haven't revised these now for about three months or longer. I find after three months it's terrible. (Jacob, T8 in Rose, 2003: 990)

In this excerpt, Jacob acknowledges the limitation in the approach in that the stories require quite a lot of review, but fails to recognize that the lack of memorizing the *kanji* might be more connected to a shallow attempt at encoding the *kanji* (using nonsensical associations), rather than a failure to retrieve. After all, in the this example, Jacob recalls the story perfectly, because his retrieval practice has created a strong memory trace between the *kanji* and the story, but has neglected to create a strong memory trace between the *kanji* and its meaning (or its reading in Japanese).

In summary, mnemonic devices, whether nonsensical or not, were seen as important strategies for most learners. There is strong evidence that a mnemonic strategy provides a powerful tool to link *kanji* and *kanji* components to their meaning. However, sole reliance on mnemonics can lead to limitations such as a de-emphasis on pronunciation and difficultly in creating memorable mnemonics, which often can lead to confabulation. Based on my own studies, and on evidence from others, I would disagree with Heisig's (2007/2008: 7) assertion that his approach can help students attain their goal of 'native proficiency in writing the Japanese characters'. I think such claims give students a false understanding of the usefulness of mnemonics. Instead, mnemonic strategies should be viewed as one tool in a repertoire of strategies necessary to memorize all *kanji* types, which have multiple pronunciations and meanings depending on the context of their use.

Implications

Implications for the *kanji* learner

Previous studies have provided contradictory findings of the benefits of mnemonic strategies in *kanji* learning. Such research has revealed some benefits of mnemonic strategies for *kanji* learning, but also indicated that an exclusive application of this strategy causes a limitation in *kanji* knowledge, in that learners are often unable to recall the pronunciation of the *kanji*, as most mnemonics rely on making a meaningful link between a *kanji* and its meaning. This means that students who overuse a mnemonic approach may have difficulty understanding both the meaning and pronunciation of the *kanji* when it is used in combinations with other *kanji*, as both meaning and pronunciation are subject to change when combined.

In addition to this, research has highlighted an issue of 'losing the meaning in the mnemonic', where stories used become separated from the original meaning of the *kanji* and learners are able to recall the story, but not the meaning. Therefore, research has suggested mnemonics provide both benefits and limitations in the *kanji*-learning task. Certainly mnemonics help learners make sense of *kanji* that contain reoccurring components, but an exclusive use of a mnemonic based strategy causes limitations in knowledge when applied broadly and ineffectively.

Implications for the *kanji* instructor

Research into mnemonic approaches to learning also have clear implications for the Japanese language instructor, especially considering that mnemonics are seen as problematic when associations are particularly convoluted or complex. While my own research (Rose, 2013) warns against the implementation of a pure mnemonic approach, it does concur with previous studies (e.g. Lu *et al.*, 1999; Toyoda, 1998), which show mnemonics to be a useful strategy for students of Japanese. My own research, however, qualifies this finding by emphasizing that a mnemonic approach is only useful when meaningful associations can be made, especially those which connect a *kanji* to both its meaning and the reading. Logically, mnemonics might prove less useful for *kanji* that are not connected to their etymological origin, not connected in a clear way to its components, or are semantically abstract when presented in isolation, as is the case for many advanced *kanji*. Therefore, instructors should be wary of promoting a mnemonic-based approach for all *kanji*.

Furthermore, in my own studies, I found that many students were heavily influenced by the mnemonic strategies taught to them by their own teachers, in both positive and negative ways. Some learners were quick to defend the usefulness of mnemonic stories taught to them by their teachers, even when they were clearly convoluted. Other learners seemed very quick to dismiss mnemonics altogether, as the ones they had been taught were seen as childish. These learners had refused to employ mnemonic strategies at all in their independent study of *kanji*, regardless of the benefit they could bring to learning *kanji* that had clear semantically or phonologically linked components.

Implications for the researcher

In my own studies into mnemonic strategy use I tried to situate the use of mnemonics within a wider context of learning *kanji*, in order to examine how students applied this strategy alongside other strategies. A wider research lens is essential, as mnemonics are rarely used in isolation and are inclusive of other cognitive strategies outlined in this chapter, such as pictorial associations and component analysis. Future studies might also consider an approach where use of mnemonic strategies can be measured in conjunction with (and not in opposition to) such strategies.

In terms of research methods for measuring mnemonic strategy use, I have previously made the following recommendation of further research:

> In terms of data collection, stimulated recall data shed light on the types of mnemonic strategies employed by learners, concurring with recent recommendations for the inclusion of this instrument in strategy research (Dörnyei, 2005; Rose, 2012b; Tseng *et al.*, 2006). Qualitative interview data revealed the impetus behind choosing or avoiding mnemonic strategies, and the self-perceived impact they had on learning. By comparing data from the questionnaire and interview with the stimulated recall task, limitations to self-report instruments were also revealed in the form of learners who reported not using mnemonic strategies but that were nevertheless observed in stimulated recall and vice versa. This concurs with previous studies that have warned against the reliability of self-report data in strategy research. (Rose, 2013: 989)

Thus, I am an avid campaigner of the importance of multiple methods to measure strategy use, as previous research has tended towards the questionnaire and interview approach, through which learners are encouraged to self-report their own strategy use. The nature of self-report measures causes one to question the legitimacy of such data as valid representations of the actual strategies used. Furthermore, studies are needed that examine the effectiveness of mnemonic strategies for different *kanji* types in order to confirm or refute my claims here that certain semantically-oriented *kanji* lend themselves to mnemonic strategies than other, more abstract, *kanji*. At the moment this is an assumption I have made based on a small, qualitative study into mnemonic strategy use, and the variables that affect such strategy usage has still to be empirically tested.

Part 3
Psychology and Self-regulation

8 Learner Psychology, Self-regulation and Language Learning

Self-regulation as an Alternative to Language Learner Strategy Research

In addition to the importance of cognitive strategies in language learning, SLA research has suggested that we need to examine learners' capacity to regulate the study of language and control their motivation to learn (e.g. see Dörnyei, 2001, 2005; Dörnyei & Ryan, 2015; Tseng *et al.*, 2006). Self-regulation refers to the degree to which learners are active participants in their own learning and are proactive in their pursuit of language learning (Dörnyei, 2005).

Self-regulation was a term borrowed from psychology and was proposed by Dörnyei (2005) as a replacement for the existing notion of language learner strategies. It is important to note that, at this time, other applied linguists had also highlighted problems with the theoretical construct of language learner strategies. Criticisms of language learning strategies came from many SLA researchers, including the observations that are outlined in Table 8.1 (see Rose, 2015 for a more detailed discussion).

It is also important to note that researchers from within language learner strategy research had also been concerned with the unresolved issues surrounding the theoretical underpinning of much strategy research. Perhaps the most important critical review of the area was carried out by Macaro (2006), around the same time as Dörnyei (2005) proposed the replacement of the construct of language learning strategies with self-regulation. A summary of Macaro's (2006: 325) noted problems with the field of strategy research are shown in Table 8.2. Macaro (2006: 325) concludes the summary by stating that 'There is clearly a need to revise the theoretical underpinnings of learner strategy research'.

Much of these issues centered on research into language learning strategies in the Oxford era in the 1990s; however, since this time, there have

Table 8.1 Criticisms of language learning strategies

(1)	There are conflicting results and methodologies (Skehan, 1989).
(2)	Definitions of learning strategies are 'ad hoc and atheoretical' (Ellis, 1994: 533).
(3)	Past studies have attempted to describe and quantify strategies rather than to incorporate them into a model of psycholinguistic processing (Ellis, 1997).
(4)	The conceptualization of learning strategies is 'rather inconsistent and elusive' (Dörnyei & Skehan, 2003: 608).
(5)	The 'term has been used in far too broad a sense, including a number of different things that do not necessarily belong together' (Dörnyei & Skehan, 2003: 610).
(6)	The construct of learning strategies, while useful for researchers, is less helpful when conducting in-depth analyses of what it consists of (Dörnyei, 2005).
(7)	There has been no coherent agreement on the defining criteria for a language learning strategy, which is still the situation today (Tseng et al., 2006).

Table 8.2 Issues with the field of language learning strategies

(1)	There is no apparent consensus about where learner strategies occur, inside the brain or outside it.
(2)	There is no consensus about what learner strategies are. Do they consist of knowledge, intention, action or all three?
(3)	It is unclear how general or abstract learner strategies are and whether there exist substrategies as well as strategies and, as a consequence, if they can be classified in a framework or a hierarchy.
(4)	A lack of clarity also exists about whether their integrity survives across learning situations, tasks and contexts.
(5)	There is no consensus about what they do, especially whether they are always facilitative and effective.
(6)	It is unclear whether they are integral to language processing or if they are some kind of extra facility that speeds up learning.
(7)	Strategy definition in the literature is arrived at through the use of equally undefined terms.
(8)	There is a lack of consensus on a strategy's relationship to skills and processes.
(9)	A lack of consensus remains on how strategies lead to both language learning and skill development over the long term.

Source: Macaro (2006: 325).

been some notable re-theorizing of language learning strategies. In fact, even during the upsurge of language learning strategy research in the 1990s, other taxonomies were also being explored. Pintrich *et al.* (1991) and Vanderstoep and Pintrich (2003, 2008) emphasized a taxonomy that categorized strategies in two groups: (a) cognitive and metacognitive and (b) resource management. Each of these groups consisted of a number of subgroups of strategy use. Weinstein *et al.* (2000) argued for a categorization that embraced a segregation of affective, behavioral and cognitive factors. This distinction is of particular interest to *kanji* learning as it allows a differentiation between cognitive processes students apply to memorize the *kanji* and behavioral practices students use to review and recall *kanji*. Schmidt and Watanabe (2001) conceptualized learner strategies into four groups, based on a previous six-group model proposed five years earlier by Schmidt *et al.* (1996). The four categories included cognitive, social, study skills and coping. Cohen and Chi (2002) created a strategy inventory that was divided in terms of four language skills plus vocabulary and translation strategies, in order to create a more practically based system. However, all of these taxonomies were more a *re-organization* of strategy use rather than an answer to the calls to 'step back' and *re-theorize* made by Skehan in 1989 and Dörnyei in 2005. They also did not address many of Macaro's (2006) concerns, and in fact may have supported his assertion that there was a lack of clarity regarding whether strategies could be classified in a framework. In addition, each of the above systems lacked the research conducted within their framework that the Oxford or O'Malley and Chamot (1990) taxonomies offered, so their adequacy as suitable replacements was very uncertain.

Thus, when Dörnyei called a re-theorization of language learning strategies in the form of self-regulation, the idea received much attention in SLA literature, (e.g. see Dörnyei, 2005; Oxford, 2011; Rose, 2012b; Tseng *et al.*, 2006). This re-theorization culminated in a proposed model that incorporated self-regulation within the motivation control strategy taxonomy (Dörnyei, 2005), which examines the strategies students use to control their own learning. It has since been noted by self-regulation researchers (e.g. Ranalli, 2012) and even Dörnyei himself (see Dörnyei & Ryan, 2015), that this conceptualization of self-regulation is just one of many ways to view self-regulation. However, it is the one I used in my exploration of the self-regulation of learners of the Japanese language in *The Self-regulation Study*, and is therefore the model of self-regulation that I will outline in this book.

Dörnyei's Model of Self-regulation

Dörnyei's model of self-regulation is based in the framework of motivation control strategies (Dörnyei, 2001) and consists of five categories. Dörnyei (2005) notes that his system was based on Kuhl's (1987) and Corno and Kanfer's (1993) taxonomy of action control strategies (see Dörnyei, 2005). The categories are defined below:

(1) *Commitment control strategies* for helping preserve or increase the learner's goal commitment.

(2) *Metacognitive control strategies* for monitoring and controlling concentration and for curtailing unnecessary procrastination.
(3) *Satiation control strategies* for eliminating boredom and adding extra attraction or interest to the task.
(4) *Emotion control strategies* for managing disruptive emotional states or moods and for generating emotions that are conducive to implementing one's intentions.
(5) *Environmental control strategies* for the eliminating of negative environmental influences by making an environment an ally in the pursuit of a difficult goal. (from Dörnyei, 2005: 113)

In a later publication, Tseng *et al.* (2006) applied the conceptualization to the task of vocabulary learning in the form of a questionnaire designed to measure the self-regulatory capacity of vocabulary learning (SRCVoc). In that study, items on the questionnaire were developed from focus groups with students and fitted into the above framework, 'because of the theoretical problems surrounding the existing learning strategy taxonomies' (Dörnyei, 2005: 186). The study concluded that the questionnaire was a psychometrically accurate measure of a learner's underlying self-regulatory capacity, rather than a measure of actual strategy use (Tseng *et al.*, 2006). The authors also make the following claim:

> For the sake of conceptual clarity, we have decided to model the self-regulatory system proposed in this paper on one particular language learning domain, vocabulary learning, but at the same time we offer a detailed description of the procedures used to develop our instrument so that this can serve as a template for other content areas as well. Thus, we believe that our suggested approach is transferable to researching other facets of second language learning. (Tseng *et al.*, 2006: 79–80)

Therefore, when I was deciding on the conceptual framework for *The Self-regulation Study*, I reached a conclusion that the same template could be used for *kanji* learning, which was an area yet to be explored in this new paradigm. However, use of this instrument alone would only provide an understanding of the underlying self-regulatory capacity of a learner's *kanji* learning, rather than strategy use itself. Dörnyei (2005: 84) explains: 'the SRCVoc does not measure strategy use but rather the learner's underlying self-regulatory capacity that will result in strategy use'. Such observations suggested that models of strategy use and Dörnyei's model of self-regulation were not incompatible as they measured the beginning and end product of the same event. Thus, in *The Self-regulation Study*, self-regulation was seen as a tool to measure the cognitive processes of learning Japanese, which was an equally important part of my understanding of how learners learned the language.

Self-regulation as an Additive to Language Learning Strategy Research

Since the introduction of self-regulation as a replacement of language learner strategies, scholars have noted that the two concepts are not mutually exclusive, thus questioning whether one can replace the other. Gao (2006), in a response to Tseng *et al.* (2006), argued the emergence of self-regulation did not mean language learning strategy research was being marginalized. Self-regulation is looking at the initial driving forces, while learning strategies examine the outcome of these forces. This suggests that the two models are complementary, thus Gao (2006) suggested the emergence of models such as those proposed by Tseng *et al.* (2006) and Dörnyei (2005) did not mean the end to language learning strategy research, but instead broadened the perspective of future research into the field. This has also been the stance of a number of other researchers, including myself (Rose, 2012a, 2012b, 2015), Oxford (2011) and Gu (2012). A number of prominent researchers in the field have also examined the possibility of merging the two frameworks. Oxford (2011) created a model of strategic learning that incorporated self-regulation into a framework that examined strategic learning from psychological and socio-cultural theories from micro and macro perspectives. This model is of interest because it appears to draw upon theories from both educational psychology and traditional theories of strategic learning from second language learning research. Oxford's adoption of the term self-regulation in her revised model clearly indicates the impact that Dörnyei's criticism had on the field. It also serves as an illustration that language learner strategy researchers had recognised the value that self-regulation theory could offer their field of study.

Thus, in order to understand the bigger picture, participants in *The Strategies Study*, which examined the language learning strategies used by Japanese as a foreign language learners, also took part in a complementary study (*The Self-regulation Study*), which examined the self-regulation of these learners within the framework of Dörnyei's self-regulation. In this study, 12 learners of Japanese formed a multiple case study of learners within which to examine the self-regulatory capacity of learners from a range of proficiency levels when studying *kanji*.

The 12 participants were L1 speakers of an alphabetic language and had native or near-native proficiency in English. All participants were undertaking language studies in the Tokyo metropolitan area. In order to include a wide range of learners in the study, a spread of participants were chosen from a range of levels: four were on a beginner course (knowledge of less than 350 *kanji*); four were on an intermediate course (350–750 *kanji*); and four were on an advanced course (more than 750 *kanji*). These levels were pre-determined by a *kanji* placement given at the beginning of their studies. As with *The Strategies Study*, this study also aimed to sample participants who exhibited good and poor self-regulation, as determined by an initial screening interview. Because aspects of self-regulation would not be easily or accurately measured in a single interview or at a single time, participants were interviewed 10 times throughout the year in order to gain a fuller picture of each student's self-regulation of *kanji* learning.

The following three chapters will examine the results of this study, but will also situate it within other literature of self-regulation. This is important, as *The Self-Regulation Study* was one of the first studies to be conducted into self-regulation and language learning in general, and thus specific research into Japanese language learning and self-regulation was too sparse to discuss the results of the study.

Self-regulating Capacity of *Kanji* Learning

One of the biggest contributions to the field of SLA made by self-regulation was arguably the data collection instrument called the SRCVoc questionnaire, designed by Tseng *et al.* (2006). Due to issues surrounding the lack of reliability of strategy-based questionnaires, these researchers devised a new questionnaire grounded in self-regulation that was intended to measure a learner's underlying self-regulatory capacity thought to result in strategy use. By doing so, the researchers argued that the instrument could bypass many of the theoretical problems that had riddled defining, categorizing and measuring strategies. The SRCVoc was concerned with the sole task of vocabulary learning, as previous research had also highlighted the importance of situating research into strategic learning into context specific tasks (e.g. a student would use a different set of strategies and thus have a different underlying capacity to learn vocabulary compared to another aspect of language such as phonology or grammar). The SRCVoc was theorized within Dörnyei's motivation control taxonomy, mentioned above, and consisted of 20 items, listed in Table 8.3. In the application of this instrument, it was found that the SRCVoc had good psychometric properties. The instrument was also applied to other learning contexts such as in Japan, where the instrument once again proved to be robust (Mizumoto & Takeuchi, 2012).

Thus, because of the usefulness of the SRCVoc in previous research, an element of *The Self-Regulation Study* aimed to explore whether similar statements in the SRCVoc could be transferred to the task of *kanji* learning. As the SRCVoc examined the underlying self-regulatory capacity rather than the strategies themselves, it was assumed that the capacity to self-regulate for vocabulary might not be dissimilar to the capacity for learning of *kanji*, which represent lexical items in the language, albeit in a different manner. In order to match the task, some statements in the SRCVoc were adapted so that they referred specifically to *kanji* learning and the result was an adapted

Table 8.3 Self-regulatory capacity for learning vocabulary

(1) Once the novelty of learning vocabulary is gone, I easily become impatient with it.
(2) When I feel stressed about vocabulary learning, I know how to reduce this stress.
(3) When I am studying vocabulary and the learning environment becomes unsuitable, I try to sort out the problem.
(4) When learning vocabulary, I have special techniques to achieve my learning goals.
(5) When learning vocabulary, I have special techniques to keep my concentration focused.
(6) I feel satisfied with the methods I use to reduce the stress of vocabulary learning.
(7) When learning vocabulary, I believe I can achieve my goals more quickly than expected.
(8) During the process of learning vocabulary, I feel satisfied with the ways I eliminate boredom.
(9) When learning vocabulary, I think my methods of controlling my concentration are effective.
(10) When learning vocabulary, I persist until I reach the goals that I make for myself.
(11) When it comes to learning vocabulary, I have my special techniques to prevent procrastination.
(12) When I feel stressed about vocabulary learning, I simply want to give up.
(13) I believe I can overcome all the difficulties related to achieving my vocabulary learning goals.
(14) When learning vocabulary, I know how to arrange the environment to make learning more efficient.
(15) When I feel stressed about my vocabulary learning, I cope with this problem immediately.
(16) When it comes to learning vocabulary, I think my methods of controlling procrastination are effective.
(17) When learning vocabulary, I am aware that the learning environment matters.
(18) During the process of learning vocabulary, I am confident that I can overcome any sense of boredom.
(19) When feeling bored with learning vocabulary, I know how to regulate my mood in order to invigorate the learning process.
(20) When I study vocabulary, I look for a good learning environment.

Source: Tseng *et al.* (2006).

questionnaire called the *SRCKanji* (self-regulatory capacity in *kanji* learning). This questionnaire is shown in Table 8.4. As with the SRCVoc, students answered these statements according to a six-point Likert scale ranging from strongly agree to strongly disagree.

It is important to note, however, that due to the small sample size of *The Self-regulation Study*, the *SRCKanji* could not be verified in terms of whether it was a robust fit with the data and thus the reliability of it as a measure of

Table 8.4 Self-regulatory capacity for learning *kanji* (*SRCKanji*)

Commitment control strategies

- When learning *kanji*, I have special techniques to achieve my learning goals.
- When learning *kanji*, I believe I can achieve my goals more quickly than expected.
- When learning *kanji*, I persist until I reach the goals that I make for myself.
- I believe I can overcome all the difficulties related to achieving my *kanji* learning goals.

Metacognitive strategies

- When learning *kanji*, I have special techniques to keep my concentration focused.
- When learning *kanji*, I think my methods of controlling my concentration are effective.
- When it comes to learning *kanji*, I think my methods of controlling procrastination are effective.
- When it comes to learning *kanji*, I have my special techniques to prevent procrastination.

Satiation control strategies

- Once the novelty of learning *kanji* is gone, I easily become impatient with it.
- During the process of learning *kanji*, I am confident that I can overcome any sense of boredom.
- During the process of learning *kanji*, I feel satisfied with the ways I eliminate boredom.
- When feeling bored with learning *kanji*, I know how to regulate my mood in order to invigorate the learning process.

Emotion control strategies

- When I feel stressed about *kanji* learning, I know how to reduce this stress.
- I feel satisfied with the methods I use to reduce the stress of *kanji* learning.
- When I feel stressed about *kanji* learning, I simply want to give up.
- When I feel stressed about my *kanji* learning, I cope with this problem immediately.

Environment control strategies

- When I am studying *kanji* and the learning environment becomes unsuitable, I try to sort out the problem.
- When learning *kanji*, I know how to arrange the environment to make learning more efficient.
- When learning *kanji*, I am aware that the learning environment affects my learning.
- When I study *kanji*, I look for a good learning environment.

Source: Adapted from the Self Regulatory Capacity in Vocabulary Learning by Tseng *et al.* (2006).

self-regulation in the *kanji* learning task could not be measured. This is a suggested goal for future researchers in the area.

In addition to the *SRCKanji*, an interview was included to gather qualitative data on the self-regulation of the participants. This decision was in response to Tseng *et al.*'s (2006) call for more qualitative methods to investigate self-regulation. An interview guide was established, which included the questions and follow-up probes outlined in Table 8.5. Data from the interviews were coded using NVivo software. The researcher organized data into appropriate categories and subcategories initially based on Dörnyei's self-regulation taxonomy, but then expanded into other themes as they emerged as important in the first pass of the data. This generated the following additional themes: goals, procrastination, boredom, interest, stress and place.

The interview guide proved to be a powerful tool to gain insight into learners' self-regulation in *The Self-regulation Study* and it was revealed that learners' struggles with learning the Japanese writing system took an

Table 8.5 Interview guide for investigating self-regulation in *kanji* learning

Question	Follow-ups/probes
Question 1 What *kanji* learning goals, if any, did you set for yourself in the past week? What do you think of your willpower this week in achieving these goals?	Did you feel satisfied/confident about your willpower? Did you feel the methods to control your willpower were effective/useful? Any other reflections on the methods used?
Question 2 Think back to your last Japanese *kanji* lesson or study period dedicated to learning *kanji*. How did you feel during this lesson/period?	Did you feel bored/afraid/impatient about this situation? If so, what did you do about this feeling? Did you feel satisfied/confident about your methods to control this negative feeling? How effective/useful were the methods?
Question 3 Think about the last *kanji* test you had to take. How did you prepare for it?	Did you procrastinate in reviewing the words? If so, what made you procrastinate? Comment on the methods used to stop procrastination. Did you feel easily distracted? If so, why did you feel easily distracted? Comment on the methods used to enhance concentration.
Question 4 How did you feel when learning a new group of *kanji* this week? Did you feel easily bored?	If so, why did you feel easily bored? Comment on the methods used to get rid of the feeling of boredom. If not, how do you maintain interest?
Question 5 Where and when did you study *kanji* in the past week?	How did you select a conducive time and place for your learning? (e.g. waiting for a bus, during a classroom break, your own room.) Which environments were best/worst for you? Comment on the methods used to control the learning environment.

immense psychological toll on the Japanese language learner. The results of this study will be discussed in the following three chapters.

Implications

Implications for the Japanese language learner

The implications of self-regulation theory on learning the Japanese language are more conceptual rather than something that can be directly applied to learning. It is important that learners are aware that strategies are not something that can be easily applied to learning with a positive outcome such as easy acquisition of the writing system. Self-regulation, in examination of the underlying forces that exist in all learners, highlights the importance for learners to develop a capacity for regulating and managing their own learning, for long-term results, as opposed to strategies which learners often take at face value as 'quick-fix', short-term solutions. As the acquisition of the Japanese writing system is a lifelong learning task for learners of the Japanese language, it is perhaps a worthy investment for students to proactively consider how they regulate their learning in terms of:

- setting short term and long-term goals so they are achievable;
- managing their study behaviors to study more efficiently;
- controlling and maintaining interest in studying Japanese;
- containing negative emotional aspects of study such as stress;
- choosing appropriate learning environments to facilitate learning.

If a learner is able to improve their capacity to self-regulate in their language learning, theory seems to suggest that this will have a long-term positive effect on their acquisition of the Japanese language, in both its written and non-written forms.

Implications for the Japanese language instructor

Instructors are in a unique position to support learners in their development of self-regulation in learning Japanese. Specifically, instructors can play a crucial role in the setting of goals in Japanese language learning, which can affect learners' ability to control their learning commitments. In the setting of short-term and long-term goals in a syllabus, an instructor can place benchmarks for performance, which can be worked into a reasonable timeline for language development. This is particularly important when setting set numbers of *kana* and *kanji* that need to be learned at various stages of the language syllabus. Instructors can also play a crucial role in the reduction of stress in learning, by setting achievable and believable goals in learning, although it can be, at times, difficult if they are working within a prescribed curriculum. In regards to the other types of self-regulation, the instructor can act as a mentor for learners who are struggling with mastery of the Japanese script. It is important for instructors to reflect on their own challenges in learning foreign languages so as to best offer advice to learners who may find difficulty in managing their learning.

Implications for the Japanese language researcher

This chapter has shown there has been a wane in confidence for numerous taxonomies of strategic learning. In the construction of the conceptual framework for research into the area language learning, there are clearly benefits of examining strategies from an educational psychology perspective. As self-regulation measures the underlying regulatory capacity of the learner, rather than actual strategy use, we also see further importance of developing a model that incorporates the strengths of this theory. In addition to borrowing the concept of self-regulation, I can also see merit in including further concepts from the field of self-regulation into future research frameworks. Furthermore, it is clear that any model of strategic learning must be task specific, as there is general agreement that strategies are task dependent (Cohen & Macaro, 2007). Just as Tseng *et al.* (2006) developed a framework to examine vocabulary learning, a framework must also be developed to examine the specific task of Japanese learning. While *The Self-regulation Study* has made inroads into this need for research, much more can be done. The *SRCKanji* has yet to be tested and remains a crude adaption that assumes *kanji* learning is similar in properties of self-regulation as vocabulary learning; it is currently a theoretical idea that needs further investigation. Thus, there is an opportunity for a future researcher to test the properties of this instrument and make changes where needed.

In addition to this, there is an opportunity to take self-regulation in yet unexplored directions. In fact, the SRCVoc takes one view of self-regulation where many others exist. For example, the conceptualization of self-regulation by Dörnyei (2005) takes a volitional view of self-regulation, which views self-regulation in terms of a learner's persistence in maintaining attention to learning in the face of negative distractions, such as procrastination, stress and boredom. In fact, many alternate conceptualizations of self-regulation exist (see Zimmerman & Schunk, 2001), which are yet to be explored fully in the context of language learning. Ranalli (2012: 372–373) for example has stated:

> Dörnyei and colleagues have proposed a volitional, trait-based model, which they position as a necessary antecedent to the creative search for and use of individualized learning mechanisms, and which they suggest could allow us to circumvent the problematic study of such mechanisms themselves. My counter argument is that such a model will be insufficient for explaining phenomena of primary interest to L2 strategy researchers,

in contrast to models that view self-regulation as an adaptive process and allow learners' specific strategic choices, as well as other important individual-difference factors, to be contextualized and related to each other.

In light of this narrow view of self-regulation as depicted Dörnyei's motivational control theoretical framework, which was used in *The Self-regulation Study*, there is an opportunity to return to self-regulation archetypes and explore how they might also be relevant to the task of Japanese language learning. Ranalli (2012), for example, illustrates how an alternative model of self-regulation (Winne & Hadwin, 1998) can applied to language learning. A similar exploration could be done with the task of *kanji* learning. Key researchers in the field of self-regulation (Zimmerman & Schunk, 2001) have also outlined a number of other alternative models, of which a volitional perspective is just one of many possible constructs. These include:

- Operant
- Phenomenological
- Information Processing
- Social Cognitive
- Volitional
- Vygotskian
- Constructivist

Thus, the scope to explore Japanese language learning within any of these constructs is yet an unexplored area of research.

9 Metacognition and Language Learning

Metacognitive strategies involve those used to control one's own cognition through the coordination, planning, organization and evaluation of the learning process. In Chapter 4, we saw that successful memorization from a cognitive point of view requires two complementary processes: encoding, which involves integrating new information into the memory; and retrieval practice, which involves frequent retrieval of this new information to strengthen the memory trace to the newly stored information. In addition to this, Part 2 of the book has examined the process of encoding, through various strategies such as mnemonic associations, visual association and component analysis. This chapter deals with the managing and organizing of metacognitive strategies used in the process of retrieval practice. It will also examine the underlying processes of metacognitive control, which is conceptualized within self-regulation theory, as outlined in the previous chapter. Metacognitive processes are of vital importance when learning Japanese written characters, because a learner will often have to learn upwards of 100 *kana* in the beginning stages of language learning and then long lists of *kanji* each week as they progress into the intermediate and advanced stages, while ensuring they are maintaining knowledge of up to hundreds (or thousands) of previously studied *kanji* and *kana* through regular review. Therefore, the coordination and management of the study of written Japanese is probably even more important than the initial encoding itself for long-term success in reaching a functionally literate level in Japanese writing.

In some learning strategies studies, the term *indirect strategies* has been used to categorize those strategies that are not applied directly to the learning process; indirect strategies are used to describe those strategies that are concerned with the management of the learning process. This book prefers the term metacognitive strategies, which have been defined as 'controlling cognition through the co-ordination of the planning, organization and evaluation of the learning process' (Oxford, 2001: 166). The concept of metacognitive strategy use has also been described under the umbrella term metacognitive control strategies in the self-regulation conceptual framework. However, self-regulation examines overall self-regulatory capacity of a learner, rather than the strategies themselves. Both notions will be dealt with in this chapter.

First, under the umbrella of language learner strategies, this chapter will outline three categories of metacognitive strategies, which are planning learning, evaluating learning and engaging in collaborative learning. Each of these is defined below, alongside the notion of metacognitive control strategies, conceptualized in self-regulation. There is, of course, much overlap between these conceptualizations; for example, the strategies for planning learning, evaluating learning and engaging in collaborative learning may be used to maintain control over a learner's concentration and to monitor one's language development.

(1) Planning learning strategies involve the management of the *kanji* learning in terms of time and process.
(2) Evaluation learning strategies involve the evaluation of progress through self-testing and review.
(3) Collaborative learning strategies involve the study of *kanji* through use of peers and teachers.
(4) Metacognitive control strategies for monitoring and controlling concentration and for curtailing unnecessary procrastination.

Planning Learning

This section will look at strategies used by learners in the planning of their *kanji* learning. It will draw on previously published research as well as original data. Successful learners have often been attributed as being good metacognitive strategy users; that is, successful learners can better plan their learning to reach their desired outcome. Thus, it is somewhat unsurprising that good Japanese language learners also have a strong ability to manage the learning process.

In *The Strategies Study*, it was revealed that good Japanese language learners exhibited an expert ability to plan their learning of *kanji*. In this study, two highly self-regulated learners used computer spreadsheets, wall posters and flashcards to systematically plan their learning and track their progression in *kanji* study. I have included two excerpts below, which I find very illustrative of this systematic approach.

Excerpt 9.1

If I had a list of *kanji* to learn with associated vocab words, first I'll probably take the list and write down the meanings and the readings I know. Then I'll make flashcards. Checking and writing down other readings that I need to know as I'm doing that. I also look them up in here [referring to an electronic dictionary] ... I'll also add them to my notes. I have a set of notes on a computer in a text file so I can keep that well organized, so I have a list of all the *kanji* I've learned, which is handy at least some of the time. At least it lets me keep count of all the *kanji* I've learned. (Learner Interview, *The Strategies Study*)

Excerpt 9.2

What I do is I made an Excel spreadsheet – I've still got all my Excel spreadsheets containing two years' worth of *kanji*... I would select, say, 10 words for each *kanji*, 10 compounds, put it all in an Excel spreadsheet with definitions, readings and all that. I would then print that out and I would carry it around with me for a week. Specifically what I did is I would sit – I used to do some voluntary work which involved sitting in the car for about two hours on a Saturday waiting for some children. I had flashcards just like this and I would simply have those and I'd just go through them again and again. Three at a time actually. Again and again and again until I knew all the readings and I could do that. With 10 *kanji* I could do that in about two hours. Then I had a big sheet on the wall and I'd add 10 new *kanji* each week and then I would just go through that list, just look at the wall, go through the list doing the readings. I had the *kanji* and next to it I had written a number that represented a number of readings. So I just had to list that number of readings. (Learner Interview, *The Strategies Study*)

In these excerpts, we can see the great lengths learners go through to maintain control of their *kanji* study. The learner in Excerpt 9.1 illustrates the amount of effort required to even maintain knowledge of previously learned *kanji*; other interviews with learners revealed that without constant review, knowledge of previously learned *kanji* could easily be lost. This was due to a break down in the original memory trace, which can only be maintained and strengthened through constant retrieval practice.

Other participants in this study integrated more nuanced methods of learning and retrieval practice, utilizing less structured approaches where they consciously incorporated *kanji* study into everyday routine. About half of the learners in *The Strategies Study* could be placed in this group. One participant in *The Strategies Study*, for example, tried to use *kanji* as much as possible in his written assignments rather than relying on the *hiragana* as he had done in the past. This approach is described in the following interview excerpt:

Excerpt 9.3

Well, I've had a lot more writing homework recently, and you get tired of writing out *hiragana* for words that you know there are *kanji* for, and so I just, like, a couple of words I've just learned the *kanji*, 'cause I'm tired of writing out the *Hiragana* for particularly long words. So, every time now that I write I try to use all the *kanji* I can – all the ones… And text messages I always when I send them, I use the *kanji* for the ones I know, and for the ones I don't, I kind of look up the *kanji*, and save it for later and see if I can – which is a consequence, I can recognize a lot more *kanji* than I can write. (Learner Interview, *The Strategies Study*)

Another participant experimented with popular media in his review of *kanji* learning to aid in a more natural approach to retrieval practice. This participant started to read manga (Japanese comic books) with the idea that it would not only help him review known *kanji*, but also that he could record new *kanji* he came across in a study notebook. However, this student found that they became so engrossed in the story that they read the *furigana* [*hiragana* written above *kanji* in children's books] above unknown *kanji* and guessed unknown words from context, as the writing and looking up of *kanji* distracted from enjoyment gained from reading. The participant indicated that the method itself seemed to be good for improving reading proficiency, but was perhaps not as good for *kanji* study unless a reader was very disciplined.

Other participants in this study experimented with a number of programs on their Nintendo DS, smartphones and tablet devices. They stated that such programs were very powerful tools for the systematic study of *kanji*. All of these *kanji* learning programs were exclusively designed for the native Japanese market and students stated they were always organized according to either levels of native Japanese school years or according to a widely used test of *kanji* in Japan, The *Nihon Kanji Noryoku Kentei* [日本漢字能力検定] (see Chapter 10 for details). Although the structure of different software was slightly varied, almost all programs involved activities to study the *kanji*, test the *kanji* and retest *kanji* that were not recalled correctly before the user completed that level and moved on to the next. Participants in *The Strategies Study* stated that such programs helped to add a structure to learning and removed the onus of planning *kanji* study from the learner. Programs such as these meant the learner was also no longer required to make flashcards, spreadsheets or keep notebooks to track their *kanji* progression. The inbuilt stylus or touch functionality on many of the hardware devices that ran these programs also meant that the writing of *kanji* could be tested, including the use of correct stroke order. One participant in the study noted that if a *kanji* was drawn with the incorrect stroke order, often the software could not recognize it, so it forced the learner to learn and use the correct stroke order.

Another participant noted one major downside of using these programs was that the best programs were written for Japanese people, so all instructions were in Japanese and the programs assumed an advanced knowledge of vocabulary before the studying of *kanji*. This meant that foreign language learners of Japanese had to work harder to read the *kanji* in a wider range of combinations than typical at the second language learner level in order to answer test questions correctly. Therefore, the programs were designed to test *kanji* for learners of a greater vocabulary size (e.g. a native level), than for learners who were in earlier stages of second language development. Another issue was that the order of the *kanji* in all programs followed that used in Japanese schools, which was often very different from the order *kanji* are presented in foreign language textbooks. This is problematic, seeing as some studies have shown that the ordering of *kanji* in most textbooks is unique (Paxton, 2015).

However, despite the limitations of the self-directed, naturalistic and computer-assisted planning of learning, this type of systematic study is clearly a necessary step to progress in a learning task as taxing and long-lasting as *kanji* memorization. In *The Strategies Study*, although it was not a focus of the study, I observed that students who did not study *kanji* in a systematic way seemed to make very little progress in their learning throughout the year of the study. This highlights the importance of planning in learning. Thus, a discussion point of *The Strategies Study* was that students who used a high level of indirect strategies in the planning of their *kanji* learning progressed in language development more than those who displayed little use of planning strategies. Such findings would be in line with general theory into learning strategies and self-regulation, which show metacognition to be important for learning and *kanji* are no exception.

Evaluating Learning

Interview data from *The Strategies Study* into learning *kanji* indicated that evaluation of learning of *kanji* becomes inexplicably intertwined when put into practice by the participants. Interview and stimulated recall data indicated that study strategies and self-testing strategies happened simultaneously; that is, for most participants, the study of new *kanji* involved the immediate self-testing and review of these *kanji*. Therefore, testing was seen by some students as the only way to review their learning. In the terminology of memory strategies introducing in Chapter 3, learners were engaged in *retrieval practice*, before devoting time to *encoding*. The result is constant practice in retrieving poorly encoded information, which puts in danger the degree to which the information is adequately stored in proper knowledge structures.

Furthermore, the interview data indicated there were far less emphasis on the act of reviewing previously studied *kanji* (such as making use of lists of previously learned *kanji* for future reference), compared to the immediate study and review of more recently learned *kanji*. Interview data with participants over the year revealed the reason behind this observation was related to the manner in which *kanji* was constantly tested in the Japanese curriculum. Frequent *kanji* tests rewarded knowledge of recently learned *kanji* lists, without requiring extensive review of previously studied lists. This relationship is outlined in the following statement from one of the participants.

Excerpt 9.4

> It's part of the education system really whereby in a way the Japanese language course is a bit like the Japanese education system as a whole whereby it's all geared towards exams. So I know what I need to know for exams which essentially at the end of the day it's going to be *kanji*. (Learner Interview, *The Strategies Study*)

Furthermore, in a later interview this same participant outlined how the exam-oriented nature of Japanese *kanji* courses had a detrimental effect on long-term retention of *kanji*, in that study for exams often involved last minute cramming, and thus, for this learner, the learning of *kanji* never cemented into his long-term memory. In fact, most participants in *The Strategies Study* reported clearly devised strategies for learning new lists of *kanji* for tests, but also reported struggling with the long-term review and retention of *kanji* that were previously learned.

It is important to draw the following conclusion here: there is a close relationship between testing and review of *kanji*. It is clear that the traditional exam-oriented Japanese language curriculum has had an impact on metacognitive strategy use by *kanji* learners. It is also clear that without testing of previously learned *kanji* that learners will inevitably turn to cram session as opposed to meaningful memorization techniques.

Collaborative Learning

Previous studies into *kanji* learning have highlighted the benefits some students find in working with their peers during Japanese language study (Bourke, 1996). In *The Strategies Study*, students drew attention to the benefits of studying with a partner. These included an increase in enjoyment, productivity and motivation when studying with someone, compared to studying alone. However, students also mentioned negative outcomes related to working with peers in that study sessions could quickly lead to procrastination through distraction or could impact on the quality of study. Other students commented that due to the cognitive processes required for learning *kanji*, which is a highly individualized learning activity, the study process did not lend itself to the same type of peer collaboration as other aspects of language learning. This attitude is nicely illustrated by the following two interview excerpts.

Excerpt 9.5

I can't do something visual with something else – with someone else. If it's like practicing, conversation, with someone else is a preferable way to study, but with writing, I really can't study with someone else. (Learner Interview, *The Strategies Study*)

Excerpt 9.6

I generally study with others, but for *kanji*, I never study with others ... Because I think everybody has their own way of studying *kanji*, and you just need to find like – especially since I work visually. So if someone tells me it looks like a dog, and I don't see it, then that's useless to me. (Learner Interview, *The Strategies Study*)

In these excerpts, we see learners reporting that *kanji* learning, unlike some other types of study, is very visual and individualistic and thus it is difficult to work with a partner. Thus, working with a partner seems to hold both benefits and problems from the viewpoint of Japanese language learners.

A solution to managing these benefits and problems emerged in a later interview with one of the same participants. During a discussion on study environment, the participant explained how he often studied with friends of his, but maintained it as an individual activity.

Excerpt 9.7

Interviewer: So normally you study with a group?
Learner: Not together. Independently, but just in a group. We'll all be in the coffee shop near my dorm. We don't really help each other study but we're just together. So if we have questions we can ask each other.
Interviewer: And does that help motivate you a little bit more to –
Learner: Yeah, it's a big motivator. It's the same as like working out. It's good to have a workout buddy or study buddy or anybody to motivate you when you don't feel like going. It's better just being with someone. You don't feel like the only person doing it. I study a lot more. Like if all my friends are going to study, then there's a much higher chance of me going to study.

In this excerpt, the learner applies a study method that maximizes the benefits of studying with a partner (of increasing motivation and increasing enjoyment and productivity) without incorporating the reported problems (of working at varying paces or solving individual differences in approaches to *kanji* study). This illustration may offer a type of compromising solution for learners of the Japanese writing system that struggle with procrastination, a topic that is discussed next.

Metacognitive Control Strategies

Metacognitive control refers to the ability to control procrastination and concentration in study. In interview data, controlling procrastination and concentration in *kanji* learning was a reoccurring problem cited by most participants. All participants in *The Self-regulation Study* expressed some difficulty in the control of concentration during *kanji* learning. Some students expressed trouble controlling procrastination to severe degrees, as evident in the following interview excerpt.

Excerpt 9.8

I just can't concentrate when it comes to *kanji*. It's really strange, you know. Anything else is ok. Conversation, I love… vocab study… no problem… even grammar is kind of fun, but I just can't sit down and study *kanji*. When I try, I'll always find something else to do or some program on TV to watch, or just surf the Internet. (Learner Interview, *The Self-regulation Study*)

This type of reflection on metacognitive control was typical of many of the intermediate learners of Japanese in *The Self-regulation Study*. It seemed that this coincided with a period of Japanese language study where *kanji* started to play a pivotal role and learners struggled with ability to 'keep on top' of *kanji* knowledge. The case of the learner in Excerpt 9.8, who we will call Jonathon, was distinguishable from the other participants in *The Self-regulation Study* in terms of metacognitive control, because of his explicit awareness of his procrastination. However, Jonathon was not the participant who was most lacking in concentration nor did he seem to procrastinate the most, but he seemed most aware of how procrastination affected his goals in *kanji* learning and of his need of strategies to cope with this negative force. Jonathon frequently and openly discussed his issues with metacognitive control as can be seen in the following excerpt.

Excerpt 9.9

Well, this is a big battle with procrastination—not just *kanji* but in all things. Recently, I'm trying to tackle it through positive thinking to reading various books about getting things done and believing that you can actually do it. And listening to various sorts of motivational CDs and things. I've actually found it really useful. Having said that, if I think back to this weekend, all day yesterday right from the start I knew that I had to do this homework. I had a Japanese essay to write and I knew I had to do it. And yet, I'd find myself doing anything possible to not do it. And essentially, the only way for me to stop that is just to say, 'Right, [Jonathon], come on. Let's sit down and do it.' And actually I find that once I start doing it, I enjoy it. So I still haven't figured out any proper way of actually making myself do these things. And I've been thinking really seriously for the last few days, okay, maybe if I introduce some kind of reward system for myself. So if I study the *kanji* for an hour or whatever, then I can do this or whatever. Because I know that I have to stop this. I have to stop right here because otherwise I'm stuffed when I get back in September. I'll be absolutely stuffed. (Learner Interview, *The Self-regulation Study*)

Jonathon understood that procrastination was having a severe effect on his achievement of goals by the set deadline. To deal with this effect, he later experimented with a number of strategies to control his concentration from positive reinforcement, self-talk and rewards, but felt he was making little progress in finding a suitable solution.

For this learner, the deadline of September seemed to cause anxiety rather than motivation to achieve goals and stop procrastination. This was in stark contrast to other participants in *The Self-regulation Study*, who seemed to believe a deadline was enough to motivate them to concentrate on their studies. One participant argued that 'there's no better motivator than something that has to be done' (Learner Interview, *The Self-regulation Study*), and that 'If I want to learn, I can concentrate' (Learner Interview, *The Self-regulation Study*). A quarter of the cases either found the *kanji* learning task itself motivation enough to control procrastination or did not suffer enough that strategies were necessary. This indicates that metacognitive control is highly individualized to the extent that some students suffer from a lack of strategies to deal with procrastination, while others did not suffer from procrastination at all, as their self-regulatory capacity is high enough to compensate for the negative impact of forces that might lead to procrastination.

Implications

Implications for the Japanese language learner

The implications of metacognition research for the language learner highlight the importance of managing one's learning in order to find success in learning the Japanese writing system. *The Strategies Study* and *The Self-regulation Study* revealed that learning the Japanese writing system is a highly individualized task; however, this does not mean that it has to be a challenge that is taken on without support and friends. The students in *The Strategies Study* and *The Self-regulation Study* outlined a number of strategies they implemented to effectively organize and manage their study.

First, *The Strategies Study* highlighted the benefits of using software that organizes learning (of not only *kanji*, but also *kana*) for the learner. All of the software mentioned in the study encouraged the re-learning of difficult and new items, and even allowed for the systematic review and self-testing of reading and writing (when hardware allowed for a stylus or touch input). For example, if a learner incorrectly recalled a *kanji* in one of the self-tests, the software would automatically flag that *kanji* for re-testing in the next phase of study; other programs would not allow learners to move on to a next level until a new *kanji* was recalled in a random self-test more than three times; some programs mixed in a review of previously learned *kanji* with self-tests of new *kanji* to ensure periodic memory retrieval. The usefulness of such software should not be underestimated or seen as a 'gimmick', as the learning principles that underpin these programs fit into our understanding of best practices in cognitive strategies; these programs facilitate effective memorization and systematic review, which should result in stronger memory traces.

Second, *The Strategies Study* also highlighted the benefits of creating and using a network of fellow students to engage in collaborative learning. The study revealed that many students saw the advantages of study groups, even if these group meeting involved independent learning activities conducted in groups. It seemed too many of the participants that the act of studying together helped to organize learning, control procrastination and increase enjoyment of the learning task. Thus, the use of groups might also be seen as an effective metacognitive control strategy to avoid the type of procrastination highlighted in *The Self-regulation Study*.

Implications for the Japanese language instructor

At the advanced level, the onus to retain previously learned *kanji* in addition to newly taught *kanji* is usually shifted from the language instructor to the learner. At the advanced stages, it is often assumed that learners have developed the kinds of strategies necessary to review and maintain their knowledge of previously taught *kanji*, so that instructors are able to focus on the task of introducing new language, and *kanji*. However, *The Self-regulation Study* revealed that without structured review, some learners have difficulty in measuring progress, to the point that some learners in this study saw their knowledge of the Japanese writing system to be moving in the wrong direction. These learners reported forgetting previously known *kanji* at a greater rate than the learning of new *kanji*. Learners, therefore, may benefit from a system to track their progress of *kanji* learning, as well as a system of review. In order to facilitate this, teachers could implement classroom assessment that places value on the learning process and review of *kanji*, rather than the focus on weekly quizzes on new *kanji* that populate many university curricula. They might also benefit from a systematic way to record progress in learning, so students can see what they knew at the beginning of a term compared to what they know at the end.

In many ways, when a pattern emerges of students learning new *kanji* at the expense of devoting time to maintaining knowledge of previously learned *kanji*, it is usually the result of a washback effect. Washback effect refers to the influence that language tests have on teaching practices and learning behaviors (see Bailey, 1996; Wall, 2012). Language tests directly impact the choices of learners and teachers in Japanese language classrooms; for example, if an upcoming test focuses on a new list of *kanji* attached to a chapter set in the curriculum, instructors will give more attention to these *kanji* and learners will focus on the content of the upcoming test. If an instructor is in a position to adapt the curriculum, I feel students would benefit from a shift of focus from the introduction of new *kanji*, to the mastery of previous introduced *kanji*. It is my conviction that half of any regular *kanji* quiz should be devoted to testing previously learned *kanji* so the importance of review is made clear to students from the outset of study.

Implications for researchers

Considering the huge metacognitive challenges associated with the learning of thousands of characters in a writing system that consists of four scripts that represent language differently, it is surprising that very little research has been conducted into the strategies students deploy in the management of this formidable task. Furthermore, considering the task of *kanji* learning at the more advanced levels is often carried out as an autonomous task with light instructor guidance, it is even more surprising that next to no research has examined the self-regulated learning of students of the Japanese writing system. I feel there is a need for two types of studies.

First, there is a need for an exploratory study of the types of strategies that learners engage in to manage the metacognitive load placed on them when learning written Japanese. It would be useful also to see whether there are patterns in the data that show certain strategies correlate with success in the long-term mastery of this writing system. Such research could inform teaching practices as well as those exercises that underpin teaching materials and emerging software study programs.

Second, there is a need to explore the notion of metacognition from the viewpoint of self-regulation. As mentioned in the preceding chapter, *The Self-regulation Study* built on the theoretical concepts of Dörnyei's model of motivational control, which takes a volitional view of self-regulation; that is, self-regulation is viewed in terms of the actions learners take to minimize the negative effects on metacognition, such as procrastination. An alternative conceptualization of self-regulation might open up new avenues to explore what learners do to manage the large task of Japanese language learning.

10 Goal Setting and Commitment Control Strategies

Commitment Control Strategies

Commitment control strategies refer to the strategies learners apply to their language learning in terms of the setting of short- and long-term goals, and in terms of controlling their ability to achieve these goals. It is unsurprising that commitment control is a major facet of self-regulation in the learning of the Japanese written language. Students must organize their learning so that they can learn more than 100 *kana* and 2000 *kanji* to become functionally literate in the language. Mastery of the Japanese writing system is not an easy or quick task, thus it is an outcome that needs to be broken down into short-term goals over a long period of time in order to achieve success.

Before we examine to motivational control strategies of setting and reaching goals, it is first important to analyze what constitutes a 'good' goal in learning. McCombs and Pope (1994) explain that a goal needs to have four attributes in order to have success:

(1) Achievability (the learner must possess the ability to reach the goal).
(2) Believability (the learner must believe they can reach the goal).
(3) Conceivability (the goal must be clearly stated and measureable).
(4) Desirability (the goal must be desired by the learner).

In this framework, there is a connection between commitments in learning and a learner's abilities, beliefs, desires and their understanding of the goal.

In terms of achievability, goals must be of the nature that learners are able to reach them. A learner that expects to become literate in the Japanese language to an extent that they can engage with authentic texts within two semesters of study (a true case in *The Self-regulation Study*), may not be setting a realistic goal. Such a goal would require a learner to memorize upwards of 80 new *kanji* per week, as well as to stay on top of the vocabulary attached to them. This is also discounting the toll on the learner to even maintain knowledge of previously learned *kanji*, which – for many learners – is a struggle in itself at the more advanced stages of *kanji* knowledge. Thus, learners of Japanese need to be realistic when setting goals and ensure they are within the realms of achievability within the set time.

In terms of believability, goals must be of the nature that learners believe they can be attained. In short, if a learner does not believe they can reach a goal, the possibilities of them reaching this goal are diminished. It may seem surprising to some readers that beliefs can affect actual progress in learning, but this is a concept that is well documented in research into learner psychology. Motivational research, for example, has shown that low self-confidence in a learner's language development can be a major demotivating factor in language learning (Dörnyei, 2001). Similarly, Chambers (1993) identified a lack of belief of one's own capabilities as a major characteristic of a demotivated student according to language teachers. Research into self-efficacy highlights a relationship between learners' beliefs in their own capabilities and language learning development, that is, low self-efficacy is related to low achievement and low achievement is related to low self-efficacy. Thus, a breakdown in believability of goals seems to result in a downward spiral, where a lack of confidence demotivates students and then this further affects a learner's ability to believe they can reach their goals.

In regards to conceivability, it is important that learners understand the nature of the goals in terms of how progress can be measured against them. The setting of short-term goals is of paramount importance here. Learner psychology research shows that a lack of short-term goals has been found to affect progress (Bandura & Schunk, 1981), in that if learners do not have measurable short-term benchmarks with which to compare their progress, then the ability to reach a long-term goal is severely compromised. This may seem obvious, but it is a point missed by many learners and instructors of Japanese. For example, if a teacher sets a goal that students have to learn all *hiragana* within the first term of Japanese language studies, many learners might delay their progress in reaching this goal until the long-term goal at the end of the term approaches. Many learners in this class may fail to reach this long-term goal as a result. If an instructor, instead, sets short-term goals that students must learn and review one five-vowel set of *hiragana* and their diacritic alternatives (e.g. か, き, く, け, こ, が, ぎ, ぐ, げ and ご) per week for 10 weeks and sets review benchmarks such as weekly quizzes throughout the term, it is more likely that all learners in this context will reach the long-term goal. A similar situation could be argued for *kanji* learning, where a long-term goal, such as the passing the *kanji* sections of the Japanese Language Proficiency Test (日本語能力試験) would be more conceivable to a learner if this progress were benchmarked with smaller, short-term goals. (Japanese language proficiency exams are discussed in more detail in the section below.)

In regards to desirability, the goal must be desired by a learner. This concept ties in with much literature in learner psychology and motivation, particularly Dörnyei's (2005) L2 Motivational Self System. This system places the learner at the center of his or her system of language learning motivation, where learners depict their future selves in terms of being a language user. These selves, termed possible selves, 'denote a powerful and at the same term versatile motivational self-mechanism, representing individual's ideas of what they might become, what they would like to become, and what they are afraid of becoming' (Dörnyei & Ryan, 2015: 87). This self-system, therefore, consists of multiple versions of one's future self, termed as the Ideal Self (the type of learner one ideally wants to become) and the Ought to Self (the type of learner one thinks they should become to meet external expectations or to avoid negative outcomes). If a learner's current language ability is different from either of these future selves, the learner might develop a desire to learn and therefore be motivated to develop their ability to learn a language (Dörnyei & Ryan, 2015). The opposite is also true: if the future self is not that different, then the goal cannot be said to be desirable to the student and then an issue will occur with a learner's ability to reach that goal.

> The future self must differ from the current self: Put simply, if the future self-image is too close to the current self, the individual is unlikely to feel any great need to make efforts to realize the vision. (Dörnyei & Ryan, 2015: 92)

Thus, if a Japanese language learner does not have an image of their future self as being literate in written Japanese, then there will be an issue with that learner in reaching their goals in language learning. This future self could manifest as either an ideal self (e.g. a learner wishes to pass a level of proficiency in Japanese to be a better user of the language) or an ought-to self (e.g. a learner must pass a level of proficiency in Japanese to pass a course). In short, if a learner does not desire to reach a goal (whether for intrinsic, extrinsic or instrumental reasons), motivation will reduce and the likely outcome will be that the learner will fail to reach it.

The L2 Motivational Self System is also a useful way to explore the other aspects of goal setting discussed above (achievability, believability and conceivability). Dörnyei and Ryan (2015: 92) state that:

> The future self-image must be perceived by the individual as plausible; Possible selves must be both realistic and perceived to be within the individual's competence. Plausibility is an essential pre-requisite for motivation since implausible self-images are likely to remain at the level of unregulated fantasy without any motivational response.

This ties in with the achievability of a goal for a learner, in that if the goal is not plausible it cannot possibly be regarded as achievable and thus the goal would naturally need to be reassessed. It also ties in with the believability of a goal, in that if a learner does not perceive that the goal is within their competence, they will not believe they are able to reach it. Also of interest here, is the notion that 'a desired future self-image must be available to the learner' (Dörnyei & Ryan, 2015: 92), in that if a learner does have a clear image in their mind of the proficiency they want to attain, it will be very difficult for them to establish conceivable goals. Also related to conceivability is the necessity of short-term goals to benchmark progress against, which is also supported through L2 Motivational Self System research. Dörnyei and Ryan (2015: 92) argue that:

> The future self-image should be accompanied by relevant and effective procedural strategies. These strategies, often in the guise of proximal sub-goals or specific action plans, serve as a roadmap towards the future state and distinguish between motivationally relevant future self-images and empty daydreams or fantasies.

Thus, in order for goals to be conceivable, a learner must be motivated by a clear understanding of the desired outcome of the goal, what the journey to reaching this goal entails and also will need to be aided by specific sub-goals, which are organized in a procedural manner to ensure the learner is able to reach the set long-term goal (future self).

Typical Goals and Benchmarks for Japanese Study

The most popular Japanese language proficiency examination used by learners is the Japanese Language Proficiency Test (日本語能力試験) (JLPT). This test has been offered to learners since 1984, since which time test-takers have grown in number from 7019 examinees in 1984 to a peak of 768,113 examinees in 2009 (JLPT, 2016a). In 2015 there were 652,519 examinees, slightly lower than the peak number. The Japanese Language Proficiency Test is divided into five separate levels, each with a set level of linguistic competence needed to pass it. These levels are shown in the list below, with summaries of reading competence described at each level.

- N5: One is able to read and understand typical expressions and sentences written in *hiragana*, *katakana* and basic *kanji*.
- N4: One is able to read and understand passages on familiar daily topics written in basic vocabulary and *kanji*.
- N3: One is able to read and understand written materials with specific contents concerning everyday topics. One is also able to grasp summary information such as newspaper headlines. In addition, one is also able to read slightly difficult writings encountered in everyday situations and

understand the main points of the content if some alternative phrases are available to aid one's understanding.
- N2: One is able to read materials written clearly on a variety of topics, such as articles and commentaries in newspapers and magazines, as well as simple critiques and comprehend their contents. One is also able to read written materials on general topics and follow their narratives as well as understand the intent of the writers.
- N1: One is able to read writings with logical complexity and/or abstract writings on a variety of topics, such as newspaper editorials and critiques, and comprehend both their structures and contents. One is also able to read written materials with profound contents on various topics and follow their narratives as well as understand the intent of the writers comprehensively. (JLPT, 2016b)

It is important to note that older versions of the test were divided into four levels. The descriptors for the older tests were considerably more prescriptive in terms of how many *kanji* were tested at each level. The older benchmarks are shown in Table 10.1, alongside the current test's approximate levels. Due to the considerable gap in proficiency between levels 2 and 3 on the older test, an additional level was added as a bridging level, and thus there is no equivalent of the current N3 Level on the older test.

An alternative to the Japanese Language Proficiency Test is the *Business Japanese Proficiency Test*. This test is less popular than the JLPT, with 4107 examinees in 2012 (BJT, 2016), but is aimed at non-native Japanese people who are working in, or plan to work in, Japanese companies. While the focus of this test is on business situations, there are also a number of other fundamental differences between it and the JLPT. First, all test-takers sit the same test, rather than different tests designed to test people at different levels of proficiency (as is the case with the JLPT). This test, therefore, is more similar in design to other widely used language proficiency tests such as IELTS (International English Language Testing System) or TOEFL (Test of English as a Foreign Language). Test scores are given out of a maximum of 800 points,

Table 10.1 *Kanji* knowledge recommended at each level of the Japanese Language Proficiency Test

Current test level	Old Test levels	Kanji *knowledge*
Level N1	Level 1	2000 *kanji*
Level N2	Level 2	1000 *kanji*
Level N3	(N/A)	(N/A)
Level N4	Level 3	300 *kanji*
Level N5	Level 4	100 *kanji*

Source: JLPT (2016c).

and results allocate a proficiency level to the test taker, ranging from J1+ to J5. These are summarized below:

- J1+ (600–800 points): Able to communicate successfully in Japanese in any business situation.
- J1 (530–599 points): Able to communicate appropriately in Japanese in a wide range of business situations.
- J2 (420–529 points): Able to communicate appropriately in Japanese in a limited range of business situations.
- J3 (320–419 points): Able to achieve some degree of communication in Japanese in a limited range of business situations.
- J4 (200–319 points): Able to achieve a minimal degree of communication in Japanese in a limited range of business situations.
- J5 (0–199 points): Virtually no ability to communicate in Japanese in business situations. (BJT, 2016)

A third test that is widely used by learners to benchmark knowledge of *kanji* is the Japan Kanji Aptitude Test (*Nihon Kanji Noryoku Kentei*), which unlike the above two proficiency tests, solely focuses on *kanji* knowledge and is marketed to native Japanese speakers. As a result, Japanese as a Foreign Language (JFL) learners only really encounter this test at the higher proficiency levels, where aspects of the test such as reading and listening to test instructions in Japanese is not as daunting as it would be for lower proficiency learners. This test is broken into 12 levels, each with a recommended number of *kanji* to be mastered (Kanken, 2016). These levels are:

- Level 1, testing mastery of approximately 6000 *kanji* and aimed at Japanese university students and other adults.
- Level pre-1, testing mastery of approximately 3000 *kanji* and aimed at Japanese university students and other adults.
- Level 2, testing mastery of the 2136 *joyo kanji* and aimed at high school graduates, university students and other adults.
- Level pre-2, testing mastery of the 1940 previous *joyo kanji* list and aimed at high school students (first two years of study) and others who have studied under older high school curricula.
- Level 3, testing mastery of approximately 1607 *kanji* and aimed at learners who have graduated junior high school.
- Level 4, testing mastery of approximately 1322 *kanji* and aimed at junior high school students.
- Level 5, testing mastery of approximately 1006 *kanji*, which corresponds to the *kanji* learned at graduation of elementary school in Japan.
- Level 6, testing mastery of approximately 825 *kanji*, which corresponds to the *kanji* learned at the end of Year 5 of elementary school in Japan.

- Level 7, testing mastery of approximately 640 *kanji*, which corresponds to the *kanji* learned at the end of Year 4 of elementary school in Japan.
- Level 8, testing mastery of approximately 440 *kanji*, which corresponds to the *kanji* learned at the end of Year 3 of elementary school in Japan.
- Level 9, testing mastery of approximately 240 *kanji*, which corresponds to the *kanji* learned at the end of Year 2 of elementary school in Japan.
- Level 10, testing mastery of approximately 80 *kanji*, which corresponds to the *kanji* learned at the end of Year 1 of elementary school in Japan.

The Japan Kanji Aptitude Test is not widely taken by JFL learners, but some learners, who are looking for a structured approach to learning *kanji* that follows the standard Japanese national curriculum, see it as a structured alternative to other proficiency tests which follow a 'can do' approach to evaluation. Unlike the JPLT and the Business Japanese Proficiency Test, each level contains pre-determined lists of *kanji* that need to be mastered. Numerous books, websites and software, which also follow this structured approach to learning, are also widely available.

Commitment Control of Participants in *The Self-regulation Study*

Interviews with the participants in *The Self-regulation Study* revealed a range of abilities to self-regulate commitment for the Japanese language-learning task. Some learners had specific *kanji*-related goals in mind, some had non-specific *kanji*-related goals and many had no set goals for *kanji* learning. Students with no set goals for *kanji* learning tended to focus their language study on improvement of oral communication skills, of which *kanji* were a minor or unnecessary part. In order to compare the goals of each learner, participants were assigned a rating according to the magnitude of the goal. Participants with clear goals involving improvement in *kanji* learning were assigned a high level rating by the researcher (and verified by a second researcher). Participants with no goals related to learning *kanji* were assigned a low rating. To illustrate how these ratings were assigned to each of the participants, sample comments from the participants in interviews are outlined in Table 10.2.

For example, one participant with a 'high' rating had very specific and established goals in his *kanji* learning, with specific timeframes and deadlines. Comments such as those below illustrate the reason this participant was assigned a high goal level rating alongside others who portrayed a similar projection of their future self.

Excerpt 10.1

I've set myself a goal several times now of learning – mastering this book, *Remembering the Kanji*. And I have actually been through the whole

Table 10.2 Examples of goal levels of participants in *The Self-regulation Study*

Participant	Goal	Goal level
1	To enter graduate school in Japan and study political science in Japanese.	High
2	To pass the final exam of his master's program, which requires knowledge of 1500 *kanji*.	High
3	To complete his master's in Japanese studies and become a Japanese high-school teacher in his home country.	High
4	To enter a Japanese firm in Japan or Singapore.	High
5	To pass *kanji* exams as part of autonomous study, plus possible use in future employment.	Moderate-High
6	To work in a manga-related field, perhaps in translation.	Moderate-High
7	To become as fluent as he can, to add to his skills in business.	Moderate
8	To become fluent as a personal goal.	Moderate
9	To build-up conversational ability in Japanese including minor *kanji* study.	Low-Moderate
10	To build-up conversational ability in Japanese including minor *kanji* study.	Low-Moderate
11	To build-up conversational ability in Japanese including minor *kanji* study.	Low
12	To build-up conversational ability in Japanese, without a focus on *kanji*.	Low

thing once creating stories. So my stories are all there. I've got them already created on my iPod and all that. But my goal now is by September to at least master the first 1,500 and I think the way I'm going to have to do that is through using this as a basic – remembering the *kanji* as a foundation and then using the basic *kanji* books 1, 2 and 3. So that's 1,500 to learn the readings. I have to do that by September (Learner Interview, *The Self-regulation Study*)

This participant clearly had a conceivable and desirable goal, with measurable procedural strategies and sub-goals to get him there.

In the next grouping of participants (labeled as having moderate-high goal levels), one illustrative participant had a long-term goal related to *kanji* learning, although this goal was less concrete than the previous exemplary participant, as she was more focused on oral skill development. She also lacked the specific short-term goals to work toward this long-term goal when compared to the four participants in the first grouping. For these reasons she was assigned a goal level rating of 'moderate-high'. An illustration of this participant, discussing her goals, is shown below.

Excerpt 10.2

> My long-term goal over all is to be able to graduate with a degree in Japanese and work as a translator. Mainly because I started out when I was younger watching anime and going, 'Are they really saying that?' and had no clue what they were saying so I've been wanting to learn how to be able to know what they're saying without depending on subtitles. Now I've gotten to the point where I do recognize words and different phrases. My short-term goal is basically just to pass the course. Right now. (Learner Interview, *The Self-regulation Study*)

Other participants in this group expressed a similar long-term goal, without steps needed to achieve it.

In a group labeled moderate in goal setting, an illustrative participant wanted to study Japanese as an additional skill for employment. Mastering Japanese, therefore, was not a top priority for his overall university studies, but he was still motivated to learn the language well, which included an element of reading and writing *kanji*. This earned him a goal level rating of moderate. This participant's attitude toward goal setting is illustrated in the following comment:

Excerpt 10.3

> I would like to be fluent in the language as best I can for a non-native speaker. In the short term, I'd just like to travel. I would like to have a skill that a lot of people don't. I'm an economics major, and I figure it would be a reasonably good idea to know Japanese in the future. It'd probably be better to know Chinese, but I'm content with knowing Japanese for now. (Learner Interview, *The Self-regulation Study*)

In interviews, other participants had a similar commitment to *kanji* learning, for example, another learner had personal goals set, although out of interest in *kanji* learning, rather than for future university study or work.

Further along the commitment level continuum (at moderate to low) of Japanese language study, an illustrative participant had a long-term goal of getting better at conversational Japanese during her time in Japan, of which *kanji* did not play an important role. She did, however, see a place for *kanji* in her studies after her return to the USA, as explained in the following excerpt. Thus, she was given a rating of moderate to low.

Excerpt 10.4

> Hopefully by end of semester I'll be able to get better at *kaiwa* [conversational Japanese] and when I go back and have to take Japanese classes more I will focus on writing, because this is really a lifelong process to learn it better so. (Learner Interview, *The Self-regulation Study*)

Other participants within this rating band also chose to focus on conversational Japanese.

Finally, another participant serves as an example of a learner with low goal setting for Japanese language learning. This participant had no goals set for *kanji* learning, except an informal desire to be somewhat communicative in the language by the end of her year in Japan, thus earning a low rating. This attitude is illustrated in the following comment.

Excerpt 10.5

Short-term I have [no goals] but from what I plan to get from a year is at least be fluent enough to carry a casual conversation. I know I won't be able to speak and giggle yet or like a business level Japanese so hopefully I can make my way from survival Japanese to something more – something brag-able. So I can tell people I can just chat with like any Japanese now. But that's it. (Learner Interview, *The Self-regulation Study*)

Learners such as this in *The Self-regulation Study* were assigned a goal level rating of 'low' and unsurprisingly, these students had progressed very little in their language studies at the end of the study, after one-year of living in Japan and studying Japanese at the university level.

The level of goals assigned by learners can be seen in these cases as highly related to the desirability of goals; if a learner does not wish to become more literate in the Japanese language, the progression towards the goal of literacy is severely affected. In terms of describing this within a framework of L2 Motivational Self System theory, a learner's future self is not so different from their current self and thus motivation to learn is not generated. This concurs with Dörnyei and Ryan's (2015: 92) assessment that 'the individual is unlikely to feel any great need to make efforts to realize the vision'. Of course, it is hard to problematize a situation where a learner is not motivated to reach a goal and therefore does not reach it. What is more problematic is when learners set themselves goals and are unable to reach them, thus destroying their commitment control strategies, which has detrimental effects on a learner's self-regulation.

This issue of an inability to reach long-term goals was particularly noticeable at the higher proficiency end of the spectrum. This is illustrated by one learner, whose inability to reach his goals had the effect of re-adjusting the learners desirability to reach them (and re-adjusting their ideal L2 self in the process).

Excerpt 10.6

Tests? I always somehow manage to do the minimum to pass, but then forget everything after the test cause I don't review. Also it's just sheer time. The amount of Japanese study, I've done, I should know 2000 *kanji* by now. I've probably learned them all at one stage but forgotten 75% of them. I could pass *ikkyu* if it weren't for the *kanji*. But I just don't care anymore. I figure I know enough to do what I want to, so the drive is no longer there. (Learner Interview, *The Self-regulation Study*)

There were two other participants in *The Self-regulation Study* who, like the learner above, had incredible issues with commitment control strategies to the point that at the end of the study they expressed desire to give up on *kanji* study. In fact, an argument could be made in all three cases that an inability to deal with metacognitive control in terms of the study management necessary to set and reach sub-goals lead to them all to give up on *kanji* learning, to re-assess the goals they had set and to re-adjust their ideal L2 self. This is particularly evident in the above learner's case where in previous interviews he once expressed a desire to pass the Level 1 Japanese Proficiency Test (*ikkyu*), but felt it was unachievable due to the *kanji* component of the test. As a result, this learner adapted his long-term goal for *kanji* study from becoming a teacher of Japanese at the university level to teaching it at the high school level. This was due to an inability to control commitment to the reach the goal the learner had set, which led him to re-assign his L2 self so that his current self-matched his ideal self, therefore dissolving the 'gap' where the motivation to learn would usually emerge. Cases such as this demonstrate the detrimental effects that poor goal setting, and a lack of strategies to deal with reaching these goals, can have on motivation to learn. They also highlight the implications of an inability to reach long-term goals on construction of one's future self. This is highly relevant in the case of goals surrounding mastering literacy in Japanese, which research has shown is a lifelong learning task.

The results of *The Self-regulation Study*, however, also highlighted positive cases where participants were able to control their commitment to *kanji* learning. Commitment control was generally not an issue for many of the lower level students, even those with lofty long-term goals. For the lower-proficiency participants, commitment to *kanji* learning remained minimal and shorter-term with more manageable goals such as the passing of *kanji* tests. Even though many of these lower-proficiency participants also had longer-term goals, repercussions for not reaching these commitments were not as immediate as for the higher-proficiency learners, whose education and future employment hung on their success. It seemed the existence of regular *kana* and *kanji* tests was manageable for learners. This was also the case for some higher-level students who seemed to display good regulation over commitment control strategies by breaking down *kanji* learning and review into regular self-study tasks. Some participants took part in a self-study *kanji* program, which involved the study of sets of 100 *kanji* tested by monthly examinations. Although for the higher- proficiency students, these examinations were a form of reviewing previously learned *kanji*, participants reported these short-term goals helped them to gain control and confidence over the *kanji*-learning task. Therefore, there was considerable evidence that a regular review system aided students in setting shorter-term, manageable goals, even for higher-proficiency learners.

Implications

Implications for the language learner

The implications for language learners in regards to commitment control and goal setting are probably unsurprising to most readers; learners need to set conceivable and believable goals, and need to break down any long-term goals into sub-goals, which will help a learner judge whether a goal is achievable. Such implications concur with literature in the field of motivation and goal setting. An important study by Bandura and Schunk (1981), for example, found that learners who set short-term and specific goals made 50% more progress than learners with general goals or distant goals. This study is of particular significance, as the setting was a self-directed program that involved sets of materials not dissimilar in organization to the self-study *kanji* materials used by learners in *The Self-regulation Study* with reported success in managing their commitments to learning Japanese. In short, language learning theory emphasizes that breaking down a goal into small achievable steps with clear deadlines is an essential part of goal setting (see Dörnyei, 2001). Thus, some of advanced Japanese language learners may experience a breakdown in commitment control because they focus only on distant goals. These learners are especially in need of a structured study plan, where sub-goals are organized to help learners not only study new *kanji*, but to review of previously learned *kanji* an a systematic way to support them in reaching their goals. Because commitment control is a known problem for most learners of Japanese, particularly higher-proficiency learners whose future L2 selves may be more general and undefined, it is important to add elements to support and track progress in more explicit and measurable ways. These implications are supported by notions of previous research into motivation of the importance of short-term and specific goal setting for the language learner (Bandura & Schunk, 1981; Dörnyei, 2001).

Implications for the language instructor

The instructor can play an important role in avoiding breakdown of self-regulation in Japanese language learning by discussing with their students the difficulty of learning from the outset of their study of the Japanese language. *The Self-regulation Study* highlighted a number of students with clearly unrealistic goals; one of these students expected to pursue a career in Japanese and English translation by the end of her two years of Japanese language studies. Such a goal, while not completely unrealistic for exceptional students in immersion settings, was clearly questionable for a zero-beginner student who was only just embarking on her language studies. The instructor must navigate the fine line between inspiring their students to learn the language and also being realistic with them regarding their likely progress. Japanese is a hard language and learners need to calibrate their goals with a realistic trajectory of their future selves.

I often impart an anecdote when learners of Japanese ask me whether learning Japanese is difficult. I tell them the story of a friend of mine who arrived in Japan with a goal of becoming fluent in the Japanese language. This friend had an aptitude for learning language and had acquired a number of European languages within a year or two of living in each country, to the point that she could work in translation for two of the European languages and was functionally proficient in another. She immersed herself in the Japanese language and although she used English as the language of her workplace, she placed herself in a homestay situation so as to increase exposure to the language at home. She took Japanese language classes and studied hard for two years, but was disappointed at her lack of progress in the language. Despite her best efforts, she estimated that after two years of intensive study, her Japanese was not as proficient as her European languages were after just six months of similarly intense study. This story is not intended to deter students from studying Japanese, as I also go on to explain the wonders of learning a language that is so linguistically distant from English, but I feel it is important that students understand that the road to fluency (and literacy) in Japanese will be very different than other languages that are closer (both linguistically and culturally) to English. Everson (2011: 265) argues, 'teachers serve as powerful purveyors of both language and culture, and can influence students' views that their difficulties in learning *kanji* are not because they are somehow ill-equipped for the learning task which is somehow beyond them'. Thus, it is important that such discussions are for the purpose of reducing learners' perceptions that they are unable to reach goals, but instead are for the purpose of setting achievable goals.

In addition to this reality check, instructors can also support students to set realistic short-term or sub-goals in order for them to better reach their long-term goals. By providing students with a systematic way to measure progress and to review previously learned *kanji*, they can help them to better observe their progress in the language. It is also important that the usefulness of learning *kanji* is constantly in the forefront of learners' minds so they can see the purpose of learning is not just to meet these short-term goals, but to apply their knowledge of the writing system in meaningful and useful ways. This helps to cement these goals as integral to realizing their ideal L2 selves. In an earlier publication, I made the following observation:

> The *kanji* instructor can help students overcome barriers associated with *kanji* learning from the outset of their program of studies. The instructor needs to be aware that frequent quizzes, while a necessary part of *kanji*

learning, detract from the importance of maintaining knowledge of previously taught *kanji* and using *kanji* to read authentic and meaningful texts. Instructors could make use of assessment techniques that shift the focus from testing knowledge of new *kanji* through *kanji* quizzes to learning *kanji* for communicative purposes. Such purposes include reading for pleasure and to reinforce and increase content knowledge, and to learn about cultural practices, products, perspectives, and points of view and provide informal opportunities for review. Doing this also emphasizes the importance of the learning process and ultimate usefulness of *kanji* learning, rather than regurgitation of knowledge that often is crammed into short-term memory before a student takes a test and then is soon forgotten. (Rose & Harbon, 2013: 103)

Thus, there is a delicate balance for instructors to find between setting short-term goals, in order for learners to measure progression, while making sure the long-term goal does not appear too far out of reach.

Implications for language researchers

The impact of goal setting and commitment control strategies in language learning is a thoroughly unexplored area in the teaching and learning of Japanese. In this chapter, I have had to refer to language learning literature in general, as well as the wider topics of self-regulation in educational psychology studies. This is because no research has been carried out into the goal setting aspects of self-regulation in Japanese, apart from the Rose and Harbon (2013) study, which forms part of the research outlined in *The Self-regulation Study*. There is great scope, therefore, to investigate the relationship between the setting of short-term goals and progression in acquiring the written Japanese language. There is also much scope to explore goal setting and the commitment control strategies that learners apply to reach these goals. *The Self-regulation Study* examined goal setting of just 12 participants in a university setting, where opportunities to use the language were in the learners' direct environment. It is fair to assume that the goals of learners in a foreign language learning environment or in different educational contexts would be very different to those outlined in this chapter – as too would their ability to reach them – and the strategies they deployed in their journey towards success. Our knowledge of the effects of goal-setting and Japanese language learning is still largely in its infancy.

11 Affective Factors in *Kanji* Learning

Emotion and Affective Factors in Self-regulation

As defined by Larsen and Prizmic (2004), *emotion* or *affect regulation* is the process of monitoring and evaluating feelings experienced by the learner at any given time. Emotion control examines how learners cope with emotionally charged feelings such as stress, which may hinder their language development (Dörnyei, 2005). There have been hundreds of studies that have looked at affective factors in language learning and most theories of SLA agree that affective variables on a learner have some effect on second language attainment. In regard to self-regulation and language learning in general, focus groups with ESL learners in previous research projects have at least highlighted the issue of stress in the vocabulary-learning task (Tseng et al., 2006); however, those focus groups did not highlight other affect-related emotions.

In terms of affect and *kanji* learning, there have been few studies that have examined the emotional aspects of learning *kanji*. This is surprising, seeing as a recent study of mine (Rose & Harbon, 2013) has shown the emotional stress of learning *kanji* to be particularly complex, especially at advanced levels. This study, and follow-up studies, revealed a complex network of emotions, including self-criticism, frustration and defeatism, which had a massive impact on learning. This indicates the task of learning *kanji* to be far more emotionally taxing to the learner than other language learning tasks. Because emotion seems to play an important role in the regulation of a learner of Japanese, such as goal setting and metacognition discussed in previous chapters, it, too, is deserving of a chapter in this book in order to fully explore this construct.

Anecdotally, I have always found JFL learners to become quite stressed over the act of learning the Japanese writing system. In the earlier stages, students worry they will not be able to cope with reading texts written entirely in *kana*. At the later stages, learners become concerned that they will not have mastered the necessary *kanji* needed for an upcoming examination.

Many learners, while motivated by the unique nature of the writing system, become anxious over prospects of being tested on and through it. Most JFL learners in my studies have also consistently indicated some degree of anxiety and stress over *kanji* learning and usually associated this stress with a commitment such as an examination or quiz. A study by Shimizu and Green (2002) into the beliefs of Japanese language teachers revealed that teachers of Japanese believe in rote learning strategies, which involve the frequent giving of *kanji* quizzes, as well as repeated writing and practice drills. Thus, in order to cope with these quizzes and drills, not only do students need to manage their learning as outlined in the previous chapter, but they also need to manage the emotional weight of stress placed on them by this continued evaluation of *kanji* acquisition that follow students throughout years of their Japanese language learning.

Emotion Control in *The Self-regulation Study*

In *The Self-regulation Study*, some of the participants offered coping strategies to deal with this stress, such as tackling the task instead of putting it off. These strategies would not be dissimilar of strategies to manage the stress of studying for any type of exam, irrelevant of the content. One student I encountered in this study had a particular strategy that resonated with me, and I thought it may prove useful to others:

> As stressed as I might be about studying *kanji*, it doesn't matter. You do what you got to do. And you know, a little bit of that stress, a little bit of the adrenaline, a little bit is good – sometimes I like to study *kanji* when I'm on an exercise bike, because the adrenaline pumping usually helps me memorize them a little more quickly. Like when I'm on an exercise bike, I'm doing it – because I'm stationary, I can usually get done the 30 [*kanji*] in 35, 40 minutes, and then I can go back over the other ones.

Here, the participant turns emotional energy caused by stress into a tool to study *kanji*, while dealing with the stress through physical exercise. While these ideas might at first appear unorthodox, the use of exercise as means of self-regulation has been reported in research in the field. Larsen and Prizmic (2004: 48) write: 'It may seem ironic that the use of energy (to exercise) actually elevates energy, but the impact of exercise on affect and felt energy has been reliably demonstrated in a number of studies'. A study by Stevens and Lane (2001), for example, found exercise to be an effective strategy for regulating depression, tension and fatigue. In any case, students will probably have developed their own strategies for dealing with stress and these strategies will probably be similar regardless of the content being covered.

While it is clear that *kanji* learning and the constant testing of *kanji* knowledge has a stressful impact on the *kanji* learner, the 'stress' factor is just scratching the surface of the depths of emotions faced by the *kanji* learner. Emotions of disillusionment, disappointment, self-criticism and loss of self-efficacy are immense affective factors for the *kanji* learner. *The Self-regulation Study* highlighted some examples where these emotions can cause learners to give up on Japanese language study entirely. In this study, disillusionment and self-criticism over a lack of progress in *kanji* study was most evident at the intermediate and advanced levels of language proficiency, where students expressed the desire to stop learning Japanese due to frustration at a perceived lack of progress in learning. This desire is illustrated by the following excerpts.

Excerpt 11.1

The main problem of course is always time – so many demands. It's quite a challenge. And if I don't do it, then I'll be really disappointed with myself. I'm a bit of a perfectionist. So that's why in a way I found the *kanji* so difficult because I'm not succeeding, as I'd like to. (Learner Interview, *The Self-regulation Study*)

Excerpt 11.2

Especially the *kanji* [is most depressing]. It's just so demoralizing to be still studying *kanji* I was supposed to have learned three years ago! (Learner Interview, *The Self-regulation Study*)

It seems quite interesting that *The Self-regulation Study* highlighted that more highly proficiency participants subjected themselves to harsher self-criticisms and disillusionment due to lack of progress. There seemed to be a clear link with level of proficiency and a lack of emotional control; that is, the higher-level participants' inability to reach goals set for them led to a decline in emotional control. Gamage (2003: 3) offers an explanation of this phenomenon:

Firstly, the gradual increase of new *kanji* to be learnt and retaining the already learnt *kanji* seem to be an endless memory-load on the part of the learner at this [intermediate] stage. Secondly, it is at the intermediate stages that the learners are exposed to authentic material other than *kanji* textbooks, and frustration builds up when learners realize they are still unable to read an authentic text such as a newspaper.

The emotional impact of *kanji* learning on the learner also explains the high attrition rates at Japanese courses at universities, as reported by Kato (2002).

The Self-regulation Study also found it was the advanced students who were under the greatest emotional stress. In this study, I found advanced learners who talked about giving up after years of intensive study because of the difficulty of learning *kanji,* as illustrated by the following excerpts.

Excerpt 11.3

I want to give up learning Japanese – so I give up studying sometimes, and do other things. And then I – think of all the time I have invested in it, so I have to – go back to study it. It's too late. (Learner Interview, *The Self-regulation Study*)

Excerpt 11.4

It's a real struggle. And yesterday, I must admit – it wasn't just yesterday – recently I've been saying, 'Stuff this bloody course and learning Japanese!' I mean my plan is to – after I've graduated is to come back here and live in Japan anyway. So hey, you know, I can speak basic Japanese and I'll pick up the rest if I live here for a while. Bugger it. But then – that's a really bad attitude. (Learner Interview, *The Self-regulation Study*)

These students were frustrated at forgetting and having to review *kanji* they had learned years ago. They were disappointed at their lack of ability to interact with authentic texts in Japanese and displayed a high degree of self-criticism at their inability to overcome the obstacle to literacy and proficiency in Japanese that *kanji* creates. In this study, data showed a clear divide between participants, in that higher-proficiency participants subjected themselves to harsher self-criticisms and disillusionment due to lack of progress, although these feelings did not necessary coincide with levels of stress (some advanced learners in the study did express frustration over *kanji* learning, but still 'got on with' the learning task). There seemed to be a clear link with level of commitment and lack of emotional control; that is, the goals that higher-level participants set for themselves were more unattainable than those set by lower-level participants, and when these goals were not reached in the desired time, it led to a decline in their ability to control their emotions.

An explanation for this lack of emotional control in higher-proficiency students is that it might be connected to the magnitude of the *kanji*-learning task. For beginner level students, when students are studying a set number of *kanji* each week with regular structured assessment, learners are able to clearly see their progression in *kanji* learning. At the higher-proficiency level, however, when students no longer have formal training of *kanji* and the onus is on them to review thousands of *kanji*, the magnitude of the task seems daunting, progress is not as obviously measurable and emotional control breaks down. Therefore, better structure and support should perhaps be provided to higher-level students to ensure these negative emotional effects do not lead to a breakdown of emotion control.

Such findings fit within the wider literature of self-regulation, where researchers have found that a breakdown in regulation of emotion can lead to episodes of depression and anxiety (Nolen-Hoeksema & Corte, 2004). In *The Self-regulation Study*, advanced students reported emotions of stress, frustration and self-criticism over a lack of progress, even to the point of defeatism. In *The Self-regulation Study*, one student openly discussed his decision to 'give up' on *kanji* learning, having felt like the constant review of *kanji* and a deterioration of knowledge had defeated him. This case was different from the above two excerpts, where learners reported frustration and desire to give up, but persevered with the study task.

Excerpt 11.5

I gave up on the dream of becoming fluent a long time ago. I remember thinking... I'll be completely fluent after one year in Japan, but now it's been three, and I haven't really made that much progress since the first 6 months... I mean, I'm sure I have but it's been baby steps since then. I mean, at this point, I know it's not going to happen.

This learner also reported self-criticism at his inability to push through procrastination issues in the *kanji*-learning task and frustration over the constant review of *kanji* he had once learned, but had forgotten. He also doubted his ability to master the number of *kanji* necessary to graduate. Another student, although able to deal with the stress of learning *kanji*, also expressed defeatism in the *kanji* learning task, feeling that it was impossible to learn and remember all essential *kanji*, to the point that she also reassessed the role of *kanji* in her future career. A lack of self-efficacy in believing they could reach their long-term goals of literacy in Japanese, caused these students to reassess their life goals and future career plans. Thus, the emotional impact of *kanji* learning was a life-changing event for some students. In conclusion, it is clear that the emotional impact of *kanji* learning may be the greatest challenge to the Japanese language learner, and one of the most emotionally challenging tasks of learning any language.

Implications

Implications for the *kanji* learner

The emotional toll that *kanji* learning takes of the Japanese language learner is not a matter that should be treated lightly, nor is it a problem that is easily solvable. Perhaps the biggest implication of research into affect and *kanji* learning is the importance of a raised awareness that these emotions are shared by most learners and that the learner's struggles are a normal part of *kanji* acquisition. In *The Self-regulation Study*, where I met with learners on a regular basis, the students commented that even the act of talking about their personal struggles with *kanji* learning were helpful for their emotion control. The regular interviews where we discussed *kanji* learning gave them an opportunity to vent their frustrations, reflect upon their learning and progress, and reassess their long- and short-term goals in relation to *kanji* learning. Bandura (1989) argues that self-reflection and self-evaluation is key to the development of a healthy sense of self-efficacy. Zimmerman (2000) also stresses the importance of self-evaluation on self-efficacy beliefs. The act of reflecting on previous accomplishments and achievements, rather than focusing on goals yet to be achieved, may help the *kanji* learners' emotional state.

Research such as Rose and Harbon (2013) and Gamage (2003) suggests it is at the intermediate and advanced levels where students have the biggest breakdown of emotion control. This is due to progress being less obvious to the learner, as opposed to the beginning stages where it is easier for the learner to track quite obvious progress in *kanji* acquisition; that is, the road to the attainment of the first couple of hundred *kanji* is more easily marked by achievements. Students can see their knowledge of *kanji* double in a single semester-long basic or pre-intermediate Japanese language course. At the intermediate and advanced level, the onus to retain previously learned *kanji* in addition to newly taught *kanji* shifts to the learner and progress is not only less obvious, but can seem to the learner at times to be moving in the wrong direction, as previously known *kanji* become forgotten.

As noted in previous chapters, learners need a system to track their progress of *kanji* learning. They also need a system of review. In Chapter 9 and in the previous chapter, I discussed the notion of flashcards (both physical and in software) as a way to improve the memory trace between learned *kanji* through retrieval practice. Flashcards, if used in a systematic way, are also a useful way to visualize progress in *kanji* learning. If they are organized appropriately, students are able to physically see new *kanji* move into new collections of learned *kanji*, which then can be reviewed regularly. *Kanji* learning software often do this automatically and provide the students with tallies of current learning, learned and mastered *kanji*, which is a great way for students to track their progress. Tracking *kanji* acquisition is one way for the learner to avoid feelings of disillusionment over a lack progress in *kanji* learning, but it does not entirely solve the issue discussed in this chapter of students wanting to give-up or reassess future goals because of the emotional toll of *kanji* learning.

Learners need to be systematic about their goals of *kanji* learning. As mentioned in Chapter 10, a goal must be believable, achievable, conceivable and desirable (McCombs & Pope, 1994). A breakdown in emotion control often stems from the fact that a goal no longer seems believable to a student, which manifests in a loss of self-efficacy. According to Zimmerman (2000), self-efficacy beliefs and goal setting are strongly connected. Achieving goals improves self-efficacy and a higher self-efficacy influences future goal setting. At times, a student might set a goal that is only achievable in the long-term, such as mastering the 2000 essential *kanji* or passing the first-level of the Japanese Language Proficiency Test. Without short-term goals to measure progress toward this long-term goal, this goal will no longer seem achievable to a learner. Learners, therefore, would benefit from more realistic, achievable and believable goal setting, which would reduce the negative affect associated with the failure to reach a goal.

Implications for the *kanji* instructor

The *kanji* instructor can help their students overcome emotional barriers associated with *kanji* learning from the outset of their learning. Shimizu and Green (2002) noted that Japanese language teachers widely agree that *kanji* learning is an extremely difficult and arduous task for students. Therefore, this difficulty should not be sugar-coated for the students. Instructors have to strike the right balance of being honest with students over the difficulty of *kanji* learning, while not turning them off the study of Japanese. A lack of emotion control often stems from the fact that students set unrealistic and unachievable goals in their *kanji* learning. Students expect to become moderately fluent after a year of study at a Japanese university. They often expect to be able to pick up a *manga* or watch and understand an *anime* after a few years of study. Thus, when they find after a few years that they have not achieved this goal, it takes an emotional toll on their belief in their own self-efficacy. Students need to be aware that *kanji* learning is a lifelong task and that even native Japanese speakers spend nine years of formal education to achieve adult functional literacy.

In addition to this, the instructor needs to be aware that frequent quizzes, while a necessary part of *kanji* learning due to the extrinsic motivation they provide students, can also be quite stressful for students. Instructors can perhaps take advantage of *kanji* learning software, where they can record individual progress in regard to studying and reviewing *kanji*, as opposed to the tradition of weekly *kanji* tests. Doing this also puts emphasis on the importance of the learning process, rather than regurgitation of knowledge that often is crammed into short-term memory before a student takes a test and then is soon forgotten. Also, the constant teaching and quizzing of new *kanji* often detracts from the importance of maintaining knowledge of previously taught *kanji*. In testing *kanji*, instructors often focus too much on the producing knowledge, rather than the process of integrating knowledge. Rather than grading students on the outcome of tests, some teachers might be better off grading them on a self-study workbook or time engaged (and documented) in self-study software.

Implications for the researcher

Implications of affect and *kanji* learning for the researcher are many. A breakdown of emotion control clearly has a large impact on the *kanji* learner, but is a topic that has rarely been explored in the literature. Literature does discuss issues of affect and SLA of a general nature, examining affective factors such as anxiety and stress, but the task of *kanji* learning is a far more emotionally complex and taxing a task than other areas of language learning such as English vocabulary acquisition, which is a topic that has been investigated far more than *kanji* learning.

In fact, in my review of literature, it was difficult to find research conducted into the emotional toll that *kanji* learning has on native speakers of Japanese. Considering the enormous time devoted in the national curriculum to the learning of *kanji* in Japanese schools, and the importance of testing of Japanese knowledge in Japanese schools and universities, this lack of research is surprising. The examination of *kanji* knowledge comprises a major part of the *kokugo* (Japanese language) section of university entrance examinations for all public and private universities. Students, therefore, are not only required to study *kanji* intensively in school, but also often attend after-school *juku* to further their learning of *kanji*. In terms of foreign students coming to Japan to study or work, the Japanese Language Proficiency Test is often used as a criterion for entry into study programs and employment. *Kanji* knowledge is directly tested in the *kanji* section of the exam, as well as indirectly tested in reading and grammar sections. Thus, the study of *kanji* takes up a huge percentage of preparation time in studying for this exam. Surely then, we can surmise that *kanji* learning would take a huge emotional toll on these students whose future study and work careers hinge on their memorization of *kanji*. Surprisingly, however, this is an area that is currently under-researched and in need of attention. Thus, the scope of research in this area of *kanji* learning is enormous and has significant implications for Japanese learning and teaching.

Part 4
Implications

12 Implications for Learners

The following chapter summarizes the challenges faced by Japanese language learners who are trying to learn the Japanese writing system. It begins with an examination the notion of reform of the Japanese writing system, which is a common yearning of any foreign language learner that is struggling with the learning of *kanji*. The chapter explores the pros and cons of reducing *kanji* or getting rid of them entirely. We end this chapter with advice for Japanese as a foreign language learners based on the research presented in the first three parts of this book, with the aim of suggesting ways people can become better learners of written Japanese.

Challenges Faced by Japanese Language Learners

The previous chapters have outlined the major challenges that the Japanese writing system poses for the second language learner. First, there is an inherent linguistic challenge in the way that the Japanese writing system represents language: *kanji* – the backbone of the Japanese writing system – are a morphographic script that for the most part represents language at the morpheme level, where one *kanji* represents a single meaning. *Kana* – the writing system developed from *kanji* – are a syllabic script that for the most part represents the syllabic structure of the Japanese language. *Romaji* – the borrowed Roman script – is a full alphabet that represents phonemes or single units of sound. Currently, the Japanese writing system is the only writing system to fully integrate these three script types into a single writing system. The challenges faced by a reader in moving fluidly from decoding morphemes, syllables and phonemes is, therefore, an inherent challenge for any learner who is accustomed to reading within one type of writing system.

For alphabetic language background speakers, such as speakers of English, reading and writing *kanji* require a substantial adjustment due to a shift in decoding writing for meaning, rather than sound. For Chinese speakers, the adjustment to reading *kanji* may pose fewer issues, due a background in reading a morphographic script; however, there are also further linguistic challenges to the reading of *kanji*, even for these students. As Chapter 2 has shown, Japanese *kanji* are not always representative of meaning and many sub-types of *kanji* exist, such as those that contain phonological elements and those that have separated from their etymology. Also, unlike Chinese, a single Japanese *kanji* can be read with numerous pronunciations, due to the historical use of *kanji* to represent Chinese language and Japanese language in writing. This has resulted in an *on-yomi* (Chinese reading) and *kun-yomi* (Japanese reading) for many *kanji* in use today. Furthermore, the fact that many *kanji* can have multiple *on-yomi* and *kun-yomi* adds an extra challenge to readers who may be able to decode the meaning of the *kanji*, but can still have difficulty assigning the correct reading to them.

Second, this book has shown a challenge stemming from the sheer volume of *kanji* needed to be learned in order to become functionally literate in the Japanese language. Second language learners must learn more than 2000 *kanji* to achieve adult literacy in Japanese. In practice, many students learn a fraction of this, even after years of study in the language (e.g. after four years of study in Queensland high schools in the 1990s, students master just 200 *kanji*). In other language classes, a student would be considered an 'advanced' language learner after learning 500–1000 *kanji*, meaning that an advanced learner would still not be a literate one. It is my conviction that due to the steer volume of *kanji*, Japanese is one of the few languages I know of where highly educated, second language learners can function at a highly proficient level in speaking the language, but can still be illiterate. The barrier of the number of *kanji* required to learn is clearly an issue for Japanese SLA. The repercussions of this have been discussed throughout the book in terms of the cognitive, metacognitive and psychological strain that the learning of *kanji* can cause for the second language learner. However, before we continue to look at the implications for the learner, it is important to remind the reader that the learning of *kanji* is also a considerable strain for native Japanese speakers who approach the task with the advantage of a fully developed lexicon. For the foreign language learner, the learning and maintenance of *kanji* is a lifelong task.

A Learner's Lament: Why Can't the Japanese Writing System be Simplified?

Every learner of the Japanese language has at some point has questioned the worth of learning the writing system. This usually will occur before big examinations or during study sessions at the intermediate level, where the novelty of learning a morphographic script has begun to fade. This frustration of study usually manifests in an expressed desire to have the writing system simplified.

As outlined in Chapter 2, *kanji* was a script that was adopted from Chinese and modified for use with the Japanese language. Unfortunately, the script was an ill fit to represent Japanese syntax, which then spawned use of new scripts to plug the grammatical gaps that were unable to be represented by *kanji*. Although these new scripts were adapted from *kanji* themselves, they are a Japanese invention and perfectly represent the sounds of the Japanese language. In fact, from a linguistic perspective *kana* much more accurately represent the Japanese language than the Roman alphabet represents the sounds of the English language. This leads some people to question the need for *kanji* within the Japanese writing system, as the entire language can be represented accurately in this homegrown syllabary. Some students might go so far to ask why Japanese needs *kanji* at all? After all, if *kana* represents the language perfectly and if getting rid of *kanji* in favor of a homegrown phonetic script worked for the Korean language, then why not for Japanese?

In fact, Japanese language learners are not alone in their love–hate relationship with *kanji*, and there have been notable movements within Japan to abolish, or at least reduce, the importance of *kanji* in the writing system. The chairman of the Japanese language council from 1949 to 1961 actively explored suggestions to switch the writing system entirely to a romanized one. Around the same time there was an active group called the *Kanamojikai* that promoted the use of *kana* only to write the Japanese language. The main reasons for making this switch was that it was thought education could be improved, as time devoted to learning *kanji* could be reduced in favor of learning other subjects, such as mathematics. Also, at this time, technology was not very adaptive to *kanji* and an alphabetic or syllabic script could be better integrated with printing and emerging data storage technology. However, these movements were seen by some as being influenced by the American occupying forces and failed to generate the momentum needed to instigate actual change. Nevertheless, they stand as examples of ongoing debates for writing system reform within Japan.

One of the biggest arguments for not abolishing *kanji* is the number of homonyms within the Japanese language and this is a counterargument any reformer will likely encounter first if they suggest the abolition of *kanji*. The argument is based on the fact that in Japanese, there are an exceedingly large amount of homonyms due to the small vowel and consonant set of the Japanese language and the uniform syllabic structure of the language system. While some of these homonyms are distinguishable in their spoken forms due to slight differences in stress, when written in kana they appear the same. It is argued that use of *kanji* in the writing system allows for readers to distinguish between these homonyms. For example, without *kanji* it might be difficult to distinguish between the same sounding words that can be represented by a number of *kanji* and produce a number of different meanings such as 会 (meet), 界 (world), 貝 (shellfish), 解 (solution), 階 (floor), 回 (time) or 海 (ocean), plus several others that are read as *kai*. Of course, many of these *kanji* are not used in isolation, thus context would allow a reader to understand the meaning, but this is not always the case. If a reader were to read the following sentence in only *hiragana*, it could be interpreted in two ways:

さけがすきです

This sentence could be read as either: 酒が好きです (I like rice wine) or 鮭が好きです (I like salmon). While the word *sake*, meaning both wine and salmon, have different stresses in their spoken form, they are written as さけ in *kana* and are thus indistinguishable. If they are written with *kanji*, the reader instantly knows which *sake* the writer is referring to. This is a somewhat rudimentary example, as the reader would likely guess meaning correctly from context or automatically assume the writer was referring to rice wine (also due to the fact that salmon is often written in *katakana* when referring to the food). Nevertheless, it does make the point that the use of *kanji* automatically differentiates one homonym from another in a precise and unambiguous way. This differentiation is simply not possible in a phonological script. Considering the large number of homonyms in the Japanese language, *kanji* offers a clear advantage over other scripts because of this characteristic.

Another argument that is often made when reforming the Japanese writing system is the suggestion that *kanji* create natural breaks in written texts and therefore make reading easier. Native Japanese speakers find reading a text entirely written in *hiragana* difficult. Advanced second language learners will also find this to be the case. As *kanji* are often used to represent the morphemes (a unit of meaning) in the Japanese language and *hiragana* are used to represent grammatical items such as particles, prepositions, conjunctions, verb stems and adjective stems, the juxtaposition of the two scripts allows a reader to automatically discern the function of what is written. A fluent reader will often be unaware of this automatic reading process until something is written in an unexpected script, which will likely slow the reader down. An example of this would be the following sentence:

くるまできた

A reader might take more time to discern meaning from this sentence, as the lack of *kanji* would require them to confirm the natural breaks in the sentence. The sentence could be broken into くるま/で/きた (車で来た), meaning 'I came by car'; but a reader would also have subconsciously eliminated the possibilities of breaking the sentence into the nonsensical segments of くる/まで/きた (来るまで来た]), meaning 'I came until he came' or くるま/できた (車出来た), meaning 'I made a car'.

It could be argued that if spaces were to be inserted between word breaks, that this issue could quickly be avoided as the spaces would then act as natural divisions between lexical items; however, I would argue that *kanji* do more than merely act as spaces between words. Ask any intermediate or advanced Japanese language learner who has grown accustomed to reading in Japanese to read aloud a text written entirely in *romaji*, and they would probably find the text very cumbersome to navigate, despite the use of spaces between lexical items. It seems *kanji* do more than just segment words for a reader; they allow a reader to approach a text in a very different way to alphabetic scripts that is still not fully understood. In Chapter 3, we did explore the notion of phonological processing of *kanji*, which research suggests is very powerful, but this should not detract from the fact that different types of semantically-driven processing play an equally important role in the reading process that cannot be equated with the reading of phonetically-based scripts.

It is important to note, however, that just because *kanji* facilitates some parts of the reading process for highly literate Japanese speakers, some scholars believe this is not reason enough to suggest that they are indispensable. After all, spoken Japanese is understood despite an absence of logographs to differentiate between homonyms and to separate morphemes from grammatical items. Ezaki (2010) makes a strong moral case for second language learners in arguing that the barrier to literacy of *kanji* unfairly disadvantages foreign workers in Japan and in the educational system. In fact, you do not have to travel far in Japan to find a foreign resident who may be fluent in the Japanese spoken language, but more or less illiterate. The complexity of the writing system is such a formidable barrier to literacy for Japanese language learners that it is the main reason for students to drop out of Japanese language classes or to give up the study of written Japanese entirely.

Ezaki (2010) does, however, point to two compelling reasons to maintain *kanji* within the writing system: the artistic aspect of *kanji* in Japanese society is an integral part of creative and artistic expression; and the historical use of *kanji* means that any change to the writing system would result in an inability to read historical documents. Because of these reasons, scholars such as Ezaki do not call for the complete abolition of *kanji*, but a reduction in the use of *kanji* for non-literary works such as newspapers and other popular means of communication. Thus, *kanji* can continue in literary works and creative expression, but should be reduced or subject to compulsory *furigana* in everyday documentation.

Nevertheless, calls for simplification from scholars and lobby groups will unlikely result in changes to the writing system. At the moment, calls for radical change are just theoretical pipedreams and would require a complete overhaul of a writing system that has been in place for more than 1000 years. (Imagine the difficulties of instigating a complete overhaul of the English spelling system to one that is more phonetically representative of the language. The rationale behind such a movement might make sense, but it would be infeasible and unwanted by many users of English.) In fact, it appears that *kanji* have been more greatly emphasized in government policy, rather than simplified. The number of *kanji* included in the list of everyday (*joyo*) *kanji* [常用漢字] has increased with every revision, from 1850 *kanji* in 1946, to 1945 *kanji* in 1981 and to 2136 *kanji* in 2010. Thus, it appears that *kanji* are going to remain as an important feature of the writing system for the foreseeable future.

How to be a Better Learner: Strategies to Overcome Challenges

Often, when people talk to me about my research area, they inevitably ask me what the best way to learn the Japanese writing system is. While *kana* can be learned effectively using a single cognitive method of study such as a pictorial method, followed by review and practice, unfortunately there is no one foolproof method for learning *kanji*. That being said, there are five simple rules that I believe will make anyone a better learner of written Japanese.

(1) Learn *kana* first and use it always

This is a simple rule that might seem like commonsense, but is one ignored by many beginners of Japanese. *Romaji* is a crutch for many beginner learners of Japanese and can seem like a useful way to read and write Japanese from the early stages of language learning. Students may think it will help to progress their learning in the beginning stages, because they will not be held up by learning how to read and write *kana* when trying to study new words, and when reading texts in Japanese. Research and practice have shown the *kana* is an extremely easy script to learn, with initial encoding of the entire script taking less than an hour. Of course, this encoding needs to be strengthened through repeated use and recall of the *kana*, but relying on *romaji* will only detract from this process and actually lengthen the time that it takes for the reading and writing of *kana* to become an automated process. I would also argue, from a cognitive perspective, that reading and writing in *kana* could improve pronunciation of Japanese by eliminating any first language interference, which might occur when applying a script used for one language to another. For example, a student reading fu in *romaji*, might continue to pronounce the sound with a /f/, due to its association with the Roman letter f; a student reading 「ふ」 in *hiragana* might be more likely to adopt the correct Japanese pronunciation of this sound as /ɸ/ as the connection to prior knowledge of 'f' as /f/ is broken. Thus, even though reading and writing in *kana* in the beginning stages of Japanese might seem burdensome, it will actually pay dividends in the long term.

(2) Invest effort in cognitive strategies before moving to practice

Another rule for becoming a better learner would be to invest effort into initial encoding before engaging in retrieval practice activities. Often, when learners attempt to study a new list of *kanji*, their first instinct is to make flashcards and test themselves. While this is a useful activity to strengthen a memory trace, the learner will have failed to anchor the new *kanji* into an appropriate part of their mind's schema, which will cause greater risk of failure to recall the *kanji* at later stages. Cognitive theory suggests that effective memorization requires two processes: encoding and retrieval. Encoding requires the new information to be stored in a meaningful place in the mind by creating meaningful links to the new item with already known information. Thus, the learner would benefit from actively making meaningful links with new *kanji* and other known *kanji*, or mental items related to that *kanji* in their mind's schemata. The more meaningful links a learner makes, the more likely that the *kanji* will be memorized effectively. Once encoding takes place, then the effectiveness of retrieval practice activities such as the use of flashcards will increase substantially. Thus, learners should not rush the encoding process of learning and should invest considerable time to examine new *kanji* and actively make creative links to their meaning, sounds and use.

(3) Choose cognitive strategies that are appropriate for the *kanji* being learned

Learning strategy research has shown that everyone learns differently from one another; just because a strategy works for one person, it does not mean that it will work for someone else. In addition to this, strategy research has shown learners who use a wider range of strategies are likely to be more successful learners. As *kanji* represent language in different ways, it is also true that different *kanji* will require different strategies to memorize them effectively. As this book has shown, in the beginning stages of learning, pictographic *kanji* make up to half of *kanji* learned and thus learners may first view pictorial associations to be the most appropriate for these *kanji*. As learners progress, pictographic *kanji* become a smaller percentage of new *kanji* they encounter and thus a different set of strategies need to be applied, lest the learner will be in danger of drawing nonsensical connections to the *kanji*, resulting in a failure to recall them. *Kanji* that contain phonological clues (e.g. *keiseimoji* and *kashamoji*) may be best learned according to sound and not meaning, to maximize the benefits of such clues. *Kanji* based on semantic components (e.g. *kaiimoji* and *keiseimoji*) might be best learned with a component analysis strategy that links some or all of the components with their semantic origins. Ideographs (*shijimoji*) might be best learned using mnemonic devices or symbolic associations. It is important that learners are aware that there is not a one-size-fits-all strategy for learning *kanji* and that each *kanji* must be learned according to what makes the most sense to the learner. Books that claim that one strategy can be used to memorize all *kanji* should be treated skeptically; they may contain good advice for many *kanji*, but my own research (Rose, 2013) has suggested that one strategy simply does not work for all cases. Learners need a repertoire of strategies they can draw upon to learn *kanji* effectively.

(4) Systematize your learning

A fourth implication for learners of the Japanese writing system is the need to systematize their learning if they are going to achieve functional literacy in the language. While self-regulating one's learning is an important characteristic in studying almost anything, it is especially important for the learning of the Japanese writing system. Learners must learn 2136 *joyo kanji* (everyday use *kanji*) in order to be considered functionally literate. Many of these *kanji* have more than one reading attached to them, which complicates learning even further. Without a system to track learning, measure progress and ensure suitable revision, a learner will simply not succeed in learning the written language. The introduction of computer assisted *kanji* learning will certainly be of use to learners in the modern age. These programs systematically organize *kanji* for the learner and ensure progress is tested and tracked. This book will avoid suggesting particular programs as any suggestions are likely to become out-of-date soon after publication, as new apps come on the market and new devices are used for the learning of Japanese. I can suggest that for the initial stages of learning, learners should turn to applications and software made for learners of Japanese as a foreign language, but at the advanced level, learners might find that those geared towards the Japanese market are of better quality. (Remember: *kanji* learning is not just something that foreign language learners struggle with, so there are some top-quality programs produced for Japanese people by Japanese firms that have a lot more money to invest in the research and development of programs compared to the smaller foreign learner market.)

(5) Be realistic in your goals and do not be self-critical of a lack of development

A final suggestion is that learners need to be realistic in how much progress they can make in their Japanese studies and therefore avoid a breakdown in self-regulation. My research (Rose, 2012a, 2012b) has shown that when one element of self-regulation broke down in a learner, it had a detrimental domino effect on their entire ability to manage their learning (see Figure 12.1). The boxes represent breakdowns in the four types of motivation

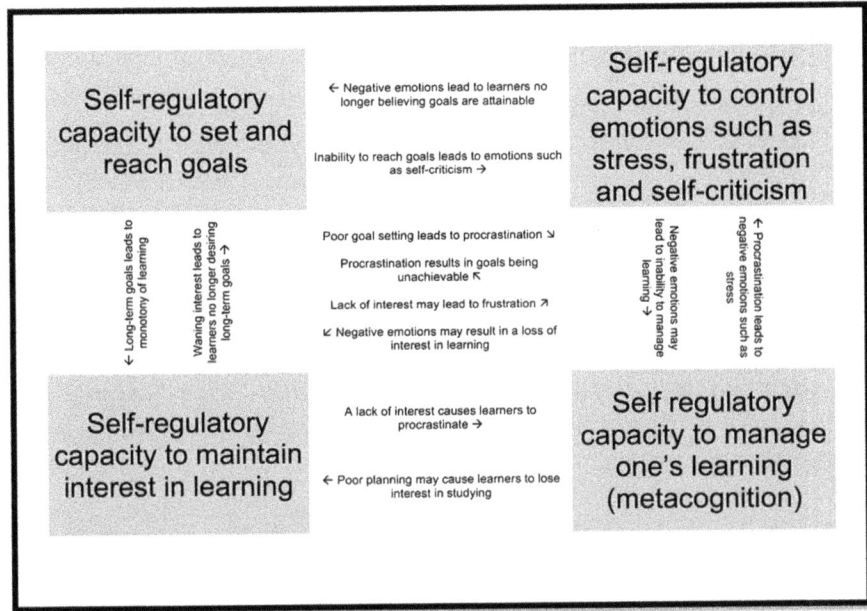

Figure 12.1 A breakdown in self-regulation for learning *kanji* of a Japanese language learner

control. The arrows indicate the effects these breakdowns can have on the other categories of motivation control.

For example, a breakdown in emotional control in terms of the self-criticism as witnessed in *The Self-regulation Study* by higher-level participants can then affect commitment one has to learning, as the believability of reaching a goal would then need to be reassessed. Likewise, a breakdown in metacognitive control manifesting in procrastination also affects the achievability of reaching a commitment as time available to achieve the goal is diminished. Furthermore, a breakdown in satiation control in terms of boredom with study can affect the desirability of achieving a goal and we saw in *The Self-regulation Study* that some participants were ready to give up on studying Japanese entirely. In terms of the other causal relationships between emotion control, satiation control and metacognitive control, *The Self-regulation Study* found a complex relationship existed. Students who expressed self-criticism and frustration also reported inability to control procrastination. Boredom with study led to procrastination, which then led to negative emotions attached to learning Japanese. This causal network is far more complex than indicated in previous explanations of motivation control taxonomy (Dörnyei, 2001, 2005; Tseng *et al.*, 2006) and thus is important for any learner of Japanese to control.

As a result, I would encourage any learner of Japanese to try to control their learning in the following ways:

(1) Set realistic short-term goals.
(2) Plan your learning to meet these goals, track your progress and reward yourself.
(3) Implement new methods of study and try new learning environments to re-invigorate the learning process.
(4) Remain positive and avoid being overly critical of a perceived lack of progress.

While this set of advice might seem 'easier said than done', it is of vital importance that learners stay on top of their learning, as only a highly self-regulated and dedicated learner will truly succeed in the learning of the Japanese writing system.

13 Implications for Instructors

The following chapter summarizes the challenges faced by Japanese language instructors who are struggling to find better methods for teaching the Japanese writing system. It examines the notion of pacing and ordering elements of the Japanese writing system in curricula, which is a fundamental issue facing all teachers, for which there is not a definitive answer. We end this chapter with advice for Japanese teachers based on the research presented in the first three parts of this book, with the aim of suggesting ways people can become better teachers of written Japanese.

Issues Surrounding the Order of Teaching Japanese Writing

The previous chapter summarized the challenges of learning the Japanese writing system for the second language learner. Teachers of Japanese play a vital role in supporting learners in their journey to read and write in their taught second language. As curriculum designers and classroom practitioners, teachers of Japanese must make a number of decisions that potentially affect the success of their learners.

First, teachers play a vital role in the selection of *kanji* for instruction, especially if they are given autonomy in curriculum design. Even if some of this decision-making is centralized in the case of a coordinated curriculum or use of a particular textbook, teachers still must make important decisions of how this is translated into a classroom context. For example, teachers often need to decide when to introduce the various elements of the writing system.

- Some curricula introduce Japanese via *romaji* and then introduce *hiragana* at a later stage after basic spoken Japanese communication is learned; other teachers discourage the use of *romaji* from the outset of study.
- Some teachers opt to teach *kanji* only after years of study; others introduce it immediately.
- Some teachers use *furigana* over newly learned *kanji*; others see it as a crutch and opt to present *kanji* on their own in a 'sink or swim' learning context.

- Some teachers introduce *kanji* that are stylistically simple first (e.g. few strokes); others introduce *kanji* that are semantically simple (e.g. the days of the week, colors or family members).

Thus, there are numerous issues that a good teacher needs to consider when teaching Japanese writing.

How to be a Better Teacher: Advice to Support Second Language Learners

When I talk to teachers about my research area, they are usually looking for advice in response to the above issues. Teachers also ask me for advice on the best methods of teaching the writing system in the classroom. In this section I will explore a number of options related to the order of instruction and the pace of introducing new *kanji*. It is important to note here, however, that the studies presented in this book look at the learning of Japanese writing from a learner's perspective. Thus, my advice here will center on the methods of teaching Japanese that are seen as beneficial from the learners' perspective, rather than drawing on original research examining the effects of various teaching methods; this is a question that would need to be addressed in additional research.

(1) *Kana* before *romaji*

Building on a point made in the previous chapter, I want to emphasize to teachers the importance of teaching *kana* in the very early stages of Japanese language learning. Some teachers may be tempted to help beginner students to read Japanese by providing worksheets, dialogues and instructions on the board that are written in *romaji*. I think although teachers have good intentions of using of *romaji* to help students access the language, an over-reliance on it means that students are likely to use it as a crutch and will take longer to make the transition to the *kana* script. Anecdotally, I have seen teachers who use *romaji* too much in the classroom and their classes are populated with students who cannot read *hiragana* effectively even after one year of instruction. If teachers do not expose students to enough *kana* and do not require students to read it, they are disadvantaging their students in the long term. It is my conviction, after dealing with many types of students in my various research projects, that learners benefit from a 'tough love' approach when it comes to the teaching of *kana* at the very start of Japanese language classes. Although teachers might feel that imposing the script on their students might seem burdensome, research says otherwise; *kana* is an incredibly easy script to learn and can be picked up with repeated opportunities to use it. In my own experience, I find that after students get through the initial steep learning curve, they enjoy the fact that they can read and

Implications for Instructors   141

write in another script. This is also supported by research into learner cognition, which emphasizes the important role of retrieval practice in strengthening the memorization of new information. In this case, repeated practice in reading and writing in a new script is necessary to learn it effectively; if a teacher is not providing opportunity for retrieval practice of *kana*, they are harming the long-term chances of their students successfully memorizing the script. Thus, I would argue that teachers should teach *kana* from the outset and avoid *romaji* almost entirely.

(2) *Katakana* before *hiragana?*

Another issue that has emerged recently in Japanese language education is whether *katakana* should be taught before *hiragana*. Although at first this notion seems to be in opposition to the natural order of learning, some curricula are making the switch. Because lexical items that come from foreign origins are written in *katakana*, and because most borrowed lexical items are taken from English, the ability to read *katakana* for English speakers can result in an added advantage to decipher a huge amount of written Japanese. After students learn *katakana*, they can decipher many everyday words, even if they have not studied the lexis in Japanese before. Everyday words such as T-shirt (Tシャツ), glass (グラス), table (テーブル) and sneakers (スニーカー) are direct phonological representations of English words written in *katakana*, as too are many sporting activities, food items and place names. Once the *katakana* script is learned, students can access items on many restaurant menus or shopping lists that can be integrated into classroom activities. To illustrate this, a restaurant from a famous Japanese hamburger chain called *Mosburger* is reproduced in Table 13.1. As can be seen, the restaurant menu is almost entirely in *katakana*. A gloss in *romaji* of decipherable menu items is provided in Table 13.2, which illustrates how a learner, even in the beginner stages of Japanese language learning, might be able to decipher most of the menu items provided they could read Japanese and had a knowledge of the English language. For example, a learner could potentially be able to enter this restaurant and order a fish burger, a side of chicken nuggets, french fries and an orange juice with a bit of creative decoding. Moreover, the ability to read *katakana* and to be able to access the wealth of lexis in Japanese that has been borrowed from English, increases the possibilities of integrating authentic resources into classroom activities. For example, this same menu could easily be used in a classroom role-play or speaking task where students have to act out the function of ordering food or expressing their likes and dislikes. In short, knowledge of *katakana* can increase students' access to reading materials that would otherwise be unreadable.

However, one possible caveat is the interference of first language phonology when learning this Japanese lexis. Teachers also have to question how beneficial this would be for students who are yet to fully comprehend Japanese

Table 13.1 Fast food menu to illustrate use of *katakana*

バーガー	ドリンク
モスバーガー 370 円 モスチーズバーガー 400 円 テリヤキバーガー 360 円 モス野菜バーガー オーロラソース 360 円 テリヤキチキンバーガー 360 円 フィッシュバーガー 340 円 ロースカツバーガー 380 円 海老カツバーガー 390 円 チキンバーガー 320 円 ハンバーガー 220 円 チーズバーガー 250 円 スパイシーモスバーガー 400 円 モスライスバーガー 340 円	プレミアムアイスコーヒー（コロンビア豆 100%） S サイズ 250 円・M サイズ 310 円・L サイズ 380 円 プレミアムアイスティー（レモン/ミルク） S サイズ 250 円・M サイズ 310 円・L サイズ 380 円 100%オレンジジュース S サイズ 250 円・M サイズ 310 円・L サイズ 380 円 コーラ（ペプシネックス） S サイズ 190 円・M サイズ 240 円・L サイズ 310 円 ジンジャーエール S サイズ 190 円・M サイズ 240 円・L サイズ 310 円 メロンソーダ S サイズ 190 円・M サイズ 240 円・L サイズ 310 円 アイスウーロン茶 S サイズ 190 円・M サイズ 240 円・L サイズ 310 円 アイスカフェラテ S サイズ 190 円・M サイズ 240 円・L サイズ 310 円 モスシェイク（バニラ/ストロベリー/コーヒー） S サイズ 250 円・M サイズ 310 円 プレミアムブレンドコーヒー（コロンビアスプレモ豆60%使用）250 円 紅茶（レモン/ミルク）250 円 カフェラテ 290 円 ホット抹茶ラテ 310 円
ホットドッグ	
ホットドッグ 320 円 チリドッグ 350 円 スパイシーチリドッグ 380 円	
サイド メニュー	
フレンチフライポテトSサイズ 220 円 フレンチフライポテトLサイズ 300 円 オニポテ（フレンチフライポテト&オニオンフライ）240 円 チキンナゲット 5 コ入り 320 円 モスチキン 270 円 モスチキンパック（5 本入り）1350 円	
ソース	スープ
チリディップソース（辛い）90 円 バーベキューソース 40 円 マスタードソース 40 円	コーンスープ北海道産コーン使用 290 円 クラムチャウダー 290 円

phonology, which would best be illustrated through the learning of traditional Japanese lexis first, which is written in *hiragana*. That is, by learning borrowed items first, a student may be unfairly influenced by the first language in the pronunciation of such items. Furthermore, many students of and

Implications for Instructors   143

Table 13.2 Fast food menu *romaji* gloss

Bāgā [Burger]	*Dorinku [Drink]*
Mosu Bāgā [Mos Burger]	Puremiamu Aisu Kōhī [Premium Ice
Mosu Chīzu Bāgā [Mos Cheese Burger]	Coffee（Koronbia 豆 100%）[Colombian]
Teriyaki Bāgā [Teriyaki Burger]	Puremiamu Aisu Ti [Premium Ice Tea]
Mosu 野菜 Bāgā Ōrorasōsu	(Remon/Miruku) [Lemon/Milk]
Teriyaki Chikin Bāgā [Teriyaki Chicken	100% Orenji Jūsu [100% Orange Juice]
Burger]	Kōra（Pepushinekkusu）[Cola (Pepsi-Nex)]
Fisshu Bāgā [Fish Burger]	Jinjā Ēru [Ginger Ale]
Rōsu Katsu Bāgā	Meron Soda [Melon Soda]
海老 Katsu Bāgā	Aisu Ūron 茶 [Iced Oolong]
Chikin Bāgā [Chicken Burger]	Aisu Kafe Rate [Ice Café Latte]
Hanbāgā [Hamburger]	Mosu Sheiku [Mos Shake]
Chīzu Bāgā [Cheese Burger]	(Banira/Sutoroberī/Kōhī)
Supaishī Mosu Bāgā [Spicy Mos Burger]	[Vanilla/Strawberry/Coffee]
Mosu Raisu Bāgā [Mos Rice Burger]	Puremiamuburendokōhī [Premium Blend
	Coffee（Koronbiasupuremo 豆 60%使用）
	[Columbia Supreme]
	紅茶（Remon / Miruku）[Lemon/Milk]
	Kafe Rate [Café Latte]
	Hotto 抹茶 Rate
Hottodoggu [Hot Dog]	
Hotto Doggu [Hot Dog]	
Chiri Doggu [Chilli Dog]	
Supaishī Chiri Doggu [Spicy Chilli Dog]	
Saido Menyū [Side Menu]	
Furenchi Furai Poteto [French Fried Potato]	
S-Saizu [Small-Size]	
L-Saizu [Large-Size] Onipote（Furenchi	
Furai Poteto & Onion Furai）[French Fried	
Potato And Fried Onion]	
Chikin Nagetto [Chicken Nuggets]	
Mosu Chikin [Mos Chicken] Mosu Chikin	
Pakku [Mos Chicken Pack]	
Sōsu [Sauce]	*Sūpu [Soup]*
Chiri Dippu Sōsu [Chilli Dip Sauce]	Kōnsūpu [Corn Soup] 北海道産 Kōn
Bābekyū Sōsu40 [Barbeque Sauce]	使用 Kuramuchaudā [Clam Chowder]
Masutādo Sōsu40 [Mustard Sauce]	

L1 English speaking background can find difficulty in reading *katakana* words of an English origin due to the differences in their phonology. The syllabic nature of Japanese phonology causes borrowed words to change considerably (e.g. shirt becomes *shatsu*, glass becomes *gurasu*, and sneaker becomes *sunika*). For some learners, some phonological differences could make borrowed words seemingly unrecognizable. Thus, there are arguments both for and against teaching *katakana* before *hiragana* and it will be up to individual teachers to decide what is best for their students.

(3) When to introduce *kanji*?

A third consideration for instructors of Japanese is the extent to which vocabulary should be taught before *kanji*. As this book has shown, cognitive theory suggests new items such as *kanji* are more effectively memorized when they can be anchored with items they are concretely associated with. For native Japanese speakers, new *kanji* can easily be linked with their prior knowledge of the lexical items they represent. Naturally, a Japanese child who begins learning *kanji* at the age of six already has an extensive knowledge of the Japanese spoken language, which includes a wide lexical base. The average six year old, after all, has expressive command of over 2000 words and a receptive understanding of more than 20,000 words. For second language learners, the situation is very different. Their spoken knowledge of Japanese is usually very limited when *kanji* are first introduced. In fact, in many curricula I have seen, *kanji* are introduced alongside new vocabulary, where *kanji* are usually paired with a new vocabulary list for each unit of study. Thus, the second language learner not only has to contend with embedding new vocabulary in its phonological form into their memories, but also new *kanji* which may need to be memorized using more semantic associations. As a result, many students find it more beneficial to link the *kanji* to their knowledge of the vocabulary items in their native languages, which can cause students to recognize the abstract meaning of *kanji*, not to know how to read it in Japanese, a recurring issues highlighted in this book when we examined mnemonic strategies.

However, one study (Rose & Harbon, 2013) looked at the self-regulation of Japanese learners, finding that beginner learners of *kanji* seemed to have a strong interest in learning *kanji* and accordingly struggled least with satiation control strategies (strategies used to maintain an interest in learning). Thus, a teacher might want to embrace an interest in learning *kanji* in the beginning stages of learning, rather than waiting until learners have a more functional control over the spoken language. In many ways, this interest in the writing system might spur on learning and have a positive effect on the learning of new vocabulary items associated with the *kanji*.

Thus, there is no clear picture of when it is best to introduce *kanji* to the learner. On the one hand, knowledge of the Japanese language's vocabulary might be beneficial before *kanji* are introduced, thus mimicking L1 acquisition and providing learners with an active L2 lexicon upon which to map *kanji*. On the other hand, if one considers the cultural interest beginner learners have in the script, it seems counterproductive to delay the teaching of it. Furthermore, it may also be merely a case of delaying the difficulties in learning the script to later stages of learning. However, from the research findings presented in this book, one thing is clear: no matter when *kanji* are introduced, it is imperative that they are frequently reviewed and used in classroom materials rather than being used as an exercise in the rote-memorization of weekly lists of *kanji*. As Rose and Harbon (2013: 13) concluded in their study of self-regulation and *kanji* learning:

> The *kanji* instructor can help students overcome barriers associated with *kanji* learning from the outset of their program of studies. The instructor needs to be aware that frequent quizzes, while a necessary part of *kanji* learning, detract from the importance of maintaining knowledge of previously taught *kanji* and using *kanji* to read authentic and meaningful texts. Instructors could make use of assessment techniques that shift the focus from testing knowledge of new *kanji* through *kanji* quizzes to learning *kanji* for communicative purposes. Such purposes include reading for pleasure and to reinforce and increase content knowledge, and to learn about cultural practices, products, perspectives, and points of view and provide informal opportunities for review. Doing this also emphasizes the importance of the learning process and ultimate usefulness of *kanji* learning, rather than regurgitation of knowledge that often is crammed into short-term memory before a student takes a test and then is soon forgotten.

Thus, it is essential to integrate *kanji* learning into the curriculum as a meaningful part of using the Japanese language, rather than an auxiliary learning activity that is carried out in addition to other aspects of language learning.

(4) Ordering of *kanji*: Frequency or simplicity?

A fourth consideration involves deciding on the best way to order *kanji* for foreign language learners. Although many textbooks contain their own unique variations, generally speaking there are four elements to a *kanji* that are considered when deciding on the order that *kanji* are presented to a learner. Many textbooks or resource materials will use one or more of these elements when deciding which *kanji* to introduce first:

(1) by frequency of use. For example, *'A New Dictionary of Kanji Usage'* (Gakken, 1982) uses this approach;
(2) by simplicity. For example, some Japanese reference lists will order *kanji* according to the number of strokes they contain (e.g. https://en.wikipedia.org/wiki/List_of_kanji_by_stroke_count);
(3) by meaning groups. For example, the *'Basic Kanji Book'* (Kano *et al.*, 2006) uses this approach for many of its chapters, with chapters on topics such as 'jobs', 'travel' and 'Japan's four seasons';
(4) by components. For example, *'Kanji ABC'* (Foerster & Tamura, 1994) organizes *kanji* around those sharing the same components.

Table 13.3 *Kanji* ordered by frequency

Order	Kanji	Meaning	Order	Kanji	Meaning
1	日	sun	11	国	country
2	一	one	12	出	leave
3	大	big	13	上	on
4	年	year	14	十	ten
5	中	middle	15	生	life
6	会	meet	16	子	child
7	人	person	17	分	minute
8	本	book	18	東	east
9	月	moon	19	三	three
10	長	long	20	行	Go

Frequency of use usually dictates those *kanji* that are used most frequently in the Japanese language are learned first. According to such an approach, the 20 *kanji* presented in Table 13.3 would be introduced first.

While the logic behind such an approach would mean that students are first learning *kanji* that they are statistically going to encounter more often, it does not always mean that they will be able to read the words they are used to represent. There are *kanji* in this list that are present because they are used in conjunction with other *kanji* to produce semantically different word items. The *kanji* for *life* [生], for example is probably so prominent, not because life is the 15th most frequently occurring word in Japanese, but because the *kanji* is used in conjunction with other *kanji* to produce other high-frequency words, such as *student* [生徒] and *teacher* [先生]. Thus, learning it in isolation might not be as useful for beginner learners. Furthermore, a frequency-based approach would mean students would be able to read the numbers one, three and ten in Japanese, but no others; they would be able to read minute, but not hour; they would understand east but not north, west or south. This seems to create a somewhat random selection of *kanji*. If we were to continue learning this way, it would also mean that words like place [地] would be taught before the *kanji* for ground [土]. Seeing as the *kanji* for ground [土] is a component in place [地] and gives a clue to its meaning, this seems somewhat counterintuitive.

A second approach would be to introduce *kanji* according to their simplicity, which would dictate that the most simple *kanji* be taught first. If this were the case, the 20 *kanji* presented in Table 13.4 would be introduced first.

With this example, we also have a semantically random selection of *kanji*, which may not be indicative of their usefulness to beginner learners. While all contain less than three strokes to write, their meanings are not always just as simple. In fact, the second *kanji* in the list, which is written with one stroke, is not commonly taught in elementary Japanese classes due to its

Table 13.4 *Kanji* ordered by simplicity

Order	Kanji	Meaning	Order	Kanji	Meaning
1	一	one	11	刀	sword
2	乙	latter	12	力	power
3	丁	city block	13	十	ten
4	七	seven	14	又	again
5	九	nine	15	三	three
6	了	finish	16	上	on
7	二	two	17	大	big
8	人	person	18	下	under
9	入	enter	19	小	small
10	八	eight	20	川	River

specialized use and its meaning is somewhat abstract. Other *kanji*, which are relatively more complex such as the one used to represent language [語], would not be taught until a more advanced level, despite the relevance of it to students who are learning the Japanese language [日本語].

A third approach would be to teach *kanji* according to their meaning groups, such as grouping the teaching of numbers, days of the week, colors, family members, adjectives and so on. An approach such as this may decide to teach the 20 *kanji* presented in Table 13.5 first.

Following this order, *kanji* are introduced with the same meaning group, which would probably coincide with a unit of study within the Japanese class. For example, the first list would coincide with the teaching of Japanese numbers and the second list would coincide with the teaching of Japanese family members. An advantage of such an approach would be that it is easier for a teacher to create opportunities to use the *kanji* in the classroom and for homework, as the *kanji* would also tie in with a classroom learning objective. From a cognitive theory point of view, presenting the *kanji* in such a way would also reflect the way we naturally categorize items in our memories and thus would likely facilitate better memorization. Disadvantages would include the introduction of somewhat complex *kanji* very early in the curriculum, such as the *kanji* for younger sister, which contains eight strokes. Furthermore, the order with which *kanji* are introduced would greatly depend on the curriculum being studied and the textbook being used. For example, a recent study by Paxton (2015) has found that there is little uniformity in Japanese language textbook's decisions on which *kanji* to present to learners, resulting in an uneven learning of *kanji* depending on what book is used. This may cause issues in learning environments where students are moving from one context (such as different high schools) to another (such as to a university). There would be no guarantee that all students would have studied the same content.

Table 13.5 *Kanji* ordered by meaning groups

Order	Kanji	Meaning	Order	Kanji	Meaning
1	一	one	11	母	mother
2	二	two	12	父	father
3	三	three	13	兄	older brother
4	四	four	14	姉	older sister
5	五	five	15	弟	younger brother
6	六	six	16	妹	younger sister
7	七	seven	17	子	child
8	八	eight	18	女	woman
9	九	nine	19	男	man
10	十	ten	20	友	Friend

A fourth approach is one suggested by Paxton (2015), who researched the order with which *kanji* is presented to learners as part of larger research project. Based on his analysis of textbooks, and student and teacher perception, he developed his own recommendation for teaching *kanji*, based on moving from single-unit *kanji* to complex *kanji*. For example, he suggests that the *kanji* for tongue [舌] be taught before the *kanji* for speak [話] before moving on to multi-*kanji* combinations such as lifestyle [生活], because tongue appears as a component of speak and in the second *kanji* in lifestyle. This approach is not dissimilar to Heisig's (2007, 2008) approach of teaching 'primitive elements' of *kanji* before the actual *kanji* they appear in. While such an approach clearly takes the view that *kanji* components are the building blocks of more advanced *kanji*, I see clear disadvantages for beginner learners. For example, students would not learn frequently occurring *kanji* such as to speak and lifestyle until well after non-frequently occurring *kanji* such as tongue. To use an example earlier in the book, this would also require students to learn the rarely used *kanji* for bird (酉), before the *kanji* for alcohol (酒), despite the fact that knowing the *kanji* for alcohol may prove of great use to any adult learner of Japanese when deciphering menus or travelling through Japan. However, I do see the merit of the approach for a learner who is planning to master all of the *joyo kanji*, because it provides a systematic approach to learning and will facilitate use of component analysis strategies, which Part 2 of this book has shown to be very powerful. However, for learners whose goal is to gain survival Japanese and who may be satisfied with knowing a few hundred *kanji*, this ordering process, which places systematicity over functionality, may result in a students' inability to read some common *kanji* and an ability to read *kanji* that may be of little use to their immediate purposes.

Strategy Instruction in the Classroom

Another area of interest to teachers surrounds the question of whether they can teach their students the strategies outlined in this book in order to facilitate better learning of *kanji* (e.g. O'Malley, 1987; Rubin *et al.*, 2007). The teaching of learning strategies for learner success is not a new concept. Indeed, seminal researchers in the field such as Rubin (1981) purported the rationale of learning strategy research lay in the potential benefits findings would have for less successful learners. In order to explore this idea fully, we perhaps need to look into research into language learning strategy instruction. Such research indicates that strategies are indeed teachable, but I would qualify this statement with findings of my own research to suggest that while strategy awareness raising is an important activity in the language classroom, the decision to ultimately adopt a repertoire of strategies that best suits each learner is entirely up to the individual.

Research into language learning strategies for reading in a foreign language has shown that students can benefit from strategy instruction. Teachers who employ strategy-based instruction in language classrooms have reported:

> Students become more efficient in completing classroom language tasks, take more responsibility for directing their own learning outside of class, and gain more confidence in their ability to learn and use language. (Cohen, 2000: 1)

For example, a study by Chamot and Keatly (2003, cited in Chamot, 2005) of strategy instruction for learners of the English language showed that students in their study adopted some of the strategies that were explicitly taught to them. Interestingly, they also found that strategy instruction was more effective when done in the students' native language. Thus, for *kanji* learning, it may be unwise to carry out strategy instruction in the target language of Japanese, due to the difficulty some students may have in following such a cognitively challenging discussion.

In regard to teaching strategies for language improvement, a study of high school and college-level Spanish and French students found a 50-minute awareness-raising session had significant effects on students' final course grades when compared to a control group in three replicated experiments (Feyton *et al.*, 1999). In a similar experiment, a group of researchers found training of reading comprehension strategies for Greek students of English improved student performance in English comprehension (Pappa *et al.*, 2003). A further study by Ikeda and Takeuchi (2003) of 210 Japanese students of

English found that only the higher proficiency learners benefited most from strategy instruction. However, these studies have all looked at English learning and not the more narrowly defined (and more cognitively challenging) task of *kanji* learning.

As there has been little research into the teaching of *kanji* learning strategies, perhaps better parallels can be drawn between vocabulary acquisition research and strategy instruction. In fact, *kanji* is much like vocabulary in that 'learning new vocabulary in a second language is a continuing process rather than a single event' (Chamot, 2005: 121). In an important study by Grenfell and Harris (1999), teachers of modern language in the UK explicitly taught memorization strategies for learning new vocabulary and found that students readily adopted them, which had positive effects on their tests. Such evidence suggests that strategy instruction for the learning of *kanji* might also prove fruitful.

There have been a number of studies that have emphasized that there is a need for strategy instruction for learning *kanji*. Toyoda (1998), for example, stresses the need for teachers to make students more aware of the differences between alphabets and *kanji* in the beginning stages of *kanji* learning. Bourke (1996) also concludes in her study that teachers need to give more guidance to beginning learners of Japanese on how to learn *kanji*, an opinion echoed by Usuki (2000), whose report criticizes teachers for not providing adequate guidance and class time to the learning of these characters. Despite these calls for provision of guidance to students on *kanji* learning, research into the raising of *kanji* learning strategy awareness remains sparse, although some work has been done.

One study, for example, examined the effect of teaching whole-*kanji* strategies compared to component analysis strategies and found that teaching component analysis strategies resulted in higher retention rates in both short-term and long-term *kanji* recall (Flaherty & Noguchi, 1998). De Courcy and Birch (1993) have also found that the teaching of reading and writing strategies in a Japanese language class resulted in students making use of a wider range of strategies and feeling more in control of their learning. One of my very first studies in the area of *kanji* learning (Rose, 2003) examined the explicit teaching of *kanji* learning strategies to primary-school aged learners of Japanese. My study found that the experimental groups that had been made aware of strategies they could use to better learn *kanji*, performed better on classroom *kanji* quizzes. Therefore, even though research in this field is still relatively sparse, preliminary findings suggest that the teaching of *kanji* learning strategies may have a positive effect on students' *kanji* learning, in terms of autonomy, language ability and control over one's learning.

Results of the studies presented in this book have also suggested that a raised awareness of strategies makes learners change their strategies. *The Intervention Study*, for example, had 25 learners take a pre-test of *kanji*

Table 13.6 Use of component analysis by an illustrative case in *The Strategies Study*

Session	1	2	3	4	5	6	7	8	9	10
Student 3	N	N	S	N	N	S	Y	Y	Y	Y

Y, Yes; N, No; S, Somewhat/unclear.

knowledge to examine their recollection of learning a list of novel *kanji* using their own preferred methods. Strategy use was measured via a simplified questionnaire. The students then engaged in a strategy instruction lesson to raise their awareness of the strategies their successful classmates (those who scored high on the tests) had used in the pre-test to some success. The following week, the same learners sat another *kanji* test on a different list of *kanji* of the same difficulty. Of the 25 learners, 23 showed an increase in *kanji* recollection, with two learners remembering one fewer *kanji* correctly in the post-test. The mean difference between the pre-test and post-test was 3.04 *kanji* and the greatest difference observed by a single learner was 11 *kanji*. This study, however, had no control group for comparison or for the measurement of a testing effort, which limits the results somewhat. Nevertheless, there seems to be some evidence that strategy instruction can improve *kanji* learning, at least in the short-term.

These results can also be illustrated qualitatively. If we take one illustrative case from *The Strategies Study* (Table 13.6), we can see that component analysis use by this student changed over the course of the study, where he became more aware of the importance of this strategy in learning *kanji*. Each session is labeled according to whether component analysis was observed in the bi-weekly stimulated recall session.

In this study, the participant expressed an explicit understanding of his adoption of a strategy he did not previously see the value in, during the initial sessions.

Excerpt 13.1

I have tried to break bigger *kanji* down to smaller parts, like – I'm not sure if that's a change, but anyway, I have been trying to do that lately… Well, just at first I didn't really bother with it because it seemed kind of like adding more complications to it than it needed. But I don't know, but it actually seemed to – in kind of talking, we talked about and everything, it kind of made sense, so I'm just sort of trying doing that… And it makes it sort of easier to remember radicals too and everything 'cause if you break it down and you kind of look at the pieces, it kind of makes it easier. (*Learner Interview, The Strategies Study*)

However, this same study also highlighted a tendency for some students to reject strategies explicitly forced on them by their teachers and thus it seems that strategy instruction, while fruitful, is best done if consciously embraced by each individual learner.

Based on the advice offered by Chamot (2005) on strategy instruction, coupled with the research that has been done in the area, I feel the following is a good guide for teachers of Japanese:

- Rather than teach strategies directly, teachers should engage in awareness raising activities, where students are encouraged to try a range of strategies, explore the benefits of using these strategies and then make an informed decision regarding which one best matches the study task at hand and their individual learning preferences.
- Teach strategies in the students' L1 so that learners fully understand what they are and how they should be applied. This is particularly important for lower proficiency students, where it might not be possible to teach them in the target language (Macaro, 2001).
- Strategy awareness raising should not be taught separately, but integrated into the language classroom.
- Each learner uses a different repertoire of strategies, so use of strategies should never be forced on the learner. Teachers may do well to remember back to their own learning experiences of Japanese when forced to do a task they did not see as beneficial (I remember having to write out each new *kanji* 30 times in my university Japanese classes, while convinced that I was not absorbing any of them into my memory).

Teachers are in a prime position to influence the way learners tackle the difficult task of *kanji* learning, so it is important that they play a positive role in the students' exposure to *kanji* learning strategies and encourage learners to adopt a system that works best for them.

14 Implications for Researchers

This book has offered a research-led examination of learners' challenges when acquiring the Japanese written language in second and foreign language learning contexts. In this examination, the book has drawn on key research in the field of applied linguistics and incorporated data from three original studies. These studies have focused on *kanji* learning strategies in particular, due to the special challenges the script poses for second language learners; however, there is scope for a much wider range of research projects drawing on theory in the fields of applied linguistics and learner psychology. This chapter aims to make recommendations for further research into the Japanese writing system so readers involved in research in the field can make informed decisions about the type of research that would be most valuable in the development of the field's understanding of how Japanese is better taught and learned.

Recommendations for Further Japanese SLA Research

(1) *Kanji* type and strategy use

A great deal of research into *kanji* learning (including those cited in this book) have paid very little attention to *kanji* type and the cognitive processes involved when memorizing different types of *kanji*. As we saw in Chapter 2, *kanji* can be classified into six categories according to how they represent language: *shokeimoji* (pictographs); *shijimoji* (logograms); *kaiimoji* (ideographs); *keiseimoji* (semasio-phonetic ideographs); *tenchuumoji* (derivative characters); and *kashamoji* (phonetic loan characters). An acknowledgement of *kanji* types challenges the basis of much research into Japanese SLA that depicts the writing system as a purely morphographic script based on morphemes and ignores the phonological aspects of many *kanji* that fall into the categories of *kashamoji* (phonetic loan characters) and *keiseimoji* (semasio-phonetic ideographs). As a result, current research in the area has not fully explored the different cognitive processes that come into play when learners encounter different *kanji* types. A study that examines the effectiveness of memory processes according to *kanji* type would shed light on how learners use both phonological and semantic processes when dealing with *kanji*. Some studies were done in the 1990s (e.g. Yamada, 1998; Sayeg, 1996), but there is scope to explore this issue in greater depth.

In addition to this, semantic-based *kanji* are also often grouped together, even though some are pictorial representations (*shokeimoji*), some are ideographic representations (*shijimoji*), others are a combination of characters (*kaiimoji*) or have nothing to do with their etymological roots (*tenchuumoji*). Thus, even though research suggests all of these *kanji* types require semantic links to aid memorization, the effectiveness of these links would surely be contingent on the *kanji* type. For example, one could assume that a pictorial association strategy simply would not be very effective for *kanji* outside the *shokeimoji* category. Nevertheless, while this is an assumption we might have as learners and teachers of Japanese, this has not been empirically tested. I see two opportunities for research in this area. One recommendation would be for a researcher to carry out an in-depth investigation of *kanji* cognitive strategy use based on the stimulated recall methodology used in *The Strategies Study*, recording both strategy use against an inventory such as that in Table 3.1, as well as *kanji* type. A researcher could then analyze the results according to the independent variable of *kanji* type to empirically show whether there is a correlation between *kanji* type and strategy use. Another recommendation for a study would be to carry out an experiment where learners are required to learn a list of *kanji* that are presented alongside pictographic clues under experimental conditions. The learners would then have to recall the *kanji* in a test and the results could be analyzed according to the independent variable of *kanji* type to see whether pictographic *kanji* are learned more successfully than other *kanji* types. This would also provide evidence that certain *kanji* are better memorized using certain strategies. A similar experiment could be designed to test other strategies, such as mnemonics and component analysis (although the latter would be harder to test due to a prerequisite that learners would already be familiar with a novel *kanji*'s components).

In short, researchers are still exploring the way learners of languages memorize written scripts, particularly in the context of second language learning. This is even more perplexing for researchers when the processes involve the learning of *kanji* whose components provide different linguistic clues, some abstract, some semantic and some phonetic. The field would benefit from in-depth experimental studies such as those described above to test the effectiveness of cognitive processes against different *kanji* types. Furthermore, there is a need for research that systematically examines strategies deployed for specific *kanji* (e.g. mapping known effective strategies for every *kanji*) so as to develop ways to better present these *kanji* to learners in textbooks. Thus, a good place to start this research would be with the most frequently occurring *kanji*, as these are most often presented first in Japanese syllabi.

(2) The role of phonology in reading Japanese

This book has made mention of some studies that examine the role of phonology in the reading of Japanese (see Chapter 3). Some studies, such as Chikamatsu (1996), have shown that second language learners from an alphabetic language background (e.g. English speakers) tend to look for phonological clues when encoding Japanese writing compared to those from morphographic writing backgrounds, suggesting that this type of approach might be problematic for learners. Other studies such as Horodeck's (1989) investigation of the role of phonology for native Japanese speakers when reading Japanese show the importance of phonological processes when decoding *kanji*. Sayeg (1996) also has argued that phonology is as equally important as semantic decoding when reading *kanji*; however, there is still a dearth of studies in the past 20 years that have examined phonological processing of *kanji* by second language learners. I think there is a current need to carry out an updated study such as that conducted by Horodeck (1989) on second language learners or to replicate the study by Sayeg (1996).

With the advancement of data collection technology since the 1990s, there is also a methodological opportunity to investigate the reading of Japanese using eye-tracking technology. Eye trackers have proved to be extremely useful for research into the reading processes of English, but the same volume of research has yet to be carried out on readers of morphographic scripts, who have a background in reading alphabetic-based written languages. Eye-tracking technology offers an opportunity to examine – in an objective manner – the parts of the written language that readers focus on to derive meaning. Furthermore, they could provide a window into how Japanese is read from a top-down perspective (e.g. utilizing the role of context in deciphering less familiar *kanji* in terms of looking at what comes before and after), rather than the bottom-up reading process that underpins most studies (e.g. viewing reading as a process of decoding each character). The opportunities afforded by eye trackers have been fully embraced in L2 reading studies of English, but have scarcely been applied to the learning of other languages and other scripts. As I argued earlier in this book, the implications for further research into the learning of a morphographic script as a second language are not only immense, but also absolutely necessary to level the playing field in our understanding of how people learn all written languages, not just alphabetic scripts.

(3) A comparative study of vocabulary acquisition strategies and *kanji* strategies

In my own investigations into *kanji* learning, I have often been interested in drawing parallels between research into L2 vocabulary acquisition and the role *kanji* in this process. I suspect that the cognitive strategies deployed in the task of *kanji* learning are quite separate from vocabulary learning; however, some metacognitive strategies are shared across the two, particularly in contexts where learners have lists of new vocabulary items to learn. This assumption has not fully been explored in Japanese to the extent it has been conducted in the learning of English as a second language. Of particular interest to researchers in applied linguistics would be studies that aim to investigate the following research questions:

- To what extent do the strategies used for learning Japanese vocabulary converge or diverge from the strategies used for learning *kanji*?
- Do learners of Japanese engage in less out-of-class reading than learners of other languages at a similar level of spoken proficiency?
- What role does *kanji* play in reducing the access of learners to reading authentic materials?
- What role does the Japanese writing system play in incidental vocabulary learning? For example, does an inability to read reduce opportunities for incidental vocabulary acquisition compared to languages written in an alphabetic script?

(4) An examination of pictorial strategy use over a period of development

A finding of *The Strategies Study* was that some learners had a tendency to over-report their use of pictorial strategies in the learning of *kanji*. The study suggested this was because pictorial analysis was a useful strategy in the beginning stages of *kanji* learning, due to the fact that most of the *kanji* introduced to the learner in the early stages of learning were simple, pictographic *kanji* [*shokeimoji*]. For example, half of the *kanji* taught in Year One of elementary school are pictographs; however, as learners progress to more difficult *kanji*, this strategy is less often applied, but this is a fact that perhaps goes unnoticed by the learners themselves. Thus, learners may have a false sense of the importance and usefulness of pictorial association for *kanji* learning in the long term. *The Strategies Study* also illustrated the dangers of continuing to apply a pictographic strategy as a student progresses in literacy and the strategy loses its ability to make significant connections between the *kanji* and its meaning. However, this is a finding that is implied by data in *The Strategies Study*, rather than being empirically tested.

In addition to the value of studies such as those already outlined previously under the heading of *kanji* type and strategy use, I see a need for a longitudinal study that examines strategy use over a long period of language development. The study's aim would be to investigate whether strategy use changes as a student progresses in literacy and encounters new challenges when introduced to more *kanji* that may represent language in very different ways.

(5) A more realistic look at mnemonics in terms of how they are used alongside other strategies

In Chapter 5, *The Strategies Study* took a critical stance against some of the mnemonic strategies outlined in commercial textbooks such as *Remembering the Kanji* (Heisig, 2007). An empirical experiment testing the strategies outlined by such methods is needed so we can better evaluate their effectiveness for learning. One study of mine (Rose, 2013: 989) concluded that data showed that an over-use of mnemonics in learning could have negative consequences for the learner:

> Data indicated that mnemonic strategies were useful when applied in a meaningful way, but were less helpful when associations became convoluted or complex. Results indicate convoluted mnemonic strategies, which link advanced *kanji* to meaning and not the Japanese reading, may result in an inability for the learner to read the *kanji* in Japanese, or recall the meaning altogether. Results also indicate adherence to a systematic approach of mnemonic strategies can lead to feelings of defeat when knowledge of *kanji* does not advance as expected.

A recommendation of this study suggested that future research should examine mnemonic use in combination with other strategies, because mnemonics are rarely used in isolation. In fact, the 2013 study showed mnemonics were often employed in conjunction with (and not in opposition to) strategies such as component analysis and pictorial association. Many previous studies of mnemonic strategy use have employed quasi-experimental designs, where learners are forced to employ an 'either-or' approach to strategy use, which is not reflective of how learners actually use mnemonics. This is an area of research where data collection techniques such as stimulated recall are essential, but also where eye-tracking technology would add a further element to providing proof as to which components learners focus on to extract meaning during the encoding and recall processes. Furthermore, studies are needed that examine the effectiveness of mnemonic strategies for different *kanji* types in order to confirm or refute my claims that certain semantically-oriented *kanji* lend themselves to mnemonic strategies than other, more abstract, *kanji*.

(6) The role of radicals and stroke order in SLA

The role of radicals and stroke order in SLA is a topic that was only briefly touched on in this book, as it was not a focus of the research questions of any of the three studies drawn upon; however, Chapter 6 illustrated mixed attitudes towards stroke order and radicals in *The Strategies Study*. Radicals and stroke order play a central role in the learning of *kanji* for native

Japanese language learners, where students are taught and tested on their correct identification of the radical for each *kanji*, as well as their correct stroke order in written *kanji* (in fact they are even tested on stroke order in some multiple-choice *kanji* examinations). As a result, radicals and stroke order are prominent in many classrooms and Japanese language learning materials that have originated from teachers who have learned *kanji* themselves in such environments. The importance of radicals for learners of Japanese as a second language and the importance of stroke order in the memorization and reproduction of *kanji* has, therefore, has not emerged out of second language teaching practice. As a teacher, researcher and learner of Japanese, I remain less convinced of their importance to the second language learner, a view that may make me unpopular with some Japanese instructors. I suspect stroke order is viewed as important because of cultural and historical value, rather than their linguistic value. Nevertheless, I must admit this is a suspicion that I have yet to prove with data. Thus, it remains an interesting question for future research.

In particular, I see the need for a study to answer the following research questions:

(1) What is the role of stroke order in memorizing and recalling *kanji*?
(2) What is the role of radicals in memorizing and recalling *kanji*?
(3) What value do second language learners place on stroke order?
(4) What value do second language learners place on radicals?

Designing a study to answer questions 1 and 2 may prove difficult because stroke order and radicals are always viewed as auxiliary information attached to *kanji*, as opposed to learning techniques in themselves (dismissing, of course, repetitive writing, which has already been proven to be ineffective). Thus, a field research approach would be necessary to record the knowledge and use of stroke order and radicals for Japanese language learners and perhaps compare these data with their test scores over time to try to test a correlation between radical and stroke order knowledge and success in remembering *kanji*. This may provide some insight into the role they play in language learning, albeit in a somewhat methodologically messy manner. Answering questions 3 and 4 would be an easier, and cleaner, study and could use questionnaires or interviews as a data collection technique. Findings for this would have to be presented as beliefs about language learning (or compared with the study that aimed to answer questions 1 and 2), since just because learners see the value in stroke order or radicals, should not suggest they are valuable. Nevertheless, I think these kinds of studies would be important in evaluating the pedagogical effectiveness of certain teaching practices that have rarely been questioned because of an assumption that they are effective.

(7) Metacognitive control and metacognitive strategies of learners

Metacognitve control is perhaps the largest area of potential research into the self-regulation of the Japanese language learner, as it ties in with a multitude of behaviors that learners engage in, during their quest to memorize *hiragana*, *katakana* and then *kanji*. For example, metacognitive control results in strategies such as using flashcards, setting study schedules, memorizing lists, writing out *kanji* and testing oneself. The effectiveness of many of these methods of control has largely been untested and continues because learners *think* they are effective, not because they have been proven effective.

It has also been noted, that 'few studies have addressed the question of metacognitive strategy training in contexts in which foreign languages are learned' (Pappa *et al.*, 2003: 773), and this is even more so for the learning of Japanese as a foreign language. Thus, following research into metacognitive methods, there would be a need to test whether they could be taught to improve learners' ability to learn language. This question is probably best answered in a series of systematic intervention studies, where groups of learners are introduced to a new metacognitive strategy and the effects of this strategy are measured against *kanji* performance on tests. Self-report measures of whether students find them effective would also add a qualitative element to the data, as test performance is just one outcome of strategy use. After all, learning strategies have been shown to help students increase confidence, motivation and enjoyment in language learning.

(8) Affect and attitude towards *kanji* learning over time

I concluded Chapter 11 with a discussion of the emotional toll of learning the Japanese writing system on the second language learner. It was noted that the study of *kanji* takes up a large amount of preparation time for learners, from which I concluded that an enormous emotional burden is placed on learners. In fact, the results of *The Self-regulation Study* indicated that learners suffer from self-criticism, defeatism and a decrease in motivation because of this emotional toll. Despite the clear emotional impact of learning *kanji* on the students, it is still an area that is currently under-researched and in need of attention. I believe further work needs to be carried out on affective strains on the language learner to fully investigate the impact *kanji* learning has on Japanese language learners. *The Self-regulation Study* took a case study approach and thus, while the sample provided an in-depth look at the issues involved, a wider ranging quantitative study needs to take place to fully survey this aspect of learning on a wider range of learners spanning a wider range of contexts and proficiencies. Data from *The Self-regulation Study* inferred that higher proficiency learners struggled the most with their control of emotion in learning;

however, in order for this to be confirmed and generalized to a wider population of learners, further research is required. The significance of this type of research is enormous in that it has direct implications for Japanese learning and teaching, in a subject area that sees huge drop-out rates of students, perhaps due to these affective factors.

Recommended Conceptual Frameworks for Use in Future Research

This book has examined the learning of the Japanese writing system from two related theoretical camps: self-regulation and language learner strategies. In constructing a research framework, the studies highlighted here were situated in my own original framework based on literature and research into self-regulation and *kanji* learning strategies, as opposed to using a generic framework that would limit the context specificity that strategy research requires. This book has examined *kanji* learning from both a cognitive (*The Strategies Study*) and behavioral perspective (*The Self-regulation Study*). A theoretical framework, outlined in Figure 14.1, illustrates such an approach.

In Figure 14.1, the arrows indicate from where a theory has been derived. For example, an examination of cognitive learning strategies, memory and recall of *kanji* (center) has been informed by theories of cognition. The theory of cognition has been, in turn, informed by research into cognitive language learning strategies (within the field of second language learning theory), but has also been underpinned by research into cognitive and memory strategies (within the fields of cognitive and educational psychology).

In constructing this framework, I argue that self-regulation alone, in its examination of learning from a behavioral and metacognitive perspective, does not allow for the full investigation of the cognitive aspects of learning. Thus, cognitive learner strategies are also drawn upon to be able to examine a fuller picture of strategic learning. Concepts of memory strategies, encoding and retrieval from the field of cognitive psychology are also incorporated into the cognitive dimension of the framework to add an additional theory to the cognitive processes being investigated. Thus, the framework takes cognitive elements from learner strategy and cognitive theory research and incorporates it with theory of self-regulation, which in is housed in Dörnyei's motivation control taxonomy.

Across the original studies highlighted this book, I have found the framework to be very beneficial in examining the intricacies of strategic learning, from the multiple perspectives of learning strategies, motivation control, self-regulation and memory cognition. Even though previous studies found some categorical issues with the motivation control framework (Rose, 2012a), overall I have found the addition of self-regulation to be useful in revealing the learning difficulties faced by learners of Japanese as a foreign language.

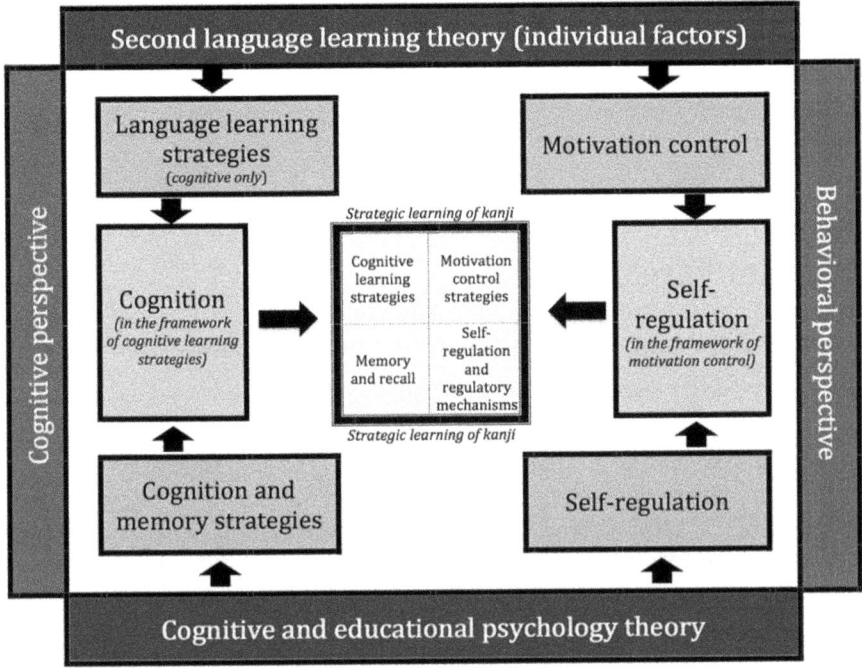

Figure 14.1 Theoretical framework for *kanji* strategy research

The addition of self-regulation into the framework revealed insights that may have gone unnoticed if pure learner strategy frameworks had been applied to the research. For example, self-regulation provides researchers with the concepts and the labels necessary to describe the problems faced by the learners who struggle with the mastery of the Japanese written language. By using these notions from the field of education psychology, it also makes it possible to compare such problems with those faced by learners in different learning situations.

This study has shown that self-regulation adds a new element to traditional frameworks that examine strategic learning. In more recent publications on individual differences in SLA (e.g. Dörnyei & Ryan, 2015), it is clear that self-regulation is an element of strategic learning that cannot be ignored in any research framework that examines strategic learning. I would concur with Gao (2006) and Gu (2012), that self-regulation and strategic learning are complementary, which is also the recent conclusion of Dörnyei and Ryan (2015). In previous work (Rose, 2012a), I have argued that self-regulation does not have to lie within the taxonomy that I used for my study, which was based on Dörnyei's motivation control taxonomy. Instead, categories can emerge from data in order to develop a system of coding, which is context appropriate to the language-learning task being investigated, in this case the learning of the Japanese writing system. However, I would argue that the framework must at least allow for the examination and description of facets of cognitive strategies (a learner's mental processes) and self-regulation (a learner's capacity to control their own learning) in order to fully investigate strategic behavior.

Recommended Methods of Data Collection for Use in Future Research

(1) A need for mixed-method approaches to examine self-regulation

The studies outlined in this book have reported on both quantitative and qualitative instruments to gather data. In regard to self-regulation, *The Self-regulation Study* employed a questionnaire called SRC*kanji*, which was based on the SRCVoc created by Tseng *et al.* (2006). However, due to the small number of participants in *The Self-regulation Study*, the results of the questionnaire were not very revealing. Thus, the study took the advice of Tseng *et al.* (2006: 98), 'to apply other, more qualitative methodologies (such as stimulated recall and structured observation) to achieve a fuller understanding of the whole picture' of self-regulation. The stimulated recall of *The Strategies Study*, while revealing, focused on the cognitive aspects of learning, rather than self-regulation, which was harder to observe. In order to conduct a deeper investigation, interviews were added to the research design to encourage learners to self-report on their self-regulation in the Japanese language learning task. These interviews were very revealing and in the initial part of *The Self-regulation Study*, the results were substantial enough to warrant publication on their own (see Rose & Harbon, 2013). Nevertheless, there is scope to examine self-regulation in *kanji* learning in much greater depth.

Thus, a potential area of recommended research is further development of the SRC*kanji* to facilitate a wide ranging look at self-regulation in the *kanji* learning task. The SRC*kanji* has yet to be properly tested and the reliability of the questionnaire needs to be confirmed. While the SRCVoc has been shown to be a valid instrument (e.g. see Tseng *et al.*, 2006; Mizumoto & Takeuchi, 2012), the same cannot be assumed for the task of *kanji* learning, where the task undertaken by students is very different to that of vocabulary learning. In the small-scale data collected in *The Self-regulation Study*, results of the instrument (which are not reported in this book due to the small sample size of the study) seem to indicate that the task of *kanji* learning poses extreme challenges for the language learner; in fact, I would argue that learners of *kanji* require different elements for learners to self-regulate compared to the task of vocabulary learning. Once the reliability of the questionnaire has been confirmed, there is scope to see whether the challenges faced by learners in *The Self-regulation Study* are representative of learners as a whole. Also, in earlier publications (e.g. Rose, 2012a, 2012b), I made claims that the current categories of self-regulation in the Dörnyei model may not be the most appropriate, arguing that environmental control did not appear to be a valid construct in my investigations. In order for this claim to be substantiated, a lot more research is needed where data is collected via quantitative instruments, such as the SRC*kanji*, and compared with data collected via qualitative instruments such as talk-alouds, journals, interviews and stimulated recall tasks.

Leading on from a need for quantitative data collection, a second area of recommended study is a wide-scale qualitative investigation of self-regulation in the *kanji*-learning task. As can be seen in *The Self-regulation Study*, while the SRC*kanji* was useful as a departure point for interviews with students on their self-regulation of *kanji* learning, the interviews allowed a much richer exploration of this relatively unexplored area. This finding concurs with recent calls from researchers into strategic learning and self-regulation for qualitative research. In Woodrow's (2005) critique of language learning strategy taxonomies and research instruments, she emphasizes the need for sample-specific data collection techniques and claims 'a more situated approach utilizing in-depth qualitative methods would be more appropriate' (Woodrow, 2005: 90). In their assessment of qualitative data analysis, Miles and Huberman (1994: 179) argue:

> Qualitative analysis, with its close-up look, can identify mechanisms, going beyond sheer association. It is unrelentingly local, and deals well with the complex network of events and processes in a situation. It can sort out temporal dimension, showing clearly what preceded what, either through direct observation or retrospection. It is well-equipped to cycle back and forth between variables and processes – showing that 'stories' are not capricious, but include underlying variables, and that variables are not disembodied, but have connections over time.

Thus, there is a great need for further research via in-depth qualitative methods, which is in line with claims of the benefits of qualitative research and analysis in general, but also in self-regulation-related research. Concurring with claims by Dörnyei (2005) that qualitative methods are necessary, the interviews in *The Self-regulation Study* helped provide a 'bigger picture' of self-regulation than the questionnaire allowed. Also, the situated approach and qualitative methods allowed the research to address sample-specific issues that the questionnaire did not, thus also supporting Woodrow's (2005) claim. Finally, the interviews revealed a complex network of associations of aspects of motivation control that were unique to the *kanji*-learning task that would not have been observable through use of questionnaires alone, concurring with Miles and Huberman's claims.

One under-utilized data collection technique that could prove very useful in the collection of data on self-regulation is learner journals or diaries. In other publications, Dörnyei (2007) has made the claim that journals can be a powerful research method to gain insight into learner practices and thoughts, which may be impossible to elicit using other data collection methods, because the participants help the researcher keep records of a learner's own thoughts, emotions and actions (Dörnyei, 2007). As journals can be used in different ways, it is important to clarify to potential researchers how I see journals being used effectively. In some recent learner strategy studies (Ma & Oxford, 2014), diaries have been used to provide a less structured narrative-like account of strategy use, but I see a more structured approach as being beneficial to provide empirical evidence of self-regulation. It has been noted (Bolger *et al.*, 2003) that there are a number of diary formats that can be used in data collection, of which an 'event-based design' is probably of most relevance to research in self-regulation. In event-based journals, participants are asked to answer questions in the diary directly after the learning event being studied. I have argued previously (Rose, 2015: 428), that this format 'helps to minimize the time between the event and the report, thus avoiding the problems of other retrospective data collection methods, but adds structure to a research project more so than a narrative account'.

In short, the benefits provided to the data generated in *The Self-regulation Study* via qualitative methods were substantial. For example, statements of commitment control by students on questionnaires alone were meaningless when compared case to case, as the type and nature of commitments differed for each student. Without an understanding of these commitments through qualitative data collection, the questionnaire data alone were an unreliable measure. Similarly, perceptions of satiation and emotion control in the *kanji*-learning task were context specific and also could not be accounted for in a questionnaire. For example, *The Self-regulation Study* highlighted one case of a learner who was not enrolled in formal *kanji* classes and who felt he was able to control stress and boredom in *kanji* learning, as his context was free of commitments. Thus, on the *SRCKanji*, this case seemed to be a highly regulated learner. In the same study, there were other cases that were required to learn 2000 *kanji* in order to graduate and the sheer weight of this commitment caused the learner to be poor at self-regulation on the *SRCKanji*. However, if the first student were put into the second students' context, it would be doubtful whether his self-regulatory capacity would have been the same, thus questioning the stability and independence of the construct of self-regulation from a learners' context. The questionnaire data alone did not account for these contextual differences in a way that the interview data did. This is further evidence of the importance of a mixed method approach.

In *The Self-regulation Study*, the *SRCkanji* yielded very little useable data compared to the rich data obtained in interviews on students' self-regulatory capacity. In the future, the generic nature of the questionnaire items in the *SRCkanji* make it more appropriate for a study that incorporates a larger number of students, rather than the small sample size of the current study. *The Self-regulation Study* makes a strong case for the necessity of qualitative research methods into self-regulation and motivation control studies in the future, as questionnaires on self-regulatory capacity alone are not adequate to understand an accurate picture of a student's self-regulatory capacity. Thus, through the *The Self-regulation Study*'s use of both questionnaires and in-depth qualitative methods, the findings support notions in the literature that qualitative methods are vital to the understanding of self-regulation and strategic learning. Future studies are encouraged to continue this mode of investigation.

(2) A need for qualitative approaches to examine learner strategies

The Strategies Study's findings illustrate a number of methodological considerations in the framing of future research, which are outlined in the following section. The main suggestion for future methodological design centers on the notion that qualitative, not quantitative, research methods are paramount to future research into strategic learning. *The Intervention Study* and *The Strategies Study* explored the concept of strategic learning both quantitatively in the form of a questionnaire and qualitatively in the form of semi-structured interviews and stimulated recall sessions. The results indicate that the qualitative data collection instruments provided a richer picture of strategic learning than the quantitative instruments.

On the one hand, while the Questionnaire of *Kanji* Learning Strategies provided a detailed description of the actual cognitive strategies employed by the participants in the study, these strategies were self-reported and at times inconsistent with the results of the stimulated recall sessions. An example of this is the over-reported use of pictorial strategies, which were presented in Chapter 5. Also, there were instances of use of strategies in stimulated recall sessions that were unreported on the questionnaire. Thus, the qualitative data collection instruments appeared to be more accurate and detailed measures of strategy use.

On the other hand, the questionnaire did provide a useful data source with which to compare qualitative data from the interviews and stimulated recall sessions. Moreover, it could be argued that self-reported strategy use on the questionnaire has the potential to provide a bigger snapshot of strategy use than is observable in a limited number of stimulated recall sessions. Thus, it is a recommendation of this book that future research continues use of questionnaires cautiously, but to also add more qualitative measures, such as interview sessions, stimulated recall tasks and learner journals as the *main* data collection instrument. Furthermore, future projects could expand the realm of qualitative data collection instruments from stimulated recall tasks to talk-aloud protocols during real study sessions that are designed to record strategy use on a frequent basis. Research instruments such as these, which are designed to collect data in real learning environments, might prove to be a useful measure of learning strategies in future research.

Conclusion

In conclusion, this book has yielded results that help better understand the strategic learning processes of students studying the Japanese writing system, which is one of the major obstacles for learners of Japanese as a foreign language. In improving understanding of how students learn this writing system – and *kanji* in particular – this book has helped to shed light on the struggles learners face with regulating their learning. This book is a key initial step to help the field of Japanese language learning and teaching to move in new directions and seek ways to better support students to learn this complex writing system.

Regarding *kanji* learning strategies, the studies reported in this book have revealed that each participant's approach to the *kanji* learning process is unique and worthy of investigation. The findings concur with past research that strategy use is an individual phenomenon; however, the findings also challenge some previous notions of strategic learning of *kanji* and have highlighted some areas of strategy use that are problematic, such as the over-reliance of mnemonics. Thus, in such ways, the study has built on knowledge in the field of *kanji* learning strategies and language learner strategies as a broader theoretical concept.

This book is also one of the first publications to apply newer models of self-regulation to the task of *kanji* learning. In doing so, this book has not only made headway into building an understanding of how learners of Japanese regulate their learning, but has also aided in theory building in the field of motivation control and self-regulation in second language learning, a largely under-researched realm. In regard to the former, this book has underscored the problems higher-level students have with commitment control, metacognitive control and emotion control. In regard to the latter, the book has highlighted the notion that commitment control is inextricably linked to emotional control in the *kanji* learning process. Moreover, it has also helped query the current models of self-regulation and opened up the field to delve into educational psychology research to explore alternative constructs of self-regulation.

In conclusion, this book has contributed to research in the field, both in its results in strategic learning of the Japanese writing system and in its exploration of motivation and self-regulation in this unexplored realm. This book has also added to a new wave of future research in both fields of Japanese language learning and self-regulation in second language learning. I hope that in its positioning of research for the three audiences of this book – the Japanese language learner, instructor and researcher – readers can move forward in positive ways in their learning, teaching and researching of this unique and fascinating writing system.

Glossary

Abstract characters are *kanji* that are arbitrary symbols for the morphemes they represent. They do not pictographically represent meaning. For example, some *kanji* for colors and numbers could be considered abstract characters in modern usage.

Alphabetic script refers to a writing system where phonemes in the language are represented by a different letter.

Cognitive strategies are strategies in which learners make mental associations between new and already known information in order to effectively store new information into memory stores.

Combination characters are *kanji* that are the synthesis of two *kanji* (or components) into one *kanji*.

Commitment control strategies are strategies for helping preserve or increase the learner's goal commitment (Dörnyei, 2005: 113).

Component analysis is the act of breaking *kanji* down into their components (or graphemes) to assist in memorization.

Components are the smallest unit a *kanji* can be broken into (also called graphemes).

Declarative knowledge is information that is stored successfully in our memory structures and can be retrieved when needed.

Direct strategies refer to the 'mental manipulation or transformation of materials or tasks, intended to enhance comprehension, acquisition, or retention' (O'Malley & Chamot, 1990: 229–232) (see also, Part 2: Cognitive Strategies).

Emotion control strategies are strategies for managing disruptive emotional states or moods and for generating emotions that are conducive to implementing one's intentions (Dörnyei, 2005: 113).

Environmental control strategies are strategies for the eliminating of negative environmental influences by making an environment an ally in the pursuit of a difficult goal (Dörnyei, 2005: 113).

Furigana are *hiragana* written above *kanji* to show the pronunciation/reading of the *kanji*. They are often used with less common *kanji* to show less common readings and in books for young learners or second language learners.

Future selves (possible selves) is a concept 'representing individual's ideas of what they might become, what they would like to become, and what they are afraid of becoming' (Dörnyei & Ryan, 2015: 87).

Graphemes are the smallest unit a *kanji* can be broken down into (also called components).

Graphemic awareness is 'awareness that *kanji* can be segmented into graphemes and that graphemes can be the subject of analysis' (Toyoda, 1998: 156).

Hiragana is one of the syllabic scripts of the Japanese writing system, which is used to represent words of Japanese origin, as well as the grammatical items in the written language.

Ideal self refers to the type of learner one ideally wants to become.

Indirect strategies are strategies that are not applied directly to the learning process and are concerned with the management of the learning process.

Joyo kanji refer to the *kanji* for official use in the Japanese writing system that have been prescribed by government policy.

Kaiimoji (or ideographs) are *kanji* that are a combination of pictographic components.

Kana is the term used to refer to the syllabic scripts of Japanese and includes both *hiragana* and *katakana*.

Kanji is the adopted morphographic script of the Japanese writing system that came from China.

Kashamoji (or phonetic loan characters) are *kanji* that have been adopted into current usage for phonetic reasons.

Katakana is one of the syllabic scripts of the Japanese writing system that is used to represent words of non-Japanese origin.

Keiseimoji (or semasio-phonetic ideographs) are *kanji* that are a combination of components, of which one gives a clue to the original Chinese pronunciation or meaning.

Kun-yomi refers to the 'Japanese' reading of a *kanji*.

L2 Motivational Self System is a framework of motivation that places the learner at the center of his or her system of language learning motivation, where learners depict their future selves in terms of being a language user.

Language learning strategies are defined as specific actions, behaviors, steps or techniques that students use to improve their skills in a second language.

Logographic scripts see Morphographic scripts.

Long-term memory is the place permanent (or semi-permanent) information is stored.

Memory encoding refers to links we make between new information and known information in our memory.

Memory retrieval refers to the process whereby information in our memory is retrieved.

Memory strategies can be defined as deliberate, goal-oriented behaviors used to improve memory (Matlin, 2005: 503).

Memory trace refers to the link to stored information in our memory.

Metacognitive control strategies are strategies for monitoring and controlling concentration and for curtailing unnecessary procrastination (Dörnyei, 2005: 113).

Metacognitive strategies refer to actions involving the controlling of one's own cognition through the coordination of the planning, organization and evaluation of the learning process (Oxford, 2001).

Mnemonic strategies refer to the making of associations between new and already known information through use of formulae, phrases or stories.

Morpheme is the smallest unit of meaning that a word can be broken down into.

Morphographic scripts are scripts that represent the morphemes (or meaning-based units) of a language.

National Japanese Language Proficiency Test is a standardized test of Japanese language broken down into five levels of proficiency.

On-yomi refers to the 'Chinese' reading of a *kanji*.

Ought To Self refers to the type of learner one thinks they should become to meet external expectations or to avoid negative outcomes.

Phoneme is the smallest unit of sound that is distinguishable in speech.

Pictorial characters are *kanji* that are stylized visual representations of the lexical item they represent.

Procedural knowledge refers to known items in our memory that are automatically and effortlessly retrieved.

Radical is a component of a *kanji* that is used to organize the *kanji* by grouping it with others that contain the root component. Called *bushu* [部首] in Japanese.

Retrieval practice refers the practice of locating and accessing stored information, by spending time actively learning and reviewing materials over multiple study sessions.

Romaji is one of the scripts of the Japanese writing system that represents the language using the Roman alphabet.

Satiation control strategies are strategies for eliminating boredom and adding extra attraction or interest to the task (Dörnyei, 2005: 113).

Schema is the network of linked information in one's memory that is usually based on experiences and knowledge of how things are connected in the world.

Self-regulation is the degree to which learners are active participants in their own learning and are proactive in their pursuit of language learning (Dörnyei, 2005).

Shijimoji (or logograms) are *kanji* that are symbolic representation of abstract ideas.

Shokeimoji (or pictographs) are *kanji* that are pictorial representations of meaning.

SILK is the Strategy Inventory of *Kanji* Learning, a questionnaire designed to measure *kanji* learning strategies and was developed by Barbara Bourke (1996).

SILL is the Strategy Inventory of Language learning, a questionnaire designed to measure language learning strategies, developed by Rebecca Oxford (1990).

SRCkanji is the self-regulatory capacity for *kanji* learning, a questionnaire designed to measure self-regulation of the *kanji* learning task. Adapted from the SRCVoc.

SRCVoc is the self-regulatory capacity for vocabulary learning, a questionnaire designed to measure self-regulation of the vocabulary learning task. Developed by Tseng *et al.* (2006).

Stroke order is the decided order in which the lines of a *kanji* are written.

Syllabic scripts (syllabary) are scripts that represent the syllables (usually consonant and vowel combinations) of a language.

Tenchuumoji (or derivative characters) are *kanji* that have been derived from an original concept that has been disassociated.

Tip-of-the-pen describes the phenomenon of a writer being unable to produce a *kanji* due to it being on the fringe of recollection.

Washback effect refers to the influence that language tests have on teaching practices and learning behaviors.

References

Anderson, J.R. (1985) *Cognitive Psychology and its Implications* (2nd edn). New York: W. H. Freeman.
Anderson, J.R. (2005) *Cognitive Psychology and its Implications* (6th edn). New York: W. H. Freeman.
Baddeley, A.D. (1997) *Human Memory*. East Sussex: Psychology Press.
Bailey, K.M. (1996) Working for washback: A review of the washback concept in language testing. *Language Testing* 13 (3), 257–279.
Bandura, A. (1989) Social cognitive theory. In R. Vasta (ed.) *Annals of Child Development (Vol. 6) Six Theories of Child Development* (pp. 1–60). Greenwich, CT: JAI Press.
Bandura, A. and Schunk, D.H. (1981) Cultivating competence, self-efficacy, and intrinsic interest through proximal self-motivation. *Journal of Personality and Social Psychology* 41 (3), 586–598.
Bialystok, E. (1979) The role of conscious strategies in second language proficiency. *Canadian Modern Language Review* 35, 372–394.
BJT (2016) Business Japanese Proficiency Test. See http://www.kanken.or.jp/bjt/english/ (accessed 10 October 2016).
Bolger, N., Davis, A. and Rafaeli, E. (2003) Diary methods: Capturing life as it is lived. *Annual Review of Psychology* 54, 579–616.
Bourke, B. (1996) Maximising efficiency in the *kanji* learning task. PhD thesis, University of Queensland.
Bramley, N. and Hanamura, N. (1998) The teaching and learning of Japanese at Australian Universities: An overview. *Australian Review of Applied Linguistics, Series S* 15, 1–10.
Chambers, G.N. (1993) Taking the 'de' out of de-motivation. *Language Learning Journal* 7, 13–16.
Chamot, A.U. (2005) Language learning strategy instruction: Current issues and research. *Annual Review of Applied Linguistics* 25, 112–130.
Chamot, A.U. and Keatley, C.W. (2003) Learning strategies of adolescent low-literacy Hispanic ESL students. Paper presented at the 2003 Annual Meeting of the American Educational Research Association. April, Chicago, IL.
Chamot, A.U. and Kupper, L. (1989) Learning strategies in foreign language instruction. *Foreign Language Annals* 22 (1), 13–24.
Chamot A.U. and O'Malley, J.M. (1987) The cognitive approach: A bridge to the mainstream. *TESOL Quarterly* 21 (3), 227–249.
Chikamatsu, N. (1996) The effects of L1 orthography on L2 word recognition: A study of American and Chinese learners of Japanese. *Studies in Second Language Acquisition* 18 (4), 403–432.
Chikamatsu, N. (2005) L2 Japanese *kanji* memory and retrieval: An experiment on the tip-of-the-pen (TOP) phenomenon. In V. Cook and B. Bassetti (eds) *Second Language Writing Systems* (pp. 71–96). Clevedon: Multilingual Matters.

Clark, S.D. (1999) Second language acquisition and non-traditional students: A case study of strategies and achievement. Unpublished Manuscript, University of North Carolina at Greensboro.

Cohen, A.D. (2000) Strategies-based instruction for learners of a second language. *NASSP Bulletin* 84 (612), 10–18.

Cohen, A.D. (2007) Coming to terms with language learner strategies. In A.D. Cohen and E. Macaro (eds) *Language Learner Strategies: 30 Years of Research and Practice* (pp. 29–46). Oxford: Oxford University Press.

Cohen, A.D. and Chi, J.C. (2002) Language strategy use inventory and index. In R.M. Paige, A.D. Cohen, B. Kappler, J.C. Chi and J.P. Lassegard (eds) *Maximizing Study Abroad: A Students' Guide to Strategies for Language and Culture Learning and Use* (pp. 16–22). Minneapolis: University of Minnesota.

Cohen, A.D. and Macaro, E.M. (eds) (2007) *Language Learner Strategies: 30 Years of Research and Practice*. Oxford: Oxford University Press.

Corno, L. and Kanfer, R. (1993) The role of volition in learning and performance. *Review of Research in Education* 19, 301–341.

De Courcy, M. and Birch, G. (1993) *Reading and Writing Strategies Used in a Japanese Immersion Program*. Brisbane: Griffith University.

Doering, L. (2001) *Language Learning Strategies of younger Second Language Learners*. Ottawa: Bibliothèque nationale du Canada (National Library of Canada).

Dörnyei, Z. (2001) *Teaching and Researching Motivation*. London: Longman.

Dörnyei, Z. (2005) *The Psychology of the Language Learner: Individual Differences in Second Language Acquisition*. London and New York: Lawrence Erlbaum Associates.

Dörnyei, Z. (2007) *Research Methods in Applied Linguistics: Quantitative, Qualitative, and mixed Methodologies*. Oxford: Oxford University Press.

Dörnyei, Z. and Ryan, S (2015) *The Psychology of the Language Learner Revisited*. Abingdon: Routledge.

Dörnyei, Z. and Skehan, P. (2003) Individual differences in second language learning. In C.J. Doughty and M.H. Long (eds) *The Handbook of Second Language Acquisition* (pp. 589–630). Oxford: Blackwell.

Dwyer, E.S. (1997) Getting started the right way: An investigation into the introduction of kanji study to neophyte Japanese learners. PhD thesis, The University of Texas.

Ehrman, M. and Oxford, R. (1989) Effects of sex differences, career choice, and psychological type on adult language learning strategies. *Modern Language Journal* 73 (1), 1–13.

Ellis R. (1994) *The Study of Second Language Acquisition*. Oxford: Oxford University Press.

Ellis R. (1997) *The Study of Second Language Acquisition* (2nd edn). Oxford: Oxford University Press.

Ellis, N.C., Natsume, M., Stavropoulou, K., Hoxhallari, L., Van Daal, V.H.P., Polyzoe, N., Tsipa, M.-L. and Petalas, M. (2004) The effects of orthographic depth on learning to read alphabetic, syllabic, and logographic scripts. *Reading Research Quarterly* 39, 438–468.

Everson, M.E. (2011) Best practices in teaching logographic and non-Roman writing systems to L2 learners. *Annual Review of Applied Linguistics* 31, 249–274.

Ezaki, M. (2010) Strategic deviations the role of 'kanji' in contemporary Japanese. *Japanese Language & Literature* 44 (2), 179–212.

Feyton, C.M., Flaitz, J.J. and LaRocca, M.A. (1999) Conciousness raising and strategy use. *Applied Language Learning* 10 (1&2), 15–38.

Flaherty, M. and Noguchi, M.S. (1998) Effectiveness of different writing approaches to *kanji* education with second language learners. *JALT Journal* 20 (2), 60–78.

Foerster, A. and Tamura, N. (1994) *Kanji ABC*. Boston: Tuttle Publishing.

Fujiyoshi, T. (1996) Kanji learning strategies used by Australian learners of Japanese. MA thesis, University of Queensland.

Gakken (1982) *A New Dictionary of Kanji Usage*. Tokyo: Gakken.

Gamage, G.H. (2003) Perceptions of *kanji* learning strategies: Do they differ among Chinese character and alphabetic background learners? *Australian Review of Applied Linguistics* 26 (2), 17–31.

Gass, S.M. and Selinker, L. (2009) *Second Language Acquisition: An Introductory Course* (2nd edn). Marhwah, NJ: Lawrence Erlbaum.

Gao, X. (2006) Has language learning strategy research come to an end? A response to Tseng, Dörnyei. *Applied Linguistics* 28 (4), 615–620.

Gottlieb, N. (2010) The rōmaji movement in Japan. *Journal of the Royal Asiatic Society* 20 (1), 75–88.

Govea de Arce, M. (2001) Foreign language learning strategies among middle school students: An exploratory study. EdD thesis, The University of Memphis.

Grenfell, M. and Harris, V. (1999) *Modern Languages and Learning Strategies: In Theory and Practice*. London: Routledge.

Grenfell, M. and Macaro, E. (2007) Claims and critiques. In A.D. Cohen and E.M. Macaro (eds) *Language Learner Strategies* (pp. 9–28). Oxford: Oxford University Press.

Gu, Y. (2012) Learning strategies: Prototypical core and dimensions of variation. *Studies in Self-Access Learning Journal* 3 (4), 330–356.

Guruz, K. (2008) *Higher Education and International Student Mobility in the Global Knowledge Economy*. New York: SUNY Press.

Hatasa, K. (1989) A study of learning and teaching of *kanji* for nonnative learners of Japanese. Unpublished PhD thesis, University of Illinois at Urbana-Champaign. See http://hdl.handle.net/2142/23070 (accessed 24 November 2015).

Heisig, J.W. (2007) *Remembering the Kanji (Vol. 1): A Systematic Guide to Reading Japanese Characters*. Honolulu: University of Hawaii Press.

Heisig, J.W. (2008) *Remembering the Kanji (Vol. 2): A Systematic Guide to Reading Japanese Characters*. Honolulu: University of Hawaii Press.

Henshall, K.G. (1988) *A Guide to Remembering Japanese Characters*. North Clarendon: Tuttle.

Herrmann, D., Raybeck, D. and Gruneberg, M. (2002) *Improving Memory and Study Skills: Advances in Theory and Practice*. Ashland, OH: Hogrefe and Huber.

Horodeck, R.A. (1989) The role of sound in reading and writing *kanji*. Unpublished PhD thesis. Ithaca, NY: Cornell University.

Hosenfeld, C. (1976) Learning about learning: Discovering our students' strategies. *Foreign Language Annals* 9 (2), 117–129.

Ikeda, M. and Takeuchi, O. (2003) Can strategy instruction help EFL learners improve reading comprehension? *JACET Bulletin* 37, 49–60.

Jackson, F.H. and Malone, M.E. (2009) *Building the Foreign Language Capacity we need: Toward a Comprehensive Strategy for a National Language*. Center for Applied Linguistics. http://www.cal.org/resource-center/publications/building-foreign-language-capacity (accessed 18 January 2017).

Japan Foundation (2009) *A Summary of the Results for the 2008 JLPT: Statistics for the last 25 years*. See http://www.jlpt.jp/e/statistics/archive.html (accessed 24 March 2010).

Japan Foundation (2013) *Japan Foundation's Survey Report on Japanese-Language Education Abroad*. See https://www.jpf.go.jp/e/project/japanese/survey/result/ (accessed 25 November 2015).

JLPT (2016a) Changes in number of examiness (1984–2105). See http://www.jlpt.jp/statistics/pdf/suii_2015.pdf (access 10 October 2016).

JLPT (2016b) Changes in number of examiness (1984–2105). See http://www.jlpt.jp/e/about/levelsummary.html (accessed 10 October 2016).

JLPT (2016c) Changes in number of examiness (1984–2105). See http://www.jlpt.jp/e/about/pdf/comparison01.pdf (accessed 10 October 2016).

Kanken (2016) Kaku-kyū no shutsudai naiyō to shinsa [contents of each level and examination criteria]. See http://www.kanken.or.jp/kanken/outline/degree.html (accessed December 15, 2016).

Kano, C., Shimizu, Y., Takenaka, H. and Ishi, E. (2006) *Basic Kanji Book Volume 2*. Tokyo: Bonjinsha.

Kato, F. (2000) Integrating learning strategies, time management, and anxiety-free learning in a tertiary-level course in basic Japanese: An intervention study. Unpublished PhD thesis, The University of Sydney.

Kato, F. (2002) Efficacy of intervention strategies in learning success rates. *Foreign Language Annals* 35, 61–72.

Komiya-Samimy, K. and Tabuse, M. (1992) Affective variables and less commonly taught language: A study in beginning Japanese classes. *Language Learning* 42 (3), 377–398.

Kuhl, J. (1987) Action control: The maintenance of motivational states. In F. Halisch and J. Kuhl (eds) *Motivation, Intention and Volition* (pp. 279–291). Berlin: Springer.

Larsen, R.J. and Prizmic, Z. (2004) Affect regulation. In R.F. Baumeister and K.D. Vohs (eds) *Handbook of Self-Regulation: Research, Theory, and Application* (pp. 40–61). New York: The Gilford Press.

Lu, M., Webb, J.M., Krus, D.J. and Fox, L.S. (1999) Using order analytic instructional hierarchies of mnemonics to facilitate learning Chinese and Japanese *kanji* characters. *The Journal of Experimental Education* 67, 293–311.

Ma, R. and Oxford, R.L. (2014) A diary study focusing on listening and speaking: The evolving interaction of learning styles and learning strategies in a motivated, advanced ESL learner. *System* 43, 101–113.

Macaro, E. (2001) *Learning Strategies in Foreign and Second Language Classrooms*. London: Continuum.

Macaro, E. (2006) Strategies for language learning and for language use: Revising the theoretical framework. *The Modern Language Journal* 90 (3), 320–337.

Mackey, A. and Gass, S.M. (2005) *Second Language Research: Methodology and Design*. Mahwah, NJ: Lawrence Erlbaum Associates.

Matlin, M.W. (2005) *Cognition* (6th edn). USA: John Wiley & Sons, Inc.

McCombs, B.L. and Pope, J.E. (1994) *Motivating Hard to Reach Students*. USA: American Psychological Association.

Miles, M.B. and Huberman, A.M. (1994) *Qualitative Sata Analysis: An Expanded Sourcebook*. Thousand Oaks, CA: SAGE Publications.

Ministry of Education, Culture, Sport, Science and Technology, Japan (MEXT) (2004) *Outline of the student exchange programs in Japan* (Special Report). Student Services Bureau, Higher Education Division.

Mizumoto, A. and Takeuchi, O. (2012) Adaptation and validation of self-regulating capacity in vocabulary learning scale. *Applied Linguistics* 33 (1), 83–91.

Mori, Y. (1999) Beliefs about language learning and their relationship to the ability to integrate information from word parts and context in interpreting novel *kanji* words. *The Modern Language Journal* 83 (4), 535–547.

Naiman, N., Frohlich, M., Stern, H.H. and Todesco, A. (1975) *The Good Language Learner*. Toronto: Ontario Institute of Studies for Education.

Noguchi, M.G. and Fotos, S. (2001) *Studies in Japanese Bilingualism*. Clevedon: Multilingual Matters.

Nolen-Hoeksema, S. and Corte, C. (2004) Gender and self-regulation. In R.F. Baumeister and K.D. Vohs (eds) *Handbook of Self-Regulation: Research, Theory, and Application* (pp. 411–421). New York: The Gilford Press.

Nunan, D. (1994) *Research Methods in Language Learning*. Cambridge: Cambridge University Press.
Nyikos, M. and Fan, M. (2007) A review of vocabulary learning strategies: Focus on language proficiency and learner voice. In D.C. Cohen and E.M. Macaro (eds) *Language Learner Strategies* (pp. 251–274). Oxford: Oxford University Press.
O'Malley, J.M. (1987) The effects of training on the use of learning strategies on learning English as a second language. In A. Wenden and J. Rubin (eds) *Learning Strategies in Language Learning* (pp. 133–144). Cambridge: Prentice Hall International.
O'Malley, J.M. and Chamot, A.U. (1990) *Learning Strategies in Second Language Acquisition*. New York: Cambridge University Press.
O'Malley, J.M., Chamot, A.U., Stewner-Manzanares, G., Küpper, L. and Russo, R.P. (1985a) Learning strategies used by beginning and intermediate ESL students. *Language Learning* 35, 21–46.
O'Malley, J.M., Chamot, A.U., Stewner-Manzanares, Russo, R.P. and Küpper, L. (1985b) Learning strategy applications with students of English as a foreign language. *TESOL Quarterly* 19 (3), 557–584.
Oxford, R.L. (1990) *Language Learning Strategies: What Every Teacher Should Know*. New York: Newbury House Publisher.
Oxford, R.L. (1998) Anxiety and the language learner: New insights. In J. Arnold (ed.) *Affective Language Learning* (pp. 58–67). Cambridge: Cambridge University Press.
Oxford, R.L. (2001) Language learning strategies. In D. Nunan and R. Carter (eds) *The Cambridge Guide to Teaching English to Speakers of Other Languages* (pp. 166–172). Cambridge: Cambridge University Press.
Oxford, R.L. (2011) *Teaching and Researching Language Learning Strategies*. Harlow: Pearson Education.
Oxford, R.L. and Ehrman, M.E. (1995) Adults' learning strategies in an intensive foreign language program in the United States. *System* 23, 359–386.
Oxford, R.L. and Nyikos, M. (1989) Variables affecting choice of language learning strategies by university students. *Modern Language Journal* 73 (3), 291–329.
Oxford, R.L. and Schramm, K. (2007) Bridging the gap between psychological and sociological perspectives on L2 learner strategies. In D.C. Cohen and E.M. Macaro (eds) *Language Learner Strategies* (pp. 47–68). Oxford: Oxford University Press.
Pappa, E., Zafiropoulou, M. and Metallidou, P. (2003) Intervention on strategy use and on motivation of Greek pupils' reading comprehension in English classes. *Perceptual and Motor Skills* 96 (3), 773–786.
Paradis, M., Hagiwara, N. and Hildebrandt, N. (1985) *Neurolinguistic Aspects of the Japanese Writing System*. Florida: Academic Press.
Payne, D.G. and Wegner M.J. (1992) Improving memory through practice. In D.J. Herrmann, H. Weingartner, A. Searlman and C. McEvoy (eds) *Memory Improvement: Implications for Memory Theory* (pp.187–209). New York: Springer-Verlag.
Paxton, S.R. (2015) Tackling the *kanji* hurdle: An investigation of *kanji* order and its role in facilitating the *kanji* learning process. Unpublished PhD thesis, Macquarie University.
Pintrich, P., Smith, D., Garcia, T. and McKeachie, W. (1991) *A Manual for the Use of the Motivated Strategies for Learning Questionnaire (MSLQ)*. Ann Arbor, MI: National Center for Research to Improve Post Secondary Teaching and Learning.
Quackenbush, H.C. and Mieko, O. (1999) *Hiragana in 48 Minutes*. Melbourne: Curriculum Corporation.
Ranalli, J. (2012) Alternative models of self-regulation and implications for L2 strategy research. *Studies in Self-Access Learning Journal* 3 (4), 357–376.
Roediger H.L., Gallo, D.A. and Geraci, L. (2002) Processing approaches to cognition: The impetus from the levels-of-processing framework. *Memory* 10 (5–6), 319–332.

Rose, H. (2003) Teaching learning strategies for learner success. *BABEL: Journal of Modern Language Teaching Association Australia* 38 (2), 32–38.

Rose, H. (2012a) Language learning strategy research: Where do we go from here? *Studies in Self-Access Learning Journal* 3 (2), 136–148.

Rose, H. (2012b) Reconceptualizing strategic learning in the face of self-regulation: Throwing language learning strategies out with the bathwater. *Applied Linguistics* 33 (1), 92–98, doi: 10.1093/applin/amr045

Rose, H. (2013) L2 learners' attitudes toward, and use of, mnemonic strategies when learning Japanese *kanji*. *The Modern Language Journal* 97 (4), 981–992.

Rose, H. (2015) Researching language learner strategies. In B. Paltridge and A. Phakiti (eds) *Research Methods in Applied Linguistics* (pp. 421–438). New York: Bloomsbury.

Rose, H. and Harbon, L. (2013) Self-regulation in second language learning: An investigation of the *kanji* -learning task. *Foreign Language Annals* 46 (1), 96–107.

Rowley, M. (1992) *Kanji Pict-o-graphix: Over 1,000 Japanese Kanji and Kana Mnemonics*. Berkeley: Stone Bridge Press.

Rubin, J. (1975) What the good language learner can teach us. *TESOL Quarterly* 9 (1), 41–51.

Rubin, J. (1981) Study of cognitive processes in second language learning. *Applied Linguistics* 11 (2), 117–131.

Rubin, J., Chamot, A.U., Harris, V. and Anderson, N.J. (2007) Intervening in the use of strategies. In D.C. Cohen and E.M. Macaro (eds) *Language Learner Strategies* (pp. 141–160). Oxford: Oxford University Press.

Sakai, J. (2004) Imagery mnemonic versus context learning: Effects on *kanji* retention. Unpublished MA thesis, California State University.

Sayeg, Y. (1996) The role of sound in reading *kanji* and kana: A review. *Australian Review of Applied Linguistics* 19 (2), 139–151.

Schmidt, R. and Watanabe, Y. (2001) Motivation, strategy use, and pedagogical preferences in foreign language learning. In Z. Dörnyei and R. Schmidt (eds) *Motivation and Second Language Acquisition* (pp. 313–59). Honolulu: HI: University of Hawaii, Second Language Teaching Center.

Schmidt, R., Boraie, D. and Kassabgy, O. (1996) Foreign language motivation: Internal structure and external connections. In R. Oxford (ed.) *Language Learning Motivation: Pathways to the New Sentury* (Technical Report No. 11, pp. 9–70). Honolulu, HI: University of Hawaii, Second Language Teaching and Curriculum Center.

Schwartz, B.L. and Metcalfe, J. (2011) Tip-of-the-tongue (TOT) states: Retrieval, behavior, and experience. *Memory and Cognition* 39 (5), 737–749.

Selinger, H.W. (1977) Does practice make perfect? A study of interactional patterns and L2 competence. *Language Learning* 27 (2), 263–278.

Shimauchi, S. (2009) Japanese language education policy toward increasing foreign students in Japanese societies with historical perspective. Paper presented at the Annual Meeting of the 53rd Annual Conference of the Comparative and International Education Society, Francis Marion Hotel, Charleston, South Carolina, 21 March 2009. See http://citation.allacademic.com/meta/p_mla_apa_research_citation/3/0/2/7/6/p302762_index.html#citation

Shimizu, K. (1995) Japanese college student attitudes towards English teachers: A survey. *The Language Teacher [online]* 19 (10). See http://jalt-publications.org/old_tlt/files/95/oct/shimizu.html

Shimizu, H. (1999) Language teachers' attitudes toward teaching kanji in Japanese curriculum. Unpublished PhD thesis, University of Denver.

Shimizu, H. and Green, K.E. (2002) Japanese language educators' strategies for and attitudes toward teaching *kanji*. *The Modern Language Journal* 86 (2), 227–241.

Skehan, P. (1989) *Individual Differences in Second Language Acquisition*. UK: Hodder Education.

Stevens, M.J. and Lane, A.M. (2001) Mood regulating strategies used by athletes. *Athletic Insight: Online Journal of Sport Psychology* 3 (3). (Electronic publication). See http://www.athleticinsight.com (accessed 18 January 2013).
Stout, M. and Hakone, K. (2011) *Basic Japanese kanji (Vol. 1): High-Frequency Kanji at your Command*. North Clarendon: Tuttle.
Suzuki, A. (2006) English as an international language: A case study of student teachers' perceptions of English in Japan. Unpublished PhD thesis, King's College London.
Takeuchi, O., Griffiths, C. and Coyle, D. (2007) Applying strategies: The role of individual, situational, and group differences. In A.D. Cohen and E. Macaro (eds) *Language Learner Strategies* (pp. 69–92). Oxford: Oxford University Press.
Taylor, I. and Taylor, M.M. (1995) *Writing and Literacy in Chinese, Korean and Japanese*. Philadelphia: John Benjamin's Publishing Company.
Toyoda, E. (1998) Teaching *kanji* by focusing on learners' development of graphemic awareness. *Australian Review of Applied Linguistics* Series 5 (15), 155–168.
Toyoda, E. (2000) English-speaking learners' use of component information in processing unfamiliar *kanji*. *Australian Review of Applied Linguistics* 23 (1), 1–14.
Toyoda, E. and M. Kubota (2001) Learning strategies employed for learning words written in *kanji* versus kana. *Australian Review of Applied Linguistics* 24 (2), 1–16.
Tseng, W.T., Dörnyei, Z. and Schmitt, N. (2006) A new approach to assessing strategic learning: The case of self-regulation in vocabulary acquisition. *Applied Linguistics* 27 (1), 78–102.
Usuki, M. (2000) Promoting learner autonomy: Learning from the Japanese language learners' persective. Research Report. ERIC: ED450588.
Wall, D. (2012) Washback. In G. Fulvher and F. Davidson (eds) *The Routledge Handbook of Language Testing*. Abingdon: Routledge.
VanderStoep, S.W. and Pintrich, P.R. (2003) *Learning to Learn: The Skill and Will of College Success*. Upper Saddle River, NJ: Prentice Hall.
VanderStoep, S.W. and Pintrich, P.R. (2008) *Learning to Learn: The Skill and Will of College Success* (2nd edn). Upper Saddle River, NJ: Prentice Hall.
Walton, A.R. (1993) Japanese language in US high schools: A New initiative. *Modern Language Journal* 77 (4), 522–523.
Wang, A.Y. and Thomas, M.H. (1992) The effect of imagery on the long-term retention of Chinese characters. *Language Learning* 42 (3), 359–376.
Weinstein, C.E., Husman, J. and Dierking, D.R. (2000) Self-regulation interventions with a focus on learning strategies. In M. Boekaerts, P.R. Pintrich, and M. Zeidner (eds) *Handbook of Self-Regulation* (pp. 727–747). San Diego, CA: Academic Press.
White, C., Schramm, K. and Chamot, A.U. (2007) Research methods in strategy research. In A.D. Cohen and E. Macaro (eds) *Language Learner Strategies* (pp. 93–116). Oxford: Oxford University Press.
Winne, P.H. and Hadwin, A.F. (1998) Studying as self-regulated learning. In D.J. Hacker, J. Dunlosky and A.C. Graesser (eds) *Metacognition in Educational Theory and Practice* (pp. 277–304). Mahwah, NJ: Lawrence Erlbaum Associates.
Woodrow, L. (2005) The challenge of measuring language learning strategies. *Foreign Language Annals* 38 (1), 90–100.
Yamada, K. (1998) The time course of semantic and phonological access in naming *kanji* and kana words. *Reading and Writing: An Interdisciplinary Journal* 10, 425–437.
Zimmerman, B. (2000) Self-efficacy: An essential motive to learn. *Contemporary Educational Psychology* 25 (1), 82–91.
Zimmerman, B.J. and Schunk, D.H. (2001) Reflections on theories of self-regulated learning and academic achievement. In B.J. Zimmerman and D.H. Schunk (eds) *Self-Regulated Learning and Academic Achievement* (pp. 289–308). Mahwah, NJ: Lawrence Erlbaum Associates.

Index

abstract characters 20, 50–51, 64, 70, 77, 154, 157, 168
alphabetic script 7–8, 14, 25
    processing of 31, 34, 56, 129, 133, 155, 168
    also see Romaji
Anderson, J.R. 39, 40, 47, 68
attrition
    of kanji knowledge 102, 113, 121
    of learners 6, 120, 133, 160
authentic materials 104, 117, 120–121, 141, 145
automatic processing 26–28, 132, 134

Bandura, A. 105, 115, 123
boredom 84, 89, 91, 137, 164, 171
bushu
    see radical
Bourke, B. 42, 49, 58, 61, 70, 98, 150, 171
Business Japanese Proficiency Test 108–110

Chamot, A.U. 38–41, 47, 83, 149, 150, 152, 168
Chikamastu, N. 19, 29–30, 155, 173
Chinese language
    relation to Japanese language 14, 19–22, 112, 170
    learning of 4, 6
    speakers 8, 129
    writing system 7, 30, 130
Cohen, A.D. 38, 83, 91, 149
cognitive processes 8–9, 12, 25–28, 31–34, 83, 153–155, 160, 166
cognitive strategies 37–46, 77, 81, 94, 102, 135, 155–156, 160, 162, 165, 168
cognitive theory 26, 32, 39–40, 71, 75, 135, 144, 147, 160
combination characters 20, 22, 60, 154, 168

commitment control strategies
    definitions of 83, 88, 104, 168
    uses of 90, 104–117, 137, 164, 166
components of kanji 9, 20, 22–23, 29, 42, 51, 54–55, 58, 68, 71–72, 75–76, 135, 145–146, 148, 154, 168
component analysis
    definitions of 44, 58–59, 168
    uses of 60–71, 77, 93, 135, 150–151, 154, 157
computer assisted learning 17–18, 30, 44, 94–97, 136
culture (Japanese) 5, 166
culture (anime and manga) 5, 66, 96, 112, 124

declarative knowledge 26, 30, 168
decoding 129, 141, 155
diary and journal methods 163–165
dictionaries 20, 59, 73, 74, 95, 145
derivative characters
    see tenchuumoji
difficulties in learning 25, 30, 64, 76, 91, 102, 115, 121, 124, 130, 143, 149, 151
Dörnyei, Z. 8–9, 13, 39, 42, 77, 82–86, 89–92, 103–107, 113, 115, 118, 137, 160–164, 168–171

Ellis, R. 28–29, 48, 82, 174
Emotions 12, 58, 90, 120–125, 159, 164
    Depression 119, 122
    Self-criticism 118, 120–122, 137, 159
emotion control strategies
    definitions of 84, 88, 168
    uses of 118–125, 137, 164, 166
environmental control strategies
    definitions of 84, 168
    uses of 87–90, 99, 117, 138, 163

etylomogy 20, 49–50, 55, 57, 72, 74, 76, 130, 154
Everson, M.E. 6, 116
eye-tracking 34, 155, 157
Ezaki, M. 133

Flaherty, M. 58, 61, 69, 150
Flashcards 44, 73, 94–96, 123, 135, 159
Frequency 57, 58, 66, 68, 71, 145–146
furigana 96, 133, 139, 169

Gamage, G.H. 120, 123
Gao, X. 13, 85, 161
Gass, S. 12, 38
goals
  importance of 90, 123–124, 138
  long-term goals 45, 90, 104–107, 111–117, 122, 124
  short-term goals 104–105, 107, 111–117, 123–124, 138
goal setting
  achievability of 90, 104–106, 114–116, 123–124
  believability of 90, 104–106, 123–124
  conceivability of 104–107, 11, 115, 123
  importance of 117
graphemes 59–60, 69, 168
graphemic awareness 59, 61, 64, 169
Grenfell, M. 11, 38–41, 150, 175

hiragana
  charcteristics of 14–16, 169
  learning of 28–29, 47–49, 105, 134, 139–144, 159
  uses of 95–96, 107, 132
  see also kana
hanzi 7
Heisig, J.W. 66, 68–69, 73–75, 148, 157

ideographic kanji
  see kaiimoji
interview method 12–13, 42, 72–74, 95, 110, 112, 123, 158, 162–165

Japanese as a foreign language
  history of 3–6
  learners of 109–110, 118–119
Japanese as a native language 29–32, 59, 96–97, 109, 125, 130, 132, 144, 155, 157
Japan Foundation 5, 11

Japanese Language Proficiency Test 5, 105, 107–108, 114, 124, 170
joyo kanji 66, 74, 109, 134, 136, 148, 169

kaiimoji 20, 22, 64, 135, 153, 169
kana
  characteristics of 8, 18, 28, 129, 131–132, 169
  learning of 19, 48–49, 52, 56, 61, 68, 93, 102, 114, 134, 140–141
  uses of 17, 19, 90, 104, 118
  see also hiragana and katakana
kanji
  classifcations 19–22
  number of 20, 74, 109, 134, 136
  order of acquisition 139–149
  origin of 19
  simplification 21, 130, 133–134
kashamoji 20, 135, 153, 169
katakana
  characteristics of 7, 14–16, 169
  learning of 44, 47–49, 52, 54, 141–144, 159
  uses of 63, 66, 107, 132
  see also kana
Kato, F. 6, 120
keiseimoji (or semasio-phonetic ideographs) 20, 23, 64, 135, 153, 169
kun-yomi
  challenges for learners 23, 130
  origin of 21–22, 169

language learning strategies
  theory 37–42
  criticisms 40, 42, 81–85
  instruments 13, 40, 42
lexis 141, 142, 170
  lexical knowledge 19, 86, 133, 141, 144
  L2 lexicon 130, 144
literacy
  general 17, 21, 29–31, 52, 56, 113–116, 121–124, 130, 133, 136, 156
  functional literacy 8, 19, 30–32, 116, 124, 130
logographic scripts
  see morphographic scripts
logograms
  see shijimoji
long-term memory 27, 56, 63, 66, 98, 170

Macaro, E. 11, 23, 38–41, 81–83, 91, 152
Mackey, A. 12

Matlin, M.W. 27, 32, 47, 170
memory
  memory encoding 27–28, 30, 32, 39, 48, 75, 93, 97, 135, 170
  memory retrieval 27, 29, 39, 73, 93, 102, 160, 170
  memory strategies 27, 30, 32, 39–40
  memory trace 27, 32, 40, 43, 48, 63, 75, 93, 95, 102, 123, 135, 170
  see also short-term memory, long-term memory and working memory
metacognitive control strategies
  definitions of 84, 88, 93–94, 100
  uses of 101–103, 114, 137, 159, 160, 166, 170
metacognitive strategies
  definitions of 32, 39, 43–45, 82
  uses of 71, 73, 93–94, 98, 156, 170
Ministry of Education, Culture, Sport, Science and Technology (MEXT) 5–6, 54
motivation to learn Japanese 23, 98, 100–101, 113–115, 124, 159–161
motivational control 103–104, 113
motivational L2 self system 106–107, 113–114, 169
mnemonic strategies
  definitions of 26, 37, 170
  uses of 9, 52, 61, 63, 68–77, 93, 135, 144, 154, 157, 166
morphemes
  in writing systems 7–8, 19, 132–133, 168, 170
  processing of 129, 153
morphographic scripts
  linguistic representation in 7–8, 14, 19, 61, 129, 153, 169–170
  processing of 25, 29–33, 46, 130, 155

national Japanese language proficiency test
  see Japanese language proficiency test
Noguchi, M.S. 4, 58, 61, 69, 150
Nyikos, F. 40–41, 43

O'Malley, J.M. 38–41, 47, 83, 149, 168
on-yomi 21–23, 130, 170
orthography 17, 28–29, 133
Oxford, R.L. 8, 38, 40–43, 68, 81, 83, 85, 93, 164, 170–171

Paradis, M. 19–20
Paxton, S.R. 51, 97, 147–148

phoneme 7, 15, 29, 129, 168, 172
phonetic loan characters
  see kashamoji
phonology 8, 25, 29–31, 48, 56, 86, 142–143, 155
phonological processing 30–31, 57, 59–60, 65, 74, 76, 130, 133, 135, 141, 143–144, 153–155
pictorial characters
  characteristics of 20, 154, 170
  processing of 24, 42, 48–52, 56–58, 61–65, 68–69, 134–135, 156–157, 165
pictographic kanji
  see shokeimoji
Pintrich, P. 82
procedural knowledge 26–27, 30, 107, 111, 171
procrastination 12, 84, 87–91, 94, 101–103, 122, 137, 170

questionnaires 10–11, 40, 43, 57, 77, 84–87, 151, 158, 162–165, 171

Ranalli, J. 83, 91–92
readings of kanji 8, 22–24, 28, 31, 49, 94–95, 111, 169
  see also kun-yomi and on-yomi
radical or bushu 28, 31, 42, 44, 59–66, 151, 157–158, 171
retrieval practice 27, 29–33, 38–39, 43, 48, 73–75, 93, 95–97, 102, 123, 135, 141, 160, 170
Romaji 8, 14–17, 129, 172
  origin of 16
  uses of 17, 134, 139–141, 143
  Romanization movements 130–134
  types of orthography 17–19, 28
Rose, H. 9–13, 32, 45, 51, 57–58, 69–71, 73–77, 81, 83, 85, 136, 150, 157, 160–164
Rose, H. & Harbon, L. 8, 10, 12–13, 32, 117–118, 123, 144–145, 162
rote-learning 27, 71, 119, 145
Rubin, J. 37–8, 149

satiation control strategies
  definitions of 84, 88, 171
  uses of 137, 144, 164
Sayeg, Y. 31, 154–155
schema 28, 31, 33, 47, 56, 58, 60, 65, 135, 171

Schunk, D.H. 91–92, 105, 115
self-regulation (models of) 8–10, 39, 81–92, 117, 136–137, 160–164
self regulatory capacity 84–88, 91, 101, 164–165, 171
semasio-phonetic kanji
  see keiseimoji
shijimoji (or logograms) 20, 153–154, 171
Shimizu, H. 8–9, 33, 119, 124
shokeimoji (or pictographs) 14, 20, 22, 49–52, 56–57, 61, 64–65, 69–72, 135, 153–156, 171
short-term memory 33, 124, 150
SILL (strategy inventory of language learning) 40, 171
SILK (strategy inventory of learning kanji) 42–43, 171
Skehan, P. 8, 42, 82–83
SRCKanji 44–45, 87–88, 91, 162–165, 171
SRCVoc 84, 86–87, 91, 162, 171
stimulated recall 12–13, 50–51, 55, 63, 71–77, 97, 151, 154, 157, 162–166
strategy instruction 23–24, 149–152
stroke count 140, 145–147
stroke order 44, 58, 96, 157–158, 171
syllabaries 7–8, 14–19, 31, 129, 131, 171
syllabic scripts
  see syllabaries
syllables 7, 15–18, 129, 171
symbolic association 20, 49, 52, 54, 56, 63, 69, 135

Takeuchi, O. 13, 41, 86, 149, 162
Taylor, I & Taylor M.M. 15, 19
teaching
  approaches to 9, 33, 119, 158, 160, 166–167
  in foreign language classrooms 3, 6, 9, 23, 33, 58, 61, 66, 68, 114, 117, 124–125, 139–140, 144, 147–150
  in Japan 32, 96–97, 109, 124–125, 130, 157

tenchuumoji (or derivative characters) 20, 153–154, 171
testing
  for business purposes 108–109
  as data collection 12, 50–51, 58, 61, 67, 91, 150–151, 154, 158–159
  kanji kentei 110
  self-testing 45, 73, 94, 97, 102, 135
  quizzes/classroom tests 10–12, 98, 103, 113, 117, 119–120, 124–125, 145
  also see Business Japanese Proficiency Test
  also see Japanese Language Proficiency Test
textbooks 49, 58, 67–68, 72, 97, 120, 139, 145, 147–148, 154, 157
  classroom materials 17, 19, 45, 47–48, 103, 115, 141, 145, 156, 158
think-aloud protocols 42
tip-of-the-pen 29, 171
Toyoda, E. 8, 33, 49, 58–61, 69–70, 76, 150, 169
Tseng *et al* 8, 12–13, 77, 81–88, 91, 118, 137, 162, 171

vocabulary 12, 26–28, 46, 49, 83–84, 107, 118, 125, 144, 150, 162
  knowledge of 23, 32–33, 47, 56, 91, 96–97, 104
  range 97
  vocabulary learning strategies 38, 40, 155–156

washback effect 103, 172
White, C. 40, 45
whole kanji association 49, 55–56, 60, 73, 150
Winne, P.H. & Hadwin, A.F. 92
Woodrow, L. 13, 163
world writing systems 7–8, 19–22, 28–30, 54, 130

Zimmerman, B. 91–92, 123

For Product Safety Concerns and Information please contact our EU Authorised Representative:

Easy Access System Europe

Mustamäe tee 50

10621 Tallinn

Estonia

gpsr.requests@easproject.com

www.ingramcontent.com/pod-product-compliance
Ingram Content Group UK Ltd.
Pitfield, Milton Keynes, MK11 3LW, UK
UKHW021823220426
5349IPUK00003B/57